# School Choice and Social Justice

# School Choice and Social Justice

### HARRY BRIGHOUSE

**OXFORD**
UNIVERSITY PRESS

# OXFORD

UNIVERSITY PRESS

Great Clarendon Street, Oxford OX2 6DP

Oxford University Press is a department of the University of Oxford.
It furthers the University's objective of excellence in research, scholarship,
and education by publishing worldwide in

Oxford New York

Athens Auckland Bangkok Bogotá Buenos Aires Calcutta
Cape Town Chennai Dar es Salaam Delhi Florence Hong Kong Istanbul
Karachi Kuala Lumpur Madrid Melbourne Mexico City Mumbai
Nairobi Paris São Paulo Singapore Taipei Tokyo Toronto Warsaw

and associated companies in Berlin Ibadan

Oxford is a registered trade mark of Oxford University Press
in the UK and in certain other countries

Published in the United States
by Oxford University Press Inc., New York

British Library Cataloguing in Publication Data

Data available

Library of Congress Cataloging in Publication Data
Brighouse, Harry.
School choice and social justice / Harry Brighouse.
Includes bibliographical references and index.
1. School choice—Social aspects. 2. Educational equalization.
3. Education and state. I. Title.
LB1027.9.B75 2000 379.1'11—dc21 99–053195
ISBN 0–19–829586–3

3 5 7 9 10 8 6 4 2

Typeset by Hope Services (Abingdon) Ltd.
Printed in Great Britain
on acid-free paper by
T. J. International Ltd
Padstow, Cornwall

For Lynn and Maddy

with my love

# ACKNOWLEDGEMENTS

I started thinking about school choice seriously in 1992, when I wrote a long and pedantic letter to my father explaining why, whatever else was wrong with school choice, it did not fall to many of the objections that had been made. In 1994 two undergraduate students, A. J. Julius and John Cook, and two of my in-laws, Bill and Tom Glueck, persuaded me that school choice was philosophically interesting. So that summer I turned the letter into a short article. Erik Wright subsequently invited me to participate in the *Real Utopias* conference at the *A. E. Havens Center* at University of Wisconsin (UW) Madison on a paper by Samuel Bowles and Herbert Gintis called 'Efficient Redistribution'. My contribution to that conference was another essay on school choice, taking their own proposal as a starting point.

I have many other debts. Dan Hausman suggested that I write the book, on the grounds that not only might it be good, but it might even do some good. We'll see. His comments on, and editing of, earlier and unrelated work of mine helped improve my writing enormously, which improvement I hope has been sustained here. He and Andrew Levine provided extensive and valuable comments on various parts of the book: again, Dan's editing is much in evidence. Much of the final draft was written while I co-taught an undergraduate course on political philosophy and educational policy with Francis Schrag: his bemused support for a junior colleague who keeps innocently diving into waters that are much more treacherous than they look is much appreciated. Other colleagues and friends at UW Madison and elsewhere whose conversation or comments have been greatly valued are Richard Arneson, Brian Barry, Samuel Bowles, Shelley Burtt, Claudia Card, Noel Carroll, David Copp, Robert Goodin, Amy Hanauer, Darrel Moellendorf, Laura Osinski, Adam Swift, Peter Vallentyne, Geoff Whitty, Dan Wikler and Erik Wright. Herbert Gintis responded almost instantly and very graciously to a series of questions I posed in the last stages of writing.

Two readers at Oxford University Press provided extremely valuable comments: Eamonn Callan's generous continued correspondence with me has helped even more than the stimulus of his important book *Creating Citizens*. And I'm grateful to my editor, Dominic Byatt, for his help, and especially for ignoring the preface to my first communication to him about the book, which started 'I'm sure you won't be interested in this . . .'. Versions of Chapter 3 and Chapter 4 were discussed at the *Cornell Program in Ethics and Public Life* in Spring 1998, when I was a Young Scholar. I owe thanks to all who attended, but especially to the commentators on those chapters, Jeremy Waldron, and Kenneth Strike, and also Sam Freeman, Jim Dwyer, Richard Miller, Jennifer Whiting, as well as to Henry Shue and Kathy Abrams for providing me with such a fantastic opportunity. I also acknowledge financial support from the Graduate School of the University of Wisconsin, Madison for writing Chapter 6.

I've heard education policy discussed ever since I can remember: my first discussions of education vouchers were with my father, Tim Brighouse, when I was still in school. I've also discussed the British education system with my mother, Mary Brighouse, for many years. One of the deepest and most unfair inequalities in life is in the parents you find yourself born to—an unfairness from which I have benefited greatly. The taxpayers of the United Kingdom footed the bill for my schooling from ages 4 to 22, without which I would not have been able to write this book. They had no choice about it—and quite properly so for the first 14 years—but I'm grateful anyway.

My greatest debts are to Lynn Glueck and Madeline Brighouse Glueck. Lynn provides me with a vital link to the real world of public education, and hardly a day goes by when we do not discuss schooling. She also reads almost everything I write, improving both the ideas and the writing. I am lucky to live with so valuable a critic, and however bad a critic she were I'd still be unable to believe my luck. Maddy's contribution has been almost entirely negative because her contribution to my life has been only positive—since she arrived she has made the prospect of doing philosophy seem so much less urgent and important than it otherwise would have done. Still, even in delaying the book she probably improved it. I dedicate it to them both with my deepest love.

Some parts of the book are developed from articles of mine that have been published previously. I am grateful to the following publishers for permission to use material from the following articles:

'Liberal Legitimacy and Civic Education', *Ethics*, 108 (1998), 719–45. Copyright by University of Chicago Press.
'Two philosophical errors concerning school choice', *Oxford Review of Education*, 23, (1997), 503–10. Copyright by Carfax Publishing Limited. PO Box 25, Abingdon, Oxfordshire OX14 3UE.
'Why Should States Fund Schools?', *British Journal for Educational Studies*, 46 (1998), 138–52. Copyright by Blackwell Publishers.

'In Defence of Educational Equality', *Journal of Philosophy of Education*, 29 (1995), 415–20. Copyright by Blackwell Publishers
'Liberal Egalitarians and School Choice', *Politics and Society*, 24 (1996), 457–86. Copyright 1998 by University of Chicago Press. All rights reserved.

# CONTENTS

# 1

# Liberal Theory and Education Policy

## POLITICAL PHILOSOPHY AND EDUCATION POLICY

A book like this stands in some need of justification. It is a work of polit‑ical philosophy that attends closely to a question firmly on the public political agenda. It is, for the most part, conducted ahistorically and at a high level of abstraction, and it is only in about one-third of the book that I directly apply the philosophical findings to education policy. Political philosophers may be made uneasy by that third of the book, preferring in general to espouse and defend political principles without considering the messy business of how they are applied in the real world. Educationists, and non-philosophers generally, may be discomforted by the rest of the book, especially its ahistorical aspect, perhaps thinking that, as one of my critics has put it, 'policies and philosophies have to be understood in rela‑tion to the appropriate social, political and economic contexts'.[1]

When I started reading about education policy I was dismayed by two recurrent features of the literature: the lack of clarity on all sides about what counted as social justice in education, and why; and the paucity of influence that the egalitarian liberalism, which, quite rightly in my view, predominates in political philosophy, has had on theorizing about educa‑tion. The two features are connected: if egalitarian liberalism had more influence there would be more clarity and accuracy about what constitutes social justice in education. I would resist the implication that people who work on education theory and policy are to blame for these deficiencies: until quite recently very little work in analytical political philosophy has addressed educational issues in ways that are accessible and directly rele‑vant to policy issues. I hope that this book will offer a much clearer view of what constitutes social justice in education, as well as a series of argu‑ments for that conception of social justice. In doing so, I hope it will help

[1] Walford, Geoffrey, 'The Common Good: reply to Brighouse', *Oxford Review of Education*, 23 (1997), 517–21 at 518.

undermine the success of post-modern, communitarian and libertarian theories that distract education theorists from what really matters.

It is important for political philosophers to think about institutional questions, and especially about education. Political philosophy as practised in the second half of this century is not only ahistorical—not, in my view, a flaw, but more on that later—but is also somewhat skewed. Political philosophy investigates the question of what enforceable claims adults have against other adults and, especially in the mainstream liberal theories, postulates that adults should be presumed responsible for their choices out of respect for their putative autonomy. But adults do not arrive in society as fully formed autonomous individuals; at best they become autonomous through a process of education and upbringing that is shaped by the society in which they are children, and the assignments of authority over them that society endorses. The question of how institutions governing the upbringing and education of children should be structured must be considered carefully if a theory of justice is to be applicable to any world with children in it. This question is unavoidably institutional in character: we cannot just ask what would constitute a good upbringing and education for children; we must also ask how much authority the state has, to ensure that children get such education and upbringing. Yet most of the leading liberal theorists leave these questions aside.[2]

It is also important for educationists and policy reformers in all arenas to think about political philosophy abstracting somewhat from the institutional contexts in which they are ensconced. It is true that, at the abstract level that most political philosophy is currently done, its findings are not very useful for purposes of policy design and institutional critique. John Rawls's seminal book *A Theory of Justice* defends two principles of justice: a liberty principle, and a principle concerning the distribution of opportunities and resources. Rawls says almost nothing about how to implement those principles, and to know how to implement justice in any particular situation we need to know a great deal about the current configuration of institutions, how they work, which transition mechanisms work and what costs are involved.

---

[2] The most important examples of liberalism include Rawls, John, *A Theory of Justice* (Cambridge, Mass.: Harvard University Press, 1971); Dworkin, Ronald, *A Matter of Principle* (Cambridge, Mass.: Harvard University Press, 1985); Raz, Joseph, *The Morality of Freedom* (Oxford: Oxford University Press, 1986); Waldron, Jeremy, *Liberal Rights* (Cambridge: Cambridge University Press, 1992); Gauthier, David, *Morals By Agreement* (Oxford: Oxford University Press, 1986); Barry, Brian, *Theories of Justice* (Los Angeles, CA: University of California Press, 1989); and *Justice as Impartiality* (Oxford: Oxford University Press, 1995). Children are mentioned briefly in *A Theory of Justice*, but only Barry can be exempted from the generalization I have made.

But political philosophy has an important role to play in thinking about social policy. One strong tendency in debates about institutional reform is for social scientists to take the goals of the institutions for granted and to treat questions of reform as merely technical in character. If only we knew enough about how the institutions worked and how they would work if we altered them, all the important questions could be settled. Many advocates of school choice simply take it for granted, for example, that what matters is achieving the highest possible median or mean test scores at the least possible expense. But high median or mean test scores are not the only measures of excellence in a system, because schooling serves other goals than getting children to take tests well, and because all children matter: the mean and median test scores do not tell us how well children who achieve especially poorly and especially well are being educated. In order to make a proper assessment of any set of institutions or proposals to reform them we need a sense of what the proper goals of institutional design should be, and simply looking at those institutions and alternatives will not tell us that. We need to know which values ought to be implemented in social policy, and we simply cannot know that without philosophizing about it. Unless we know, for example, whether equality of opportunity is more important than parental freedom, how do we know that we ought to try to design policies that ensure that children from disadvantaged backgrounds have at least as good a chance of gaining certification as similarly talented children from more advantaged backgrounds?

Suspicion of political philosophy, at least of the kind exemplified in what follows, is fuelled by the sense that it is ahistorical. It abstracts away from the actual experiences and commitments of political actors in a given time and place, and seeks to establish values which, its practitioners claim, ought to be endorsed by individuals regardless of where and when they live. One of the reasons this arouses suspicion is the fear that the resultant universal prescriptions embody some sort of imperialistic ambition. Those who claim that their values should be shared by all others are thought to be intolerant or disrespectful in some ways.

This kind of critique emerges from two different intellectual currents, both of which have far more influence in contemporary theorizing about education than the liberalism I espouse. Most post-modernists, in so far as they have a collective view, display a radical relativism not only about morality, but about truth itself. Communitarians do not espouse so radical a relativism, but they claim that any normative claim can have moral force only for people who inhabit the traditions within which the claim is formulated and made. Both currents, ultimately, are bound to a relativism about values.[3]

But the problem with relativism is this. If we assume that there is nothing to say about goals and aims that is not already believed by political actors, or implied by their beliefs, then we lack the resources to take a critical stance toward the institutions they endorse. The best that can be done is to point out that the institutions fail to live up to the very values that those actors hold. This is not, of course, entirely trivial: as we shall see, public schooling in the US fails seriously to live up to the ideal of equality of opportunity endorsed by most American politicians, and probably by most Americans. But, having pointed this out, we have no further resources for argument if the agents seek to defend the *status quo* by rejecting or subordinating the offending value. Furthermore, in any given society at any given time, there may be widespread disagreement about what political and moral values are important and about how different values should be weighted with respect to one another. If we tie ourselves to the commitments of the society itself, we shall have no grounds for adjudicating between these disagreements. In fact, it is not clear how, if one were truly relativist in one's moral outlook, one could participate sincerely in political debate within a society. The kinds of claims one has to make are not only that one's values are one's own, but that they, unlike those of one's opponent, have a status that justifies their being the basis of the state's use of coercive force against other people. We could only believe that our values justified the use of coercive force on others if we believed they were correct, or if we thought that other people did not matter. Relativism, then, of both the post-modernist and communitarian varieties, deprives us of the ability to advance cogent moral critiques of existing institutions.

Are universalistic political theories, though, inevitably intolerant or disrespectful? Well, some undoubtedly are, or have been, but the liberalism I shall defend is neither. Liberals typically claim universal truth for their theory,[4] but avoid the charge of intolerance because the values of tolerance and respect for persons are components of the very universalism for which truth is claimed. Because it is true that we ought to respect other persons

---

[3] The most prominent communitarian theories are in MacIntyre, Alistair, *After Virtue* (London: Duckworth, 1981); Sandel, Michael, *Liberalism and the Limits of Justice* (Cambridge: Cambridge University Press, 1982); Taylor, Charles, *Sources of the Self* (Cambridge: Cambridge University Press, 1990). An influential post-modernist work on education is Aronowitz, Stanley and Giroux, Henry, *Postmodern Education* (Minneapolis, Minn.: University of Minnesota Press, 1991).

[4] The exception, of course, is John Rawls, but many Rawlsians do claim universal truth for his theory.

and tolerate many of their behaviours and beliefs that we regard as false, we should be reluctant to impose coercive restraints on them, and should do so only when there are clear values to be served by such action.

## LIBERALISM

The philosophical position from which I address questions about the goals of education policy is a version of liberalism. While outside the academy, and even within the humanities outside of philosophy, liberalism has become a marginal political viewpoint, it is the predominant view in English-speaking political philosophy. I do not intend to defend liberalism here. All of the philosophical arguments in the book stand or fall independently of the truth of liberalism, though if they all stand the book will have succeeded in making liberalism a much more appealing theory than many of its opponents take it to be. However, I do want to outline some of the features of the liberal theory I deploy, since doing so will aid those readers who are not already imbued in the philosophical literature, and will also help to avoid misunderstandings that may arise from a partial acquaintance with the theory.

### Ethical Individualism

Liberalism assumes that individual persons are the sole intrinsic objects of moral concern. It is, in that sense, and in that sense alone, individualistic. This is not to say that liberals think that there is no such thing as society, a phrase and sentiment often misleadingly attributed to Baroness Thatcher, then Prime Minister of the UK. Human beings are social beings and it is only in the context of social interactions that the basic concern of liberal theory, justice, is interesting. Liberalism recognizes society as a fact of life, and as an institution that is essential for the well-being and flourishing of individual human beings. But liberals do not believe that societies matter, morally, independently of the benefits they bring to the individuals who compose those societies. To talk of the 'good of society' is, in liberal theory, always a shorthand for talking of the good of individual persons.

There are three other senses of individualism from which it is important to distinguish ethical individualism, none of which is essential to liberalism, or even endorsed by most liberals. The first is methodological individualism, the view that all explanations of social phenomena are reducible to descriptions of the behaviour and motivations of individual members of society. Whether or not methodological individualism is true is an empirical matter, and whatever individual liberals may believe about it, it plays no role in liberal political philosophy.

The second sense of individualism might be called 'social policy individualism', and is best exemplified in certain kinds of justice-based arguments against affirmative action. Some opponents of affirmative action object that affirmative action policies wrongly take the group membership of individuals as grounds for treating them in discriminatory ways. Policies should, according to these objections, treat individuals only on the basis of their individual characteristics, not their group membership. Liberals do not typically take this view, which anyway seems to be incoherent. Any given package of social policies is bound to take group membership to be relevant to how people should be treated. For example, the race-blind admissions policies that opponents of affirmative action favour for public universities in the US take many group memberships to be relevant: the groups are defined by test scores, geographical location, age, and other commonalities. I am not trying to comment on the appropriateness or otherwise of affirmative action in particular, just to point out that this particular argument is not well motivated, and that the individualism involved has no relationship to liberalism.

Finally one might distinguish an individualism that describes the motivation of individual persons. Liberals are surprisingly often accused of holding individuals to be fundamentally self-interested, and even of thinking of this as a virtue. It is true that liberals typically think that some degree of self-interest is a normal and healthy component of individual motivation. But they also typically believe that human beings are and should be concerned about others in a wide range of ways. In fact one of the central problems in liberal theory is to work out the balance between one's duties to all other citizens and one's inclinations to help and be generous to those who are close. Not only do liberals usually deny that individuals are exclusively self-interested, but the most influential liberal theory of the second half of the twentieth century, that of John Rawls, explicitly builds on the notion that individuals have a higher order interest in being able to develop and exercise a sense of justice. Roughly speaking, this is a sense of oneself as only one among the many who matter from the point of view of social justice, and the ability to accept one's place in a just order and treat others as justice requires.[5]

---

[5] Rawls, John, *Political Liberalism* (New York, NY: Columbia University Press, 1993), 19, 77, 80.

## The Role of Neutrality

Liberals believe that the government has properly available to it a range of coercive powers including the power of taxation. Many think, however, that the government has a responsibility to use its powers, and in particular its powers of coercion, neutrally. Liberals have meant a number of different things by neutrality, so it is worth reviewing some of those meanings here. Neutrality could be understood as meaning that government actions overall must not advantage some particular ways of life. So, for example, if the establishment of national parks would make the outdoors life easier to enjoy and a life of television watching more difficult, the trees interfering with broadcasts, then it would be impermissible, unless other measures were taken to counterbalance exactly the distribution of benefits. Let us call this conception *neutrality of effect*. A different meaning of neutrality would be the claim that the government should act so as to ensure that each way of life is equally easy and difficult to achieve. Thus it would have to compensate those with expensive conceptions of the good for the fact that it is more difficult to achieve expensive conceptions: other things being equal those who love skiing would each be granted slopes, snow, and skis, while those who love soccer would be provided only with some proportion of a flat field and a ball. Let us call this *neutrality of outcome*. Finally, neutrality can be understood to mean that while it is unobjectionable that state actions will have differential effects on conceptions of the good, the government should not intend to favour some conceptions over others. So, for example, it is permissible for the government to pursue a policy of building national parks as long as its intent in doing so is not to favour 'the outdoors life' over other ways of life but, say, to provide for clean air or to ensure the preservation of a wide range of species. Let us call this *neutrality of intent*.[6]

Although liberals differ in their understanding of what should be meant by neutrality, the most common understanding is neutrality of intent. The other two understandings are both extremely hard to achieve, to say the least, and not properly connected to the fundamental concern that motivated an interest in neutrality. This is the aspiration that when the state resorts to coercion, as it often must, it should do so without expressing disrespect for the persons coerced, and that part of what it is to be disrespectful is to presume false the deepest commitments of the individuals against whom coercion is used. Only neutrality of intent refers in the

---

[6] See Arneson, Richard, 'Neutrality and Utility', *Canadian Journal of Philosophy*, 20 (1990), 215–40, for a different typology of kinds of neutrality.

relevant way to the attitude of those who use force toward the commitments of those toward whom force is used.

Two clarifications are needed. The first is that the liberal commitment to neutrality is not relativistic. Liberals do not deny that some ways of life are superior to others: this is clearly true, and denying it would be incompatible with the liberal commitment that people need to be provided the conditions in which they can rationally revise their commitments. As citizens, liberals can quite consistently campaign for and against favoured and disfavoured ways of life. Their commitment to neutrality reflects their view that the *state*, with its monopolies on legitimate coercion, is not a proper agency to do this campaigning. Second, and relatedly, neutrality is not the fundamental commitment of liberalism. It has, at its root, more fundamental values—autonomy, respect for persons, and a certain view of state legitimacy—that support it strongly but not unconditionally. So, whereas the state should be neutral among a range of conceptions of the good—the practice of which is consistent with the operation of just liberal institutions—it is no objection to the internal coherence of liberalism that it espouses its own contestable values.[7]

## The Role of Rights

Liberals are typically committed to the idea that individuals have rights—that is, that they have claims on the rest of society that must be respected regardless of the preferences of others. One of the primary functions of the liberal state is to protect these rights. Different liberal theorists justify rights in different ways, and give different accounts of what particular rights people have. The most plausible account of the rights of individuals ties the idea of rights to fundamental moral interests. Thus John Rawls, for example, identifies two highest order interests of individuals as: the interest in being able to develop and exercise their 'capacity for a conception of the good'—a conception of how to live life well—and the interest in being able to develop and exercise a sense of justice. He elaborates his account of the basic liberties in terms of their service to these two highest order interests—for example:

freedom of thought and liberty of conscience are the background institutions necessary for the development and exercise of the capacity to decide upon and revise, and rationally to pursue, a conception of the good. Similarly, these liberties allow

---

[7] I take my stance on neutrality from Rawls, *Political Liberalism* see especially 199–201. I demonstrate that liberalism could not be neutral 'all the way down' in Brighouse, Harry, 'Is There a Neutral Justification for Liberalism', *Pacific Philosophical Quarterly*, 77 (1996), 193–215.

for the development and exercise of the sense of right and justice under political and social conditions that are free.

Freedom of movement and free choice of occupation against a background of diverse opportunities are required for the pursuit of final ends as well as to give effect to a decision to revise and change them, if one so desires. (Rawls, *Political Liberalism*, 310–24.)

It is misleading to think of all rights as liberties, and it is also misleading to think of all liberties as so-called 'negative' liberties. On any plausible account of fundamental human interests, individuals have an interest in adequate sustenance and shelter: these are preconditions of the pursuit of any of our other ends. So plausible accounts of rights will include some sort of rights to material resources, though these rights are described in different ways by different theories. Left-wing rights theories often invoke welfare rights, giving them the form of a right to an equal share of resources, or a right to an unconditional basic income.[8] More libertarian theories will invoke, instead, the rights to private property and to freedom of contract, claiming that as long as we have these rights our interest in acquiring a basic level of material resources will be sufficiently protected.

Note that in no theory of rights, left or right, is the state permitted to restrict its attention to protecting individuals from the interference of others, including the state itself, as is often suggested by the metaphor of 'negative' rights or liberties. All liberal theories of rights guarantee some sort of right to equal protection before the law, and most guarantee at least some limited right to participate in competitive elections. The right to equal protection before the law requires, in practice, that a court system be established through taxation of all citizens. The right to vote similarly requires a network of publicly funded institutions for its realization. Some libertarian theorists enjoy trying to show how even these rights could be realized through private markets, but whether they are right is an empirical question: recognizing these rights involves them in accepting that, in principle, taxation and government funding are legitimate if no other mechanism could, in practice, guarantee the rights successfully.

## The Significance of the Private Sphere

Liberals are famous for their endorsement of a 'private sphere' which merits the protection of the state. The metaphor of a 'sphere' suggests, and is

---

[8] For a version of equal resources see Dworkin, Ronald, 'What Is Equality? Part 2: Equality of Resources', *Philosophy and Public Affairs*, 10 (1981), 283–345. For a right to an unconditional basic income see Van Parijs, Phillippe, *What, if Anything, Justifies Capitalism?* (Oxford: Oxford University Press, 1996).

often taken by liberalism's critics literally to mean, some sort of physical space within which individuals must be free to act however they want to. This impression is supported by the language of many liberal theorists: most famously, Isaiah Berlin talks of 'barriers . . . non-arbitrarily drawn', and says that 'if I wish to protect my liberty . . . I must establish a society in which there must be some frontiers of freedom which nobody must be permitted to cross'.[9]

But the notion of a sphere really is a metaphor. The private sphere is not literally a physical space, but describes a range of permissible options among which the individual must be the sole arbiter of how they choose. So when the liberal state protects the private sphere it does not mark out certain physical spaces—households, churches, or workplaces—and say that whatever happens in those spaces is protected—wife-beatings, heretic-burnings, or exposure of employees to nuclear waste. Instead it describes areas of individuals' lives, such as sexual mores, religious affiliations, and dietary preferences, within which a wide range of choices must be protected, although even within those areas some choices may be punished such as where direct harm will be done to non-consenting others. Describing the private sphere is really just a matter of delineating the rights that one believes each individual has.

The family has traditionally fallen within the private sphere in liberal theory, and it is for this reason that it is particularly important not to be misled by the 'sphere' metaphor. The family is an interesting case because the initial units of the family—traditionally an adult male and an adult female—are presumed to have entered into that state voluntarily, so that whatever interactions they have are presumed to be consensual. Many actual states claiming a liberal mantle for themselves have indeed treated the household as if it were a physical space within which almost all is permitted: for example, rape within marriage has often not been recognized as a crime. If the private sphere were a physical space and the family, or household, fell within it, then the private sphere would be indefensible, as would liberalism, given its commitment to it.

But marital rape *is* a moral crime and is now normally treated as a legal crime, and once we understand privacy properly, we can see why liberals have to recognize it as a crime. Privacy protects a range of options, and liberal states are therefore very protective of the choices that individuals make. But there are limits. As J. S. Mill famously argued in *On Liberty*, a contract that subjects oneself perpetually to the will of another person—to enter slavery—would not be recognized as legitimate by a liberal state,

---

[9]  Berlin, Isaiah, *Four Essays on Liberty* (Oxford: Oxford University Press, 1969), 165.

since it would represent the permanent waiver of the right to self-governance that underlies the principle of privacy. The only possible defence of non-recognition of marital rape as a crime would be that women voluntarily enter a state of matrimony in which they promise to 'obey' their husband in all things. But, first, and least importantly, it is not clear that marriage has been a truly voluntary contract for many women, given that alternatives have been so unattractive. More importantly, when the marriage contract standardly involved the promise on the part of the woman to obey her husband, it resembled in a milder form a contract to enter a condition of slavery: the promise is a promise to subject oneself permanently to the will of another. As such it could not be recognized as valid by a truly liberal state. Without the promise to obey, of course, the marriage contract cannot plausibly be said to involve agreement to endure whatever evils one's spouse can offer. From the liberal state's point of view the marriage contract should be like other contracts: one that should be enforced only in so far as it specifies what the parties have agreed to.

The proper understanding of the notion of the private sphere protects liberalism from objections that construe the private sphere literally. But it does not help us to understand why the family should be in the private sphere, or what it means for it to be there. When the family consists only of two or more spouses, then the sense in which it is private is easy to see: since all parties entered the situation voluntarily, their private choice should continue to be protected. At least their continued association is consensual on all sides, and so unless one of them infringes the rights of another, the state has no business being involved. But once the family also includes children, the case breaks down. Children cannot plausibly be said to have entered the association voluntarily, and anyway they are not people whose choices the liberal state must respect. They are vulnerable individuals, persons in the making, and unlike adults, they cannot be taken to be the best, or even most appropriate, guardians of their own interests. Their interests must be protected by other agents: they need protection from themselves as well as from others. In treating the family as part of the private sphere the state effectively presumes that the parents are the most appropriate immediate guardians of the interests of their children. The question is why this should be. Before turning to that question I want briefly to introduce two final important aspects of liberalism.

*Autonomy and Toleration*

I have focused primarily on the institutional commitments common to different versions of liberalism. But there are two closely associated values that most versions of liberalism endorse in some form, and the tension between which shows up starkly when we consider the problem of the family.

Most liberals endorse the value of personal autonomy: indeed in many versions of liberalism it is the fundamental value underlying all other claims. Definitions of autonomy differ, and I shall elaborate a more precise account early in Chapter 4, but the broad common idea is that individuals should be able to be rationally self-governing, in the sense that they should be regarded as the ultimate arbiters of what reasons they choose to act on and what evidence and reasoning they take to be compelling with respect to what to believe. The requirement that we respect the autonomy of our fellow citizens implies that we must tolerate many of their beliefs and practices that we find objectionable or perhaps even deeply wrong, as long as those beliefs and practices do not harm non-consenting others. Some liberals demur from the central place I have suggested for autonomy, but nevertheless endorse the value of toleration for other reasons, but both autonomy-based and non-autonomy-based liberalisms give toleration a central place. Toleration in turn supports many of the institutional forms already described: it requires that we provide fellow citizens with various of the rights and freedoms that liberalism supports, and supports the notion of some sort of private sphere.

If the value of autonomy implies a requirement of toleration, how could there be a tension between the two values? This is impossible to see on the model that is the basis for much liberal theorizing, where society is constituted exclusively by adult citizens who it is reasonable to presume are autonomous. But when children are added to the model, the tension is quite stark. It is universal in human cultures that most adults consider their family life, and in particular their relationships with their children to be among the most important things in their lives. Parents do not merely see themselves as servants of their children's interest in becoming autonomous, but see their lives and values as intimately bound up in their relationships with their children. But, at the same time, many of their child-rearing practices may jeopardize the prospective autonomy of their children. As we shall see, autonomy is not a state that is trivially achieved, but one into which children have to be educated to some degree. Some parents reject the idea that their children should be autonomous; other parents place a low priority on the autonomy of their children compared with other achievements that they value; and even parents who claim to place a high moral priority on autonomy, will often find, in practice, that they have other desires that conflict with their children's developmental interest.

The tension should now be clear. Often, the child-rearing practices of the parents who revile or accord low priority to autonomy will be intimately connected to their views about what constitutes a good life. If we refuse to tolerate their child-rearing practices, and license government intervention, we seem to be denying them toleration altogether. But if we do tolerate the practices, we appear to be betraying the interest of the children in autonomy, and their ultimate prospect of becoming the kinds of people whose practices merit toleration.

## LIBERALISM, EDUCATION, AND THE FAMILY

The tension we have just identified is, in my view, only a tension, and not a paradox, or a problem so severe that it should force us to abandon liberalism as our guiding theory. And it could, of course, be resolved easily. We could eliminate the problem by abolishing the family. Children could be removed from their biological parents at birth and distributed to state-licensed child-rearing institutions in which they would be properly educated and raised to become autonomous. Their prospective autonomy would be ensured as well as possible, and the non-autonomy-respecting practices of their biological parents could be tolerated without fear for the children's well-being.

It is important to emphasize that this option is not one that any participant in the public or the theoretical debate about school choice, or education policy generally, for that matter, proposes. It is simply not on the table. Opponents of school choice are not opponents of the institution of the family: they, like the proponents of school choice, take it for granted that children should be raised within their biological families and that the biological or adoptive parents should have great latitude over how their children are raised. Only in extreme cases of abuse and neglect, according to the opponents of choice, should children be removed from their families. The vast majority of school choice proponents accept that in extreme cases it is permissible to remove children from the parental home, though the two sides may disagree about what counts as neglect or abuse in particular cases. The debate about school choice is simply not a debate about the family: the family is treated by all sides as a moral given.

It is worth our while, nevertheless, to take a look at the problems involved in justifying the institution of the family. I shall not offer a theory of the family here, but a tentative sketch of why the family matters. First, though, I should say that a great deal of the philosophical debate over the family has been confounded by two distinct confusions. The first is the confusion between the *status* of the right to raise a family and its *content*. The second is between the idea of the right to raise a family and the right to authority over one's children's upbringing. Conservative defenders of the family have tended to claim the *fundamental* right to authority over one's children's upbringing on the basis of arguments that only show that there is a *fundamental* right to raise one's own family. Similarly they have tended to claim *extensive* rights over one's children's upbringing on the basis of arguments that really only show that one has a *limited* right to raise one's family.

Let us take the distinction between kinds of status first. The most usual context in which we think of rights, and the model from which other cases must be derived, is the model of rights over oneself. But there are two kinds of status that individual rights can have. Some rights are regarded as fundamental claims that are morally prior to the facts of social organization. The right to physical and psychological integrity of the person is usually thought to be of this kind: the claim to one's own body parts is one that constrains completely the design of social institutions, and any organizational framework that failed to observe it would be unjust. Similarly the right to freedom of religion or freedom of conscience is usually thought to be fundamental in this way.

But some rights, at least on some accounts, are not like this. Some rights are not regarded as fundamental in the sense that they are prior to the organization of society, but are regarded as having a secondary, or auxiliary status. For many liberals, democratic rights have this secondary status: it is not that individuals are fundamentally owed a say in how our common life is governed, but that giving all individuals such a say is the institutionally most reliable way of protecting those rights that really are fundamental, or those values that really do matter. On many theories some rights are fundamental, and others are secondary. But on other theories no rights are fundamental, but rather have this secondary status. Under utilitarianism, to give the most obvious example, what really matters is just the promotion of utility, but given the facts of human nature and social organization it can most reliably be achieved by having governments uphold a certain range of rights.

The right to raise a family departs from the standard model of rights in that it cannot be thought of as a right over oneself, but is usually thought of as a shared right over others. If parents have a right to raise a family then they have rights over their children regardless of the preferences of the children or others. As such it is extremely unusual: as James Dwyer has pointed out there are no other contexts where we normally treat individuals as having rights *over* others.[10] But it is, in our debate, nevertheless considered a right by all parties. To regard it as fundamental is to regard it as a right that directly constrains the just organization of social institutions. But it could alternatively be looked at in the following way. The family could be regarded as the most convenient and most effective institutional assignee of our general obligations towards children. This stance accepts that all adults have extensive obligations toward all children, including but not limited to the obligations to provide them with roughly equal opportunities and to ensure that they become autonomous persons; and says that no adult has any more right fundamentally to care for any child than any other adult. But the stance acknowledges that most of us are ill-positioned to deliver on those obligations directly. Instead, we deliver on them by supporting a social division of labour that assigns special responsibilities for individual children to those who are best positioned to treat those children as required. These are normally those whose activities lead to their birth, or who have made an adoptive commitment, so an arrangement whereby parents have immediate contact with their child is the most efficient way of ensuring that each child gets his or her due.[11]

When we focus exclusively on the interests of children, the case for a secondary right to raise a family seems very appealing. Even if we believe that all adults are obliged to provide for the needs of all children and none has a prior right to have a connection with any particular child recognized, it is unquestionable that each child needs to have some particular person or persons who will provide him or her with the unconditional love, support and attention that are the foundation for a successful and happy life. Each child may be entitled to the impartial concern of all adults, but that is valueless without the loving attention of some particular adult. It is, furthermore, important that this loving attention be a response to the child itself, not to some pecuniary reward offered by society. The commitment to offer this love, attention, and support for a lifetime is not something we can expect many adults to take on as a paid profession. But biological parents and, perhaps even more, adoptive parents, seem well placed to provide it. Of course, some parents will fail to provide sufficiently for their children, and where those failures are both identifiable and rectifiable, social welfare agencies are obliged to intervene, either to support and educate the parents or, at the limit, to remove the children to a more appropriate

---

[10] See Dwyer, James, *Religious Schools vs. Children's Rights* (Ithaca, NY: Cornell University Press, 1998).

[11] This kind of relationship is spelled out with respect to the relationships among co-nationals in Goodin, Robert, 'What is So Special About Our Fellow Countrymen', *Ethics*, 98 (1987), 663–86.

environment. But to accept this is not to deny the right, just to limit its scope or content.

However, the account of the right to raise a family that appeals exclusively to the interests of children seems unsatisfactory. Most of us think of the right to raise one's own children as fundamental. Parents have interests as parents that also count for the purposes of institutional design. Children may come first, but the claim parents have to a relationship with their children is not simply dependent on their ability to serve their children well—it is also related to the value they will get out of the relationship. We think that the family matters partly because families are the receptacles of many of our best experiences. It is within the family that lasting and deep bonds of affection find their greatest realization. However much we value our country, our political views, careers, sports teams and intellectual traditions, these commitments are abstract in a way that only our closest personal relationships transcend. The family is not the only institution within which such personal relationships occur, but we first learn about those relationships in the family. The love and affection parents feel for children, in particular, is for many the single greatest source of reward in their lives. This is not a quirky or eccentric human tendency, and nor is it one that has been merely socially constructed: it is widely and naturally shared.

It might be objected that many parents seem to get along perfectly well with minimal contact with their children. Many parents—fathers in particular—abandon their children and have little contact. Indeed, in the traditional nuclear family fathers have often had very limited relationships with their children. But the right response to these observations is not to accept that people can get along well without relationships with their children, but to ask whether those parents—fathers especially—really have enjoyed adequate lives in the absence of relationships with their children. Not only have they failed, in many cases, to deliver on their obligations to their children but their lives have been impoverished by their absence from their children's lives. Our most urgent moral concern is, of course, with their children, but that should not obscure our sense that their lives have been diminished.

The account I have briefly sketched supports the idea that the right to raise a family is fundamental. But establishing the fundamental status of this right does little to establish the content of that right. It is often assumed that if the right is fundamental it is also extensive, but that just does not follow. The interest in the relationship supports the conclusion that parents should be allowed to raise their children, but it certainly does not establish that there are no limits on *how* they should raise them. The fundamental right to control one's own sexual behaviour gives one discretion over whom to choose as a sexual partner, but the right to raise one's child yields no discretion whatsoever over whom to choose as their sexual partner. The right to suicide appears to follow from the right to self-governance; but there is no right to infanticide supported by the right to raise a child. To construct a potentially more controversial example, suppose that there were a drug available that would produce firm and unshakable belief in the divine right of kings. The right to self-governance might give one the right to administer that drug to oneself; but it is hard to believe that parents would have a right to administer it to their children.

The question of precisely what authority parents should have over their children's upbringing, then, is not resolved by deciding the status of the right to raise one's children. My suggestion is that we should unpack the rights involved in the right to raise a family, and recognize that some of those rights are fundamental, but conditional, while others are not. The considerations I have raised referring to the interests of parents suggest that parents have a fundamental right to have intimate relationships with their children, which are conditional on their protecting certain of the children's interests. Failure to protect those interests amounts to a forfeiture of the right, in the same way that failure to obey just laws amounts to a forfeiting of one's right to freedom of association.[12] However, a limited right to control over one's children's upbringing can be justified only by appeal to the interests of the children themselves, and is thus a secondary right, whose content is limited. If children's interests in general are best served by a division of authority between parents and some other agency, then that division is to be preferred over giving parents exclusive authority, as long as this division does not infringe the fundamental rights of parents to intimate relations with their children.

If parents had unrestricted authority over their children's education then the rest of this book would be unnecessary: it would be clear that parents had the right to choose exactly what education their children should get, including the right to choose that their children get no education at all. But the account I have given immediately supports only the right to live with, and associate intimately with the children, not the right to control their education. We shall discover that the rights of parents to control their children's education are narrow, though we shall also discover that it does not follow from this alone that parental choice should be rejected.

---

[12] And, just as when someone forfeits their right to freedom of association by breaking the law, courts may sometimes refrain from imprisoning them for the sake of the good of the rest of society, when someone forfeits their right to raise their child, courts may sometimes refrain from terminating that right for the sake of the good of the child.

## CONCLUDING COMMENTS

I have offered a brief and tentative sketch of why the family should be taken as a given when thinking about education policy and social policy in general. From the sketch it does not follow that parents have extensive rights over education, but nor does it follow that they do not. In Chapters 4–7 we shall repeatedly revisit the question of parental rights over education, and a much fuller account of what is and is not appropriate will emerge. First, though, I want to look at the main arguments for school choice, and a series of common arguments against it that ultimately fail.

# 2

# The Case for Choice

School choice is the leading idea of educational reform in the English-speaking world today. Since the late 1970s it has not only been a central policy prescription of the new right, but also one that has helped to forge the coalition of conservatives and libertarians that has kept the new right politically viable. The idea that parents should choose which schools their children attend neatly appeals to both the ideological commitment to the market of the libertarian right and the 'family values' agenda of genuine conservatives, thus helping to diffuse the profound disagreements these two groups have about the proper content and goals of the educational curriculum.

In practice, the policy has had variable success. The England and Wales—henceforth referred to as the UK, with apologies—*Education Reform Act* (ERA) of 1988 embodies a highly regulated version of school choice, which allows parents to choose among government-run schools all of which are constrained by a detailed national curriculum, and which also gives schools the power to select among applicants. In 1989 New Zealand adopted a set of reforms devolving to public schools far more responsibility for how they were run. It has recently adopted a pilot programme whereby disadvantaged children are funded by the government to attend private schools chosen by their parents. Similar reforms have been adopted by many states in Australia, and the Federal Australian government subsidizes all private schools, with the size of the subsidy determined by the mission and the resources of the school in question.[1]

---

[1] Whitty, Geoff, *et al.*, *Devolution and Choice in Education* (Buckingham: Open University Press, 1998), provide more details of choice-oriented reforms in these countries, the US and Sweden in Chapter 1. The book is also a magisterial synthesis of the evidence on choice up to that point. On the UK see also Walford, Geoffrey, 'The 1988 Education Reform Act for England and Wales: Paths to Privatization', *Educational Policy*, 4 (1990), 127–44; Edwards, Tony, and Whitty, Geoff, 'Parental Choice and Educational Reform in Britain and the United States', *British Journal of Educational Studies*, 40 (1992), 101–17. On

The United States, with its locally governed school system, has less scope for national educational reform. There are currently four identifiable versions of school choice in operation in the US. Since the early 1990s trial private voucher programmes run by non-profit charitable concerns, and mostly funded by large corporations, have been continuing in Milwaukee, San Antonio, Indianapolis, and New York City; other programmes have since been established in thirteen other cities. These programmes generally provide choice only among a certain range of private schools, and are directed at children of poor families. They are extremely small: in 1994–5 these programmes assisted 6,572 students in seventeen cities. Nor do the programmes represent any kind of policy victory: they are run not by cities or school districts, but by businesspeople, without any kind of democratic mandate.[2]

Second, there are choice mechanisms *within* the public school system itself. In part, public school choice developed in response to judicial pressure for racial integration: magnet schools in particular were often developed as a response to, or to pre-empt, integrationist court orders. Inter-district transfer programmes allowing children from inner-city schools to choose places in suburban districts have allowed suburban schools to resist pressures to merge with the inner-city districts: these programmes have been the basis for several academic studies of school choice.[3] In addition, some public school choice schemes were devised to facilitate parental involvement in the public schools and to improve already integrated facilities. Most famously, East Harlem District No. 4 has twenty-three high schools organized around different themes, application to all of which is available to all parents in the district.[4] Public school choice, however, appears radical only because neighbourhood schooling has become such an established part of the US public school system.

New Zealand see Wylie, Cathy, *Self-Managing Schools in New Zealand: the Fifth Year* (Wellington: New Zealand Council for Educational Research, 1994). On Australia see Angus, Max, 'Devolution of School Governance in an Australian State School System: Third Time Lucky?' in Carter, David G., and O'Neill, Marnie H. (eds.), *Case Studies in Educational Change: an International Perspective* (London: Falmer Press, 1995).

[2] For an account of these plans, see Moe, Terry M. (ed.), *Private Vouchers* (Stanford: Hoover Institution Press, 1995). The figures are taken from page 14 in his introduction to the volume. See also Martinez, *et al.*, 'Who Chooses and Why: A Look at Five School Choice Plans', *Phi Delta Kappan* (May 1994), 678–88.

[3] See chapter 3 of Wells, Amy S., *Time to Choose* (New York: Hill and Wang, 1993).

[4] Other districts which have abolished attendance zones include Cambridge, MA and Montclair NJ. On East Harlem see Henig, Jeffrey, *Rethinking School Choice: Limits of the Market Metaphor* (Princeton NJ: Princeton University Press, 1994), 131–44. For a more partisan account see Fliegel, Seymour, *Miracle in East Harlem: The Fight for Choice in Public Education* (New York: The Manhattan Institute, 1993).

Neighbourhood schooling has never been elevated to the level of a guiding principle in the UK for example. The *1944 Education Act* which set the framework for the contemporary state school system in the UK established that 'The Minister and local education authorities shall have regard to the general principle that, so far as is compatible with the provision of efficient instruction and training and the avoidance of unreasonable public expenditure, pupils are to be educated in accordance with the wishes of their parents'.[5] It would be a mistake to think that public school choice, in turning away from neighbourhood schooling, also turns away from the fundamental principles of public schooling.

The third form of school choice is the Charter school. Charter schools are established by educational entrepreneurs in consultation with local school districts, but are exempt from much of the regulatory burden imposed by the state on public schools. The idea is that educational innovation can be fostered in the less constrained framework established, and the schools are funded by and accountable to the State. Parents may elect to send their children to these schools, which may not discriminate except on specified grounds. By 1998 thirty-three States had passed Charter school legislation, and over 1,000 Charter schools were educating more than 250,000 children. Because support for Charter schools is in some sense, bipartisan—leaders of the largest teachers union in the US, the National Education Association, and of the Democratic party, support Charter schools—they represent the form of choice likely to be most extended in the near future.[6]

The above three forms of choice are relatively uncontroversial. Far more controversial is the form of school choice most threatening to traditional understandings of public schooling: what is usually known as public/private school choice. Currently only two public/private choice programmes operate in the US: the *Milwaukee Parental Choice Program*

---

[5] Section 76, quoted in Stillman, Andy, 'Half a Century of Parental Choice in Britain?' in Halstead, J. Mark (ed.), *Parental Choice and Education* (London: Kogan Page, 1994). A subsequent Ministry of Education 'Manual of Guidance' (1950) elaborated eight reasons parents could give when choosing an alternative school to that which they would otherwise be allocated by the local education authority (LEA): denominational reasons; educational reasons; linguistic reasons; convenience of access; special facilities at a school such as the provision of midday meals for children whose parents both work all day; preference for single-sex or co-educational schools; family association with a school; and medical reasons. As may be apparent from the list there is a greater variety of kinds of school within any given LEA than within most US school districts.

[6] On Charter schools see Wells, Amy Stuart (Principle Investigator), *Beyond the Rhetoric of Charter School Reform: A Study of Ten California School Districts* (Los Angeles: UCLA School of Education, 1999); Finn, C., *et al.*, *Charter Schools in Action: The Final Report* (Washington, DC: The Hudson Institute, 1997).

(MPCP) and the *Cleveland Scholarship and Tutoring Program*. In public/private school choice parents have a choice between a range of public schools and a specified range of private schools within the area. If a private school is chosen then the public School District pays some proportion of the tuition at that school. It is, in effect, a programme of public subsidy for private schools, and thus does break with the fundamental tradition of public schooling that the government runs exactly those schools that it pays for through tax revenues.

We shall look in detail at the Milwaukee programme in Chapter 8, so I shall describe it only briefly here. Although, as we shall see, it has recently been revised and expanded, it was initially modest; the total number of students in the MPCP was limited to 1.5 per cent of the children in Milwaukee Public Schools. Eligibility is still limited to students from households with incomes up to 1.75 times the poverty income level and below who have not attended a private school, or any other school district than Milwaukee Public Schools, in the year prior to their entry into the programme. The qualifying schools were non-sectarian—a requirement that severely limited the attractions of the programme—and are subject to weak non-discrimination requirements in their selection processes. The schools receive the Milwaukee Public School per-member state aid for each eligible student enrolled.

The Cleveland programme supports more children and is not restricted to low-income families. While the Milwaukee and Cleveland schemes are modest, there have been attempts to establish other, more radical, schemes. California's Proposition 174—defeated in 1994—would have established a public/private choice system without eligibility limits for children. Schools would have had to meet only one requirement—non discrimination on the basis of race—and no inspectorate would have been established to enforce this. Religious schools would therefore have been eligible for subsidy. The proposition would also have established almost unattainable supermajority requirements for future regulation of participating schools. It would have provided a contribution toward tuition in the form of a voucher, but the amount would have been around $1,000 less per student per year than in the Milwaukee scheme thus ensuring that fewer low-income parents would be able to take advantage of it.[7]

The variety of schemes that are reasonably referred to as 'school choice' schemes make it incumbent on me to clarify my use of the term for the purposes of my argument. I shall use the term to refer to schemes that officially and directly give substantial weight to the preferences of parents

---

[7] See Jordan, Joel, 'Is Voucher Mania Defeated?', *Against the Current* 48 (1994), 3–5.

regarding the allocation of their children to schools. There is a contrast with two different models: the US model of neighbourhood schooling, and the now largely abandoned UK model of selective schooling.

In neighbourhood schooling, children are allocated to schools solely on the basis of where they live—every child from any given neighbourhood will attend the same school. As proponents of school choice delight in pointing out, neighbourhood schooling does involve an element of choice: parents who are wealthy and attentive enough can choose their neighbourhood on the basis of which school their child would go to. But this does not qualify the model as a choice scheme, since the choice mechanism is not direct. The selective model allocates children to schools on the basis of their demonstrated achievement in some sort of test. Children who score in the top 20–25 per cent of the test at age 11 or 12 are allocated to an academic school, while the others attend a vocationally oriented school, regardless of the preferences of their parents. Again, there is usually some scope for choice at the margins of this system: children selected for the academic school could choose the vocational school instead—as, famously, did UK National Union of Mineworkers leader Arthur Scargill—and wealthy parents whose children are allocated to the vocational school can buy an academic education for them by opting into the private sector. But the model does not allow any formal role for choice in the most important allocation decision, and so does not qualify as a choice model.

Another word about usage is important. The terms 'school choice' and 'educational vouchers' are often used interchangeably in public debate. A voucher scheme is only one mechanism for guaranteeing parents some degree of choice over what schools their children attend and, consequently, what kind of education they receive. Even programmes that are usually referred to as voucher schemes rarely literally deploy vouchers: usually the government does not issue a voucher to the parents, but pays a sum directly to the school on receipt of a request from the parents.[8] The notion of a voucher scheme is to be thought of as a perspicuous device for representing the idea of school choice and constraints upon it. Vouchers are, by their nature, limited: like food stamps and rationing coupons they embody the idea of what Michael Walzer calls a 'blocked exchange'.[9]

[8] The Milwaukee Parental Choice Program, for example, involves direct payments from the State of Wisconsin to the schools involved.

[9] Walzer, Michael, *Spheres of Justice* (Oxford: Martin Robertson, 1983), see especially 100–3 for elaboration of other blocked exchanges. For further discussions see Andre, Judith, 'Blocked Exchanges: A Taxonomy', *Ethics*, 103 (1992), 29–47 and Waldron, Jeremy, 'Money and Complex Equality' in Miller, David, and Walzer, Michael (eds.), *Pluralism, Justice and Equality* (Oxford: Oxford University Press, 1995), 144–70.

When a voucher is granted it represents a sum of money that can be spent on only one thing: the schooling of a particular child. By examining the proper regulative constraints on a voucher system we can represent the proper extent of parental choice over their children's schooling. I shall usually use the terms 'voucher scheme' and 'choice scheme' interchangeably, depending on what makes the most sense in the context.

It is undeniable that school choice has a great deal of popular support in those countries that have adopted it, and especially in the laggardly US. Opinion polls consistently show that a majority of voters support public school choice, and that a majority of poor and African-American voters support publicly funded private school choice. Even as early as 1986, a Gallup poll showed that 54 per cent of non-whites in the US supported publicly-funded private school choice; in 1989 67 per cent of non-whites, and 59 per cent of whites, supported choice within public schools. More recent polls show that the popularity of choice schemes has steadily increased. Gallup polls asking 'Do you favour or oppose allowing students and parents to choose a private school to attend at public expense' in 1993, 1995, 1996 and 1997 got a positive response of 24, 33, 36 and 44 per cent respectively. When the word 'government' was substituted for the word 'public' in 1997, the positive response rose to 48 per cent. When the Gallup poll asked, in 1998, whether respondents would favour or oppose a scheme in which their State paid 'all or part of the tuition' in a proposal allowing 'parents to send their school-age children to any public, private, or church-related school they choose', 51 per cent responded in favour, with support among non-whites at 68 per cent.

What success the more radical variants of school choice have had in the US has depended on a loose and uncertain Right-Left coalition between right-wing funding foundations and the so-called Christian Right on one side, and Catholic Dioceses and urban African-American activists and politicians on the other. It would have been impossible for this coalition to have been built without the dramatic failures of the urban public schools to serve urban African-Americans well: the support of African-American politicians in particular has been essential for giving credence to the claims of market ideologues that the poor will benefit most from such schemes.[10] This is not, of course, to say that most or even many African-American politicians support choice, but the existence of a critical mass of pro-choice black politicians with left credentials has played a pivotal role in making choice respectable.

[10] For a valuable account of the Milwaukee experience see Carl, Jim, 'Unusual Allies: Elite and Grass-roots Origins of Parental Choice in Milwaukee', *Teachers College Record*, 98 (1996), 266–85.

## FRIEDMAN'S CASE FOR VOUCHERS

The contemporary school choice debate is a rare instance of a public debate that is dominated by the academic work of a single author. First published as a scholarly paper in 1955, and republished in his 1962 classic work of political economy *Capitalism and Freedom*, Friedman's voucher proposal has had unparalleled influence. The themes of his original proposal echo in every discussion of choice, including, as we shall see, the work of left-wingers who support choice. Yet it has taken several decades for the influence to take effect. One professor of philosophy of education says that when he first taught about vouchers in the late 1960s students found the subject esoteric in the extreme, and neither he nor they imagined that this abstract, quirky, proposal would ever become a matter of intense debate among policy-makers.

This is not the place to explain the emergence of choice as a serious policy issue. But it is clear that Friedman is directly responsible for its appearance in public debate. The policy synthesizers at the Cato Institute in the US, and the Institute for Economic Affairs and Centre for Policy Studies in the UK, who first introduced the idea to right-wing politicians in the 1970s repeatedly cite and laud Friedman and draw on this and other of his ideas. For this reason, but not only for this reason, it is instructive to look carefully at his original argument. My comments on Friedman's argument, which I shall postpone to the final section of this chapter, set the stage for much of the rest of the book.

Public/private school choice appears to threaten the principle of public schooling as it is commonly understood because it separates the functions of providing schooling and paying for schooling.[11] Friedman's innovation is his simple observation that these two governmental roles, which are commonly assumed to be inseparable, are both analytically and practically distinct. Advocates of public schooling argue that the government has to pay for the education of minors, and also that the government

---

[11] Friedman, Milton, 'The Role of Government in Education' in Solo, R. A., (ed.), *Economics and the Public Interest* (New Brunswick: Rutgers University Press, 1955). My discussion will concentrate the slightly more recent and updated exposition of the proposal in chapter 6 of Friedman's *Capitalism and Freedom*. Vouchers have received increased attention recently, both due to the political movements around them, and the publication of Chubb, John and Moe, Terry M., *Politics, Markets, and America's Schools* (Washington, DC: Brookings Institution, 1989). For a balanced discussion of the current state of the debate, and a contribution to it, see Henig's *Rethinking School Choice: Limits of the Market Metaphor*. See also useful discussions in Clune, William H., and Witte, John F. (eds.), *Choice and Control in American Education: Volume 1* (London: The Falmer Press, 1990).

should run the institutions through which they are educated. But Friedman claims that, while there is a perfectly good argument that the government should pay for, or contribute to paying for, schooling, this argument does not support the idea that it should monopolize provision of—or even play *any* direct role in the provision of—the institutions through which it occurs.[12]

The argument that Friedman thinks justifies the government paying for some schooling is that education of children has what he calls 'neighbourhood effects': what would now more usually be called 'externalities':

A stable and democratic society is impossible without a minimum degree of literacy and knowledge on the part of most citizens and without widespread acceptance of some common set of values. Education can contribute to both. In consequence, the gain from the education of a child accrues not only to the child or his parents but also to other members of society. It is not feasible to identify particular individuals (or families) benefited and so to charge for the services rendered. There is therefore a significant neighbourhood effect. (Friedman, *Capitalism and Freedom*, 86.)

There are two important things to notice about this argument. First, as Friedman points out, it does not in itself justify what he calls 'nationalization' of schools.[13]

The desirability of such nationalization has rarely been faced. Governments have . . . financed schools by paying directly for the costs of running educational institutions. Thus this step seemed required by the decision to subsidize schooling. Yet the two steps could readily be separated. Governments could . . . [give] parents vouchers redeemable for a specified maximum sum per child if spent on 'approved' educational services. (Friedman, *Capitalism and Freedom*, 89.)

Some public goods, such as national defence and policing, may be provided efficiently only by the government. But for most, including education, all that is needed is that the government play an essential coordinating role, which in this case could, in principle, be limited to regulation of the market, injections of financial support for the consumers, and mandating some level of education for each child. The public goods

---

[12] He appears to think that in some circumstances it is proper for the government to run some schools as long as these are subject to the same regulations as private schools, and as long as there are not significant barriers to entry into the market: see *Capitalism and Freedom*, 93. Herbert Gintis explains how the government can regulate markets in schooling to overcome the most commonly posed barriers to market-entry in 'The Political Economy of School Choice', *Teachers College Record*, 96 (1995), 492–511.

[13] 'Nationalization' is the term used by Friedman just to mean public or state ownership. Although it is an odd context for use of the term, since for the most part these schools were never nationalized, never having been privately owned, I shall retain the usage while discussing Friedman.

argument, in other words, does support state funding of education, but it does not tell us anything about who should establish and run schools.

The second thing to notice is that Friedman believes that while maintaining social stability is properly thought of as a public good, the increased productivity of future workers through education is not, since competitive advantage in the labour market to a particular worker is overwhelmingly of benefit to that very person and much less benefit if any to others.[14] The 'vocational' benefits of education to the individual, then, cannot be used as a justification for government funding though he does recognize the practical difficulties in disagreggating the vocational from the civic effects of education.

Whether schooling should be run by the government depends, for Friedman, on whether nationalization will be an efficient form of delivery. He poses a voucher system as a more efficient alternative, in which the government would provide each parent with a voucher for some substantial portion of the cost of schooling and allow them to purchase schooling from private institutions. The only role of the government would be 'insuring that the schools met certain minimum standards, such as the inclusion of a minimum common content in their programs, much as it now inspects restaurants to insure that they maintain minimum sanitary standards'.[15] He elaborates a series of efficiency and equity benefits that could be expected from a voucher system.

Vouchers would, according to Friedman, widen the range of choices available to parents by permitting the establishment of a wider variety of schools and choice among them. They would also make choice effectively available to all parents, whereas under current arrangements choice is available only to those parents who can relatively easily move between and within school districts, or afford the fees of private schools from their after-tax income.[16] Vouchers would also prevent the possibility of the vicious circle in school districts where parents who send their children to high-quality parochial schools apply political pressure to lower the taxes levied to fund public schools, thus worsening the quality of the public schools and giving the parochial schools even greater relative advantage. Since parents could 'express their views of schools directly by withdrawing their children from one school and sending them to another'[17] they would have more control than at present over the structure of the school and the

---

[14] Of course, there are public productivity benefits from the overall workforce being educated up to some threshold. Friedman seems to think that the requisite threshold could be achieved without government funding.

[15] *Capitalism and Freedom*, 89.          [16] *Capitalism and Freedom*, 91.

[17] *Capitalism and Freedom*, 91.

content of the curriculum. The influence of professional educators over
the structure of the profession would decline, and in particular the current
uniformity of teachers' salaries would be broken up, thus enticing 'the
imaginative and daring and self confident' who are currently 'repelled'
from the profession.[18] The diminishing influence of teachers unions would
probably lead to lower labour costs, and even if it did not do so, the introduction of a more flexible labour market would ensure that good teachers
would be paid well and bad teachers paid badly, thus increasing the incentive for talented people to enter the teaching profession.


## THE GENERIC CASE FOR CHOICE


As I've said, Friedman was writing over forty years ago, and for the first
twenty of those years his arguments were neglected by everyone except
free-market ideologues and a few liberals who were deeply disenchanted
with the inequities in the public school system. Since the early 1980s,
though, the ideas of choice and vouchers have gained ground. The different arguments for choice are not deeply connected; some do not in themselves justify school choice, for example the equity argument; most
proponents of choice will endorse some but not other arguments; but most
cases for choice utilize some subset of these arguments. In this section I
will briefly summarize the basic arguments.

### Parental Rights

Some argue that choice over the content of their children's education, and
hence the schools they will attend, is one of the rights parents have over
their children. There are two versions of this argument. Some think that
parents' rights over their children are fundamental, so that any direction
by the state over such things as the children's education or health, beyond
some minimal standards of non-abuse, is illegitimate. Others do not claim
that a fundamental right is at stake, but point out that *some* agency has to
make paternalistic choices on the part of children, and that parents, who
know their children well and care about them deeply, are better placed to
make good decisions than the state or any other agency. Although there is
nothing about being a parent that gives you fundamental rights over your
children, a society that genuinely wants to protect children's interests will
grant strong rights to parents.

[18] *Capitalism and Freedom*, 96.

*Parental Involvement*

The standard bureaucratic allocative model alienates parents from the school, and there is evidence that parents whose children attend private schools are more involved in their children's education. Where parents get to choose which schools their children attend, they are more likely to be involved in the educational process, which in turn will have benefits for the education of the children. Of course, the evidence that this does happen is weak—parental involvement in fee-paying private schools is no evidence that parents who will not have to pay will become involved. Although evidence is emerging from the Cleveland scheme that applicants for vouchers who received them get more involved in their children's schooling than applicants who were rejected, it may be the novelty of the experience on the one hand and irritation with a system that they had sought to abandon on the other which are at work. But the psychological assumption, that when people are allowed choice they will be more involved, has some basis in fact.

*Efficiency*

Many proponents of choice echo Friedman's theme that costs of schooling can be driven down by choice, at least when choosing private schools is an option. Private schools in the US currently provide education at a much lower per-pupil cost than do public schools. Opponents of vouchers point out, rightly, that private schools have no obligation to educate children with disabilities and special educational needs, and that they are free to expel trouble-making children without due process. They are, furthermore, free of unions, so that labour costs are lower. Even if the introduction of vouchers for private schools helped to drive down costs by weakening unions—as Friedman speculates—this would be undesirable, since it is important both for the morale of the profession and its ability to attract talented people, that teachers be paid a union wage or better.

The point about unions is important, and I shall talk more about the importance of maintaining high wages for teachers in Chapter 3. But there is another, clearly desirable, way in which vouchers might be expected to reduce costs. Parents directly involved in choosing between schools are likely to look askance at the very high costs of bureaucracy in some, especially public, schools. This effect is especially likely in the US. Wisconsin, a typical state in this and many other ways, has 427 school districts serving a population of 5 million. Many of those districts administer just a single K-12 school, which has, in addition, its own management team.[19] In other words, there are two management teams, replicating each other's work. A typical urban high school has at least 5 principals—on-site school managers who do not teach—all earning significantly more than the mean teacher's salary in the school, none of whom teaches in the classroom. Just as many charities boast of their low administrative costs in their efforts to compete for charitable contributions, schools would be forced by market pressures to disclose the proportions of their budgets spent on administration; and parents would be likely to take that into account in their decision-making. As Samuel Bowles and Herbert Gintis point out, under non-choice regimes there are three major barriers to schools being accountable to parents. A diverse set of parents often will not agree with each other; there is no incentive for the school leadership to come to agreement with parents; and when they do agree, parents have neither the information or means to enforce accountability.[20] The point about vouchers, and choice generally, is that they constitute a mechanism whereby parents can directly penalize the leaderships of schools for not meeting their expressed interests. This provides school leaderships with an incentive both to deal with parents and to implement agreements.

The concern with efficiency, it should be noted, is not typically presented as being in conflict with a concern for equality. In some areas of public policy, advocates of market mechanisms say that the redistributive ambitions of egalitarians are a drag on economic growth, so that efficiency and equality are seen as rivals and efficiency is favoured. But school choice has egalitarian defenders—like Bowles and Gintis—who argue that precisely because it is more efficient, school choice makes educational equality easier to achieve. Bowles and Gintis argue for a voucher scheme in which all vouchers are worth the same amount and in which participating providers are forbidden from accepting any top-up in addition to the voucher. Forbidding the top-up would have an equalizing effect that would be, in their view, *enhanced* by the accountability of the school management teams to individual parents.

Some opponents, and a very few proponents, are unconcerned with efficiency: the very language of efficiency echoes the language of business and industry from which the world of education is supposed to keep a respectable distance. However, although they rarely suffice to determine the proper outcome of a real-world political or moral choice, considera-

[19] See Hassler, John, *Staggerford* (New York, NY: Ballantine Books, 1985) for a fictionalized account of life in a small rural school district.

[20] Bowles, Samuel and Gintis, Herbert, 'Efficient Redistribution: New Rules for Markets, States, and Communities', *Politics and Society*, 24 (1996), 307–42 at 323.

tions of efficiency are moral considerations that are properly taken seriously in political decisions. Inefficiency is wasteful, and waste is bad, because it constitutes an opportunity cost. If we could get exactly the same results under Plan A costing $100 as under Plan B costing $150, we are morally bound to choose plan A, since that will free up resources for expenditure on other socially valuable projects. If the same level of educational achievement as the *status quo* achieves could be achieved at half the cost under some set of reforms, thus freeing up resources for expenditure on health care, medical research, anti-poverty measures, or more education for the least advantaged, then those reforms should be pursued. Opponents of choice should not dismiss the efficiency claims of proponents: they should either show that the claims are false, or that they are gained at the expense of other more fundamental values.

## Diversity and Innovation

School choice is, in theory at least, liable to produce a greater diversity of schools. Parents seeking religious education of a certain stripe can support schools giving that education. Parents who want their children to specialize in languages, science, or the arts, can patronize schools offering such programmes. Schools espousing different educational philosophies will attract clients, leading to a diversity of practices and facilitating experimentation. Some theorists value diversity for its own sake. As will become clear, I am sceptical of that position. But everyone has a reason to value diversity of schooling practices instrumentally. It is only if a diverse range of practices are pursued enthusiastically by teachers and management teams that those practices can be rationally compared for their educational effectiveness: diversity is required for improvement of our practices over time. The claim in favour of choice is that it enables schools to innovate, without forcing them to, which would detract from the effectiveness of the innovations. Deborah Meier pinpoints the mechanism by which choice allows this. Describing her experience in the establishment of Central Park East, a school in the choice-giving East Harlem District No. 4 with a commitment to progressive methods of education and democratic self-management with parental involvement, she says that at the end of the second year a schism emerged within the ranks of the staff, exacerbated by a group of parents. 'Only the steady support of the district, the backing of the vast majority of parents, and the *existence of alternative choices for the dissatisfied* cut our losses and made this brief rebellion a blip in our history' (my emphasis).[21]

[21] Meier, Deborah, *The Power of their Ideas* (Boston, MA: Beacon Press, 1995), 25.

*Equity*

There is something deeply inequitable about a system that effectively accords parental choice only to the wealthy. Under the non-choice system, as Friedman enjoys explaining, parents can express their choices, but 'in general they can now express this choice only at considerable cost—by sending their children to a private school or by changing their residence. For the rest they can express their views only through cumbrous political channels.'[22] The wealthy can get their children into desired schools simply by spending money: those without money cannot. Choice mechanisms within public schools, and even more so with a public/private choice, iron out this inequity to a considerable degree, by granting poor parents some degree of control over their children's educations. Pointing this out is one of the strongest rhetorical moves of choice-proponents. Bob Dole, defending vouchers during the first Presidential Debate in 1996, put it this way:

It seems to me that we ought to take that money we can save from the Department of education and put it into opportunity scholarships and tell little Landale Shakespeare in Cleveland Ohio . . . we're going to match what the state puts up and you're going to the school of your choice. I don't fault the President or vice president for sending their children to private schools or better schools. I applaud them for it, I don't criticize them. But why shouldn't everybody have that choice? Why shouldn't low income Americans and low middle income Americans? . . . It's going to be a big, big opportunity for a lot of people.   (First 1996 Presidential Debate, 6 October 1996, Hartford, CT, transcript on file at *Commission on Presidential Debates*, Washington, DC.)

Of course, this inequity can be eliminated without extending choice to all, by depriving the wealthy of choice. This would require the prohibition of all private schooling, and some kind of allocation mechanism within the compulsory state schools that ensured that allocation was never affected by factors over which wealthy parents had more control than poor parents. The problem is that most opponents of choice—especially in the United States, but also in most other countries—do not advocate the prohibition of private schooling. Some claim that to do so would violate the rights of parents to choose their children's schools, and draw a distinction between the right to send your child to a school of your choice, and the right to have the state pay for you to send your child to the school of your choice. Others, believing this distinction to be spurious, believe that private schools should be prohibited but remain silent, fearing that espousal of abolition would lose them whatever mainstream audience they

[22] *Capitalism and Freedom*, 91.

have. Furthermore, even those who are willing to advocate abolition would have great difficulty elaborating an allocation mechanism that would be insensitive to factors over which wealthy parents can make choices, and that would not require unacceptable levels of state intrusion into people's lives and choices. So complete removal of choice as a factor in how children are allocated to schools is probably impossible.

## Mimicking Effect

Some argue that choice can have the advantage of improving schools by less well-informed parents identifying and mimicking the decisions of better informed parents. There is some evidence from studies of choice in the UK that working class parents choose on less educationally-relevant bases than do professional class parents. But the UK experiment is relatively young, and if schools were sufficiently restricted in their ability to select children, and if sufficient information about who chooses what were available, then this effect might occur.

## Real Libertarianism

A final argument for school choice is that it is supported by the general, and now widely accepted, principle that 'the state should not deny choice to those who want it unless there are very powerful, reasonable, and well documented grounds . . . for doing so'.[23] David Hargreaves has recently claimed that this is the fundamental, and common sense, principle of a 'libertarianism' that should be shared across the political spectrum. Libertarianism in political philosophy usually refers to the family of theories that give the principle of individual liberty a central place in political morality and claim that liberty's centrality precludes the permissibility of government redistribution of material wealth and provision of other goods. But there is a more intuitive sense of libertarianism in which it just asserts the prima facie desirability of individual choice. The contrast is not with left-wing views about distributive shares, but with two positions, both of which can be found in otherwise very different parts of the political spectrum, that Hargreaves dubs quasi- and anti-libertarianism. *Antilibertarianism* flatly embraces a 'thorough-going denial of choice and diversity', claiming that other more central values, such as distributive justice, intrinsically preclude making available significant choices to

[23] Hargreaves, David, 'Diversity and Choice in School Education: A Modified Libertarian Approach', *Oxford Review of Education*, 22 (1996), 131–41 at 133.

individuals.[24] *Quasi-libertarianism*, while allowing for the possibility of deploying choice in principle, does not accord it any intrinsic value, and assumes, in the case of educational provision, that enough is known about the consequences of choice to justify immediate restrictions on any element of choice allowed in the system.


## PRELIMINARY COMMENTS ON THE GENERIC CASE


Several of the arguments in the generic case for choice appeal to empirical speculations about the likely effects of choice. Choice is claimed variously to improve outcomes by involving parents more in schooling, to reduce the costs of schooling by making school leaderships accountable through market mechanisms, to produce more innovation and a greater diversity of schooling options; and even to improve the overall performance of schools and narrow the inequality of educational outcomes. For all their apparent confidence, defenders of choice like Friedman, Tooley, and Hargreaves are quite frank about the speculative character of their case: many opponents of school choice, like those I shall consider in the next chapter, are much less frank.

It is important to understand that, while there has been a burgeoning of empirical study of choice schemes over the 1990s, none of it can answer decisively whether choice will have the effects claimed for it by its defenders or attributed to it by its detractors. This is because the choice schemes we have experience of, all have distinctive features, and each has features that can explain away its failure to live up to the desired results. Take the Milwaukee Public Choice Program for example. As we shall see in Chapter 8, a close study of this programme, commissioned by the politicians who implemented the programme, has shown fairly convincingly that it has produced no educational benefits. But supporters of the programme can, reasonably enough, say that this is not surprising, since the best low-cost private schools in Milwaukee—the Diocesan Roman Catholic schools—were not included. Now they are included, and benefits may be forthcoming.

Similarly, the most ambitious study of the operation of the 1988 ERA, which looks at several diverse LEAs (Local Education Authorities) in the Greater London area shows a cleavage between the schools that attract

---

[24] ibid., 131–41 at 137. The position and its consequences for education policy are outlined on 136–7.

and admit children from middle class and professional families and those from working class families.[25] But, choice-proponents will argue, this points to the need to educate working class parents in how to choose well, and the need to restrict further the discretion schools have over which students to admit: the Milwaukee scheme, note, gives the schools barely any discretion at all. James Tooley argues that 'it would be far better if the parents and/or children [who bring more money to the school because of their educationally relevant disadvantages] were made more aware of their added "purchasing power"' and that 'government incentives could be given to encourage the setting up of independent agencies to advise on choice of schools perhaps along the lines of *Which?* or *Consumer Reports.*'[26] It might be added that non- and quasi-governmental organizations like trades unions could be licensed or encouraged to educate working class parents in the process of choosing schools. Geoffrey Walford argues that, in the UK, oversubscribed schools should be forced to select students by lottery, constrained, perhaps, by a sibling rule.[27] A recent study of Charter schools in California has found that they often have more choice over who attends than parents have in whether their children attend; that the regulation requiring schools to reflect the racial make-up of their communities has not been enforced; and that the schools are not being held accountable for the academic achievement of their students.[28] But, again, the findings impugn the regulatory regime and its oversight rather than the institution of Charter schooling itself.

Most of this book is not concerned with the empirical evidence concerning school choice. This may seem ironic, since part of my aim in this book is to argue that the actual effects of school choice are crucial to its evaluation; and that the right baselines of comparison are with the effects of schooling either as it is currently delivered or as it would be delivered by alternative feasible non-choice-based reforms. But not only are the empirical studies inconclusive about choice, even when they are conclusive about the particular schemes they consider, there is, as I pointed out in Chapter 1, insufficient agreement about what standards the education system should be held to for there to be a consensus on the implications of empirical studies for policy. Efficiency, scope of experimentation, and equity all matter, but they are not all that matter, and trade-offs may have

---

[25] Gewirtz, *et al.*, *Markets, Choice and Equity in Education* (Open University Press, 1995).

[26] Tooley, James, 'Choice and Diversity in Education: A Defence', *Oxford Review of Education*, 23 (1997): 103–16 at 107.

[27] See for example, 'Diversity and Choice in School Education: an alternative view', *Oxford Review of Education*, 22 (1996): 143–54.

[28] Wells, *Beyond the Rhetoric of Charter School Reform*, 2.

to be made among them as well as between them and other values. Even when the empirical studies of choice schemes tell us a good deal more about choice than they currently do, political philosophy will still be indispensable for determining their implications for policy. So while I argue that the evidence is important, mainly by dampening the appeal of arguments that say that school choice should be adopted or rejected as a matter of principle, independently of its practical effects, I also elaborate the values that must be used when trying to determine the implications of the evidence for policy.

## REFUTING THE REAL LIBERTARIAN ARGUMENT

The three principled considerations in the generic case are the appeal to equity, the appeal to parental rights, and the libertarian principle. I shall consider the relevance of equity and parental rights to the issue in subsequent chapters. I want to close this chapter by explaining why the real libertarian principle, although well motivated, does not support school choice in the way that Hargreaves suggests.

As Hargreaves imagines, many theorists will reject the libertarian principle in the first place. Anti- and quasi-libertarianism both have their supporters across the political spectrum. Although Hargreaves describes libertarianism as a 'common sense' position,[29] he seems to be wrong about this. Common sense has it that prescriptive morality is about, as Trollope's Mrs Proudie would have it, 'the promotion of good and the eradication of evil'. On this view we look at sets of feasible institutional arrangements and ask which does best at promoting the best ratio of good to evil. Making choice available would be supported by common sense only in those areas of people's social and private lives where its availability will systematically encourage people to do the right thing or live well: there is no presumption in favour of choice. In other words, common sense morality supports anti- or quasi-libertarianism, and not libertarianism.

Aware that libertarianism stands in more need of defence than just the claim that it is common sense, Hargreaves invokes the language of various international human rights documents. Such documents tend to support individual rights to choice in certain spheres of civil society and, in particular, they are almost unanimous in enshrining parental rights to choice concerning the education of children. The wording of these human

[29] Hargreaves, 'Diversity and Choice in School Education, 133.

rights documents, though, does not suffice to show that parental rights to choice concerning education are 'firmly grounded in a democratic conception of rights'.[30] The documents could be flawed in any of a number of ways, and given the circumstances of their drafting and endorsement by representatives of, in many cases, far from perfect governments, it would not be surprising if they were flawed. To show that the right to parental choice is rationally grounded in a defensible conception of rights we would have to show that the proper moral foundation for human rights yields this parental right.

As I have suggested in the previous chapter and shall argue further in Chapter 5 the documents are indeed flawed in securing unconditional parental rights over education. This wrongness, though, follows from the truth in real libertarianism.

Why is real libertarianism generally a good starting point? There are two common strategies for vindicating libertarianism. The first, which I think underpins Hargreaves' use of it, is a *moral strategy*. The second, which I shall consider only briefly, might be called an *economic strategy*.

The moral strategy starts by directly asking the question: why should it matter more that people have choices about how to live their lives, than that they live their lives well? The answer is roughly as follows. It is claimed that social institutions should embody a presumption of equal respect for persons. The presumption of equal respect should make us reluctant to coerce our fellow citizens especially in matters concerning how they lead their own lives, but also even in many matters concerning the common good. Guaranteeing people individual freedom matters because freedom enables them to live their lives by their own lights: to do the good as they see it. A good life needs to be led from the inside, as it were, endorsed by the person who leads it. Unless we grant people freedom we cannot be sure that they do endorse the life that they lead.

The notion of respect deployed here is closely connected to the notion of personal autonomy. To coerce someone, especially in matters concerning their own life and not that of others, is to show disrespect for their personal autonomy. It is to presume either that they are incompetent judges of their own good, or that they are morally defective in some crucial ways. And, even if they are morally well-built and competent, it deprives them of the ability to lead their life from the inside. The idea is that, except where compelling considerations require, we should not abrogate to ourselves, or to our agent, the state, power over the lives of others, but should grant each person power over him or herself. One does not have to be

[30] 'Diversity and Choice in School Education', 133.

right-wing to endorse this libertarianism: by itself it implies nothing about the proper distribution of resources, except perhaps that everyone should have access to an adequate standard of living. Only extreme conservatives and defenders of once-existing state socialism need deny it.

Now I think we can see why libertarianism does not establish any presumption that parents be allowed to choose their children's education. First, and most obviously, libertarianism implies that people be allowed to choose in matters concerning their *own* lives. Parents are not their children. When they make choices concerning their children's education they are not making choices about how to live their own lives, but about how someone else will end up living his or her life. Granting them choice does not grant them power over themselves, but power over someone else.

The key to defending libertarianism is an acceptance of the need to respect other people's autonomy. Children are not autonomous. They are people who, if treated in the right way, can come to have personal autonomy, and hence become the kind of people whose choices and freedom it is important for us to respect. Because they are not autonomous, and not capable of becoming autonomous without some help, we should establish institutional arrangements that will, among other things, enable them to become autonomous persons. This may involve us in establishing a pattern of parental choice concerning education, but it may not. No presumption in favour of school choice is established. It might well be argued that part of becoming an autonomous person is that one becomes independent of one's parents in ways that at best make the parents uneasy. Irresponsible parents simply seek to shape the outlook of the child in their own image. But even responsible parents, whose better judgement supports libertarianism, will often find it difficult in practice to let go of their children, and will sometimes be inclined against their better judgement to frustrate their children's prospective independence and autonomy. Libertarianism thus establishes a mild presumption against choice in that it supports a hard *restriction* on school choice: that school choice can be considered only in so far as it will not compromise the opportunity of the children involved eventually to become autonomous choosers. In short, it is entirely correct to be a thoroughgoing libertarian with respect to adults but that position makes no sense unless one is a quasi- or anti-libertarian with respect to children.

Where does this leave the various international documents on human rights Hargreaves invokes, which enshrine the prior rights of parents to determine the educational direction of their children? The *Universal Declaration of Human Rights* grants parents a 'prior right to choose the kind of education that shall be granted to their children'. The *International*

*Covenant on Economic, Social and Cultural Rights* respects the liberty of parents to 'ensure the religious and moral education of their children [shall be performed] in conformity with their own convictions'. The consistent libertarian is forced to say that these provisions are simply mistaken. Parents do not have such rights, and the documents that claim that they do 'efface the distinction between the freedom of parents and the autonomy of children', to quote Elizabeth Anderson.[31] To grant parents those rights in the unconditional way stated in the human rights documents is to jeopardize the opportunities of children to become autonomous persons, something which, as I shall demonstrate in the next section, other adults do not have the right to do.

Although it holds no appeal for Hargreaves, something should be said about the alternative strategy for defending libertarianism, the economic strategy. The economic strategy appeals to the value of efficiency. The idea is that some set of predefined goals is better served by allowing individuals to make choices within some sphere of activity than by allowing some set of administrators to gather information about interests and allocate goods according to some plan. The most familiar version of this argument is that for free markets in the allocation of consumer goods, which assumes that the most important social goal is that people get the package of goods they most want, and claims that this distribution is best achieved by allowing individuals to choose among goods provided by firms that compete on a free market.

The economic strategy does not, in fact, support libertarianism. The *value* it espouses is that of efficiency, which is a real and important value, but that does not establish any presumption in favour of freely made choice. Different social goals will be served efficiently by different mechanisms depending on the institutional context. There are good empirical reasons for thinking that markets are relatively efficient with respect to the production and allocation of consumer goods. But markets do badly at allocating consumer goods *equitably*, especially if markets in consumer goods are nested within institutional arrangements including free labour markets. If equitable distribution is a valuable social goal, markets must be regulated, or some of their effects negated through redistribution. Whether choice should be favoured depends on the goals we think should be produced efficiently. The economic strategy supports neither libertarianism nor quasi-libertarianism, but agnosticism about choice: there is no presumption either in favour or against it, until the empirical evidence is in, with respect to some social good.

[31] Anderson, Elizabeth, *Value in Ethics and Economics* (Cambridge, MA: Harvard University Press, 1993), 163.

There are particular reasons for suspecting that choice is inefficient with respect to educational goals, at least if we take neo-classical economics seriously. I shall show in the next section that the purpose of state-sponsored education is to deliver on obligations that all adults in a society have to each of the children in that society. In neo-classical theory the result that markets allocate goods efficiently depends on the assumption that the consumer is also the purchaser. Yet the purchasers in a choice system are not the recipients of the schooling—the children—but third parties—the parents. Children, precisely because they are children, are presumed not to be effective choosers, and because of the content of our obligations to them it is crucial that schooling is allocated to them efficiently with respect to those obligations. To re-establish the symmetry with neo-classical theory we would have to show either that in every case parents are good proxy consumers, or that parents basically have moral ownership of their children. The latter position is both false and incompatible with libertarianism. The former position is simply implausible; many adults are not even effective consumers when deciding for themselves. That fact does not matter when judging the appropriateness of markets in consumer goods because it is often reasonable to hold poorly-choosing adults responsible for their own poor choices. But allowing a child's future prospects to be determined by her parents' bad choices is tantamount to holding her responsible for *other people's* bad choices, which is morally outrageous.

## MILTON FRIEDMAN AND THE PUBLIC GOODS ARGUMENT FOR STATE FUNDING OF SCHOOLS

In concluding this chapter I want to comment on Friedman's acceptance of the public goods argument for state funding of schools. Friedman is both diagnosing and endorsing what he takes to be the standard case, and I accept his diagnosis. Nevertheless one of the surprising themes of this book is that this almost uncontroversial case is largely irrelevant to the question of whether and how the government should fund and regulate education.[32]

Friedman's case for funding is essentially a standard public goods argument. There is no canonical definition of a public good in the economic or

---

[32] For rather different reasons than mine James Tooley also regards this case as irrelevant. See *Disestablishing the School* (Aldershot: Avebury Press, 1995), especially chapter 6.

philosophical literature. Garrett Cullity identifies seven different features of which some subset is usually included in most definitions:[33]

*Jointness in Supply*: if a public good is available to one member of the group for which it is public, then it is available to every other member at no cost to any member.

*Non-excludability (or non-exclusiveness)*: if anyone else is enjoying it, no-one else can be prevented from doing so without excessive cost to would-be excluders.

*Jointness in Consumption*: one person's consumption of the good does not diminish the amount available for consumption by anyone else.

*Nonrivalness*: one person's enjoyment of the good does not diminish the benefits available to anyone else from its enjoyment.

*Compulsoriness*: if anyone receives the good, no-one else can avoid doing so without excessive cost.

*Equality*: if anyone receives the good, everyone receives the same amount.

*Indivisibility*: there can be more than one consumer of the good and each consumes total output.

The most usual features included are the first four: the last two, equality and indivisibility, are rarely included, and since they are so clearly not true of any of the outcomes of education, I shall say no more about them.

What are some examples of public goods? Clean water is often cited: a group of people might combine to sanitize the water in the Mediterranean, but they cannot, without immense additional costs, prevent others who do not contribute to the process of sanitization from using the Mediterranean. It exhibits jointness in supply and non-excludability, and effectively exhibits jointness in consumption and nonrivalness. National Defence exhibits the first five features, and arguably the other two as well.

Is education a public good? This is not the right question, as Friedman recognizes. The right question, for him, is whether education provides goods that are, in some important sense, public, and, as Friedman recognizes, it usually provides the public good of stability for the civic polity. Social stability is valuable to everyone: it provides a framework within which different people can plan and pursue diverse ends with confidence and security. It exhibits jointness in supply and consumption, nonrivalness and nonexcludability, and compulsoriness. If some significant level of education for almost the whole population is essential for civic stability in a

---

[33] Cullitty, Garrett, 'Moral Free Riding', *Philosophy and Public Affairs*, 24/1 (1995): 3–34, at 3–4. I have followed Cullitty's rendering of these features almost word-for-word. For the sources of these features see his appendix, 32–4.

modern society, then a system of almost universal compulsory education is needed to provide this public good.

Friedman does not consider, however, the other main outcome of education, its vocational benefit, to be a public good. Yet in some sense it clearly is, and most defenders of state support for schooling regard it as such. That the vocational benefits are in some part public is easy to demonstrate. Imagine that Sidney is the only member of his society who received an education past the age of 10. As an adult, in a completely uneducated society, his Ph.D. in engineering will not earn him a decent salary—the economy on which high salaries for the well-educated depends would not exist. Everyone depends, for their economic well-being, on an economy that can only survive if peopled by a largely educated population; just as everyone depends on a civic order that is sustained only by a population that is reasonably well educated.

Friedman knows this perfectly well. Why, then, does he treat the vocational benefits as irrelevant to the case for public financing? The answer is quite simple. In the case of civic stability, assuming that most of the rest of the population is sufficiently well educated to ensure stability, any individual gets no extra civic stability benefit from being educated herself. There is, in other words, no private benefit involved. But in the case of vocational benefits, although everyone gets a benefit from other citizens being educated above some threshold, the main benefit of an individual's education is the increase in her own productivity and potential earnings. Although there is a public good produced, the main good produced is private. For that reason it is reasonable to require the private beneficiary to pay privately for the benefit, and furthermore, there is not the co-ordination problem in production that there is with public goods that do not have a private side.

One can, and many theorists do, reject Friedman's view that the state should not fund vocational education, while endorsing the public goods case for funding. For many defenders of public schools the public goods case supports funding for both the civic and the vocational aspects of education, at least up to the age of 16 or 18. What I want to show here, is that, while Friedman is right to diagnose the public goods case as underlying much thinking about public schooling, the public goods argument does not, in itself, support even government funding, let alone government provision, of education. The problem with the public goods argument is that to acknowledge that some institution produces a public good is not *sufficient* to justify having the government fund it, or even to make any effort to ensure that it is provided.

It will be useful for our purposes to distinguish between two kinds of government expenditure. First is expenditure on goods that are *required by justice*—to give an uncontroversial example, spending on a court system capable of providing the right to a fair trial for all. The state bears responsibility for providing such goods in its capacity as an agent on behalf of the individual members of society: it is as moral agents that we owe one another the right to a fair trial, and the state is the mediating body through which we deliver each other that right. A second kind of expenditure is on what we might call *'mere' public goods*—goods that are indeed public in the standard sense, but that the government would not be committing an injustice in failing to provide. There is no stricture of justice requiring that the government sponsor an interstate railroad system, even though, let us suppose, an interstate railroad system would provide a public good.

The standards of justification for expenditure on goods required by justice and mere public goods are different. As suggested, the government is required to ensure that goods required by justice are provided, and must spare no expense in making sure that they are present.

But for funding mere public goods, three conditions have to be fulfilled. First, it must be shown that no-one's fundamental rights are violated by the taxation or regulation required to ensure provision. If, for example, the public good of efficient transportation could be provided only by violating the personal property and security rights of some group of individuals, then it would not be permissible for the government to provide it: rights trump public goods. Second, it must be reasonable to think that the public good would not come about but for government action, otherwise the government activity is wasteful. For example, there is a current vogue in the US for municipal governments subsidizing sports stadia. In many cases it is quite apparent that the stadiums would be build by private enterprise regardless, and in no case is there any reason to think that the benefits brought by the sport to the city would be undermined by the absence of the subsidy.[34] Finally, it must also be reasonable to expect that the opportunity costs of ensuring that the good is provided will not exceed the benefits produced. In the case of the sports stadia, the subsidies could be used to fund healthcare, education, or to support tax cuts: unless the subsidies produce more good than those alternative uses would, the money is wasted.

In treating schooling as, in effect, a mere public good, Friedman fails to bring out the most important features of schooling. It is probably true that, up to some fairly minimal standard of provision, government funding of education as a public good passes the three tests described above.

---

[34] See Crompton, John L., 'Economic Impact Analysis of Sports facilities and Events: Eleven Sources of Misapplication', *Journal of Sports Management*, 9 (1995), 14–35.

But there are two problems. First, it is almost certainly the case that while education gives rise to a public good in a way that justifies government funding to some minimal degree, the public good does not justify universal *mandatory* provision of education. All that civic stability requires is that some large critical mass of citizens are educated to a certain threshold, not that all are. There is a good analogy with universal inoculations here. The eradication of diseases such as measles, polio, and smallpox requires that almost everybody is vaccinated against them, but not that absolutely everybody is. What matters is just that sufficient numbers are vaccinated that the disease cannot get a hold. A few people can free ride on the vaccination of the others. So large scale vaccinations produce a public good but no additional good is produced for anyone by vaccinating the final fraction of a percent of the population. What, then, justifies compelling the final fraction of a percent to receive vaccinations? Not, clearly, the public goods argument. There are a number of possible justifications, but two stand out. One is that it is unfair that the final fraction of a percent should be free from the risks taken by all the others while enjoying the same benefit. This is a fairness- or justice-based argument, not a public goods argument.[35] The other is that, while it would be more efficient to vaccinate all but the final fraction of a percent, because there is no way of selecting the exemptions that would be publicly understood to be fair, the social solidarity required for acceptance of mandating the threshold level of vaccinations would be undermined—in order to ensure the required level of vaccination we have to mandate universal vaccinations.

Of course, education is unlike vaccinations in that it delivers private benefits to the recipient that cannot be obtained any other way, in particular that cannot be obtained by having others educated. But a public goods justification is not sensitive to *these* benefits. Furthermore, unlike vaccinations, there is no risk attached to receiving an education, so there is no reason for an individual to seek to avoid it and free-ride on the activities of others. Again, a public goods justification is not interested in this; and anyway, this fact means that the social solidarity argument for

---

[35] I find this argument persuasive in this case but must confess that I cannot say exactly why. That there is free-riding is never sufficient to make even a prima facie case for government intervention. Free-riding is a pervasive and unavoidable feature of social life, and while some free-ride on the efforts of others in one area, those others free-ride in other areas. There are serious social opportunity costs to having everybody do something which only some need to do in order to produce desired good, quite independently of the social and moral costs of compulsion. So there always has to be some additional purpose to justify government intervention. See Andrew Levine 'Rewarding Effort', *Journal of Political Philosophy* (forthcoming).

making provision universal that worked in the vaccination case will not be needed in the education case. The relevant fact for the public goods justification is that each additional recipient of education adds to the cost of educating. The public good of civic stability should be bought at the lowest possible cost, which is the cost of educating just that threshold number of children that need to be educated to produce the good.

This brings me to the second, and most important, problem with the public goods justification of funding education. We have to ask ourselves what our view about government funding of education would be if we found that the public goods argument did not work for funding education. Would it mean that the government should stay out of education? My view, which I would hazard that most people who use public goods arguments for government funding of education would share, and which I shall vindicate in Chapters 4 and especially 6, is that it would not. The discovery that the public good argument was false would not lead most of us to reject government funding or regulation of education. Why? Because education is not a mere public good, but a requirement of justice.

As moral agents we each have an obligation to other people's children to ensure that they get a decent education. Having the state pay for schooling through taxation is the mechanism by which we fulfill this obligation. In other words education for minors is like the right to a fair trial in that it is a good the provision of which must be guaranteed by the state as a matter of justice: it is something that all adults are obliged to provide for each future adult. Arguments using this form constitute *individualist* justifications for state funding of education that do not appeal to the public good produced thereby. While education is a public good, it is its status as a private good to which all have a right that obliges us to provide it.

The above claim may seem surprising. In everyday politics, defenders of public schooling typically appeal to its status as a public good to justify increasing or maintaining funding for education: Friedman is right to claim that neighbourhood effects play a major role in public political arguments for public schooling. But I think this reveals a deep error in standard thinking about public schooling: the public goods argument treats children as a resource for society, whereas the proper approach treats them as vulnerable wards whose interests must guide society's approach to them. This error has, however, a fairly simple institutional explanation. The rhetoric surrounding demands for public schooling is an artifice of the political context within which funding and provision must be argued for. In order to get voters to impose taxes on themselves and on corporations to provide schooling, it seems necessary to appeal to their own self-interest: to claim that they get a benefit from the education they are forced to pay for. Sometimes the appeal is transparently false: the very elderly and the very wealthy do not get as much benefit from the education they are forced to fund as they would from the money that is taken from them. When, as it often is, the appeal is true, it is more likely to be effective than appeals to the independently justified rights of children. But even where the appeal is true, it is, strictly speaking, irrelevant to the moral justification of the funding, even though it is relevant to the possibility of getting the funding.

Accepting that education is a requirement of justice does not tell us much about how much the government should fund or how it should regulate its provision. I shall argue for two principles that should govern educational delivery in Chapters 4 and 6, and defend them against objections in Chapters 5 and 7.

# 3

# Three Red Herrings

Although, as we saw in Chapter 2, some enthusiasm for school choice has come from the political left, most of the enthusiasm in recent years has been from the right. The response of the left has largely been negative. In this chapter we shall review three arguments against school choice which have been offered by, usually left-wing, political theorists, all of which are, as we shall see, unsuccessful. They are all, also, arguments with considerable currency: certainly in the US context they are very commonly heard, in one form or another, from activist opponents of school choice. Although each of the arguments fails, reviewing them is extremely informative, because it turns out that two of the arguments rely on very common mistakes about what matters of principle are relevant to the design of education policy. One of the surprising conclusions of this chapter is that neither value of democracy nor that of a common or public good should have much to do with the design of educational institutions.

## THE ARGUMENT FROM COMMODIFICATION

One charge frequently made against school choice is that it results in the commodification of education, by making its distribution subject to, albeit constrained, market forces. Education, the charge goes, is one of those goods—like personal and sexual relationships, like children, and some other goods—which by its nature should not be a commodity. Alex Molnar puts it as follows:

Over time, market values have eroded and debased the humane values of democratic civil society. Listen closely to the language that already fills discussions about school reform. It is the language of commerce applied to human relationships. Children are defined as 'future customers', 'future workers' and 'future taxpayers' . . . When the logic of the market is allowed to dominate society, relationships are inevitably turned into commodities to be bought or sold. (Molnar, Alex, *Giving Kids The Business*, 184.)

John McMurtry goes even further:

The demand that [education] operate in terms of [the market's] opposed requirements, as has been increasingly demanded of the educational process, implies the
negation of education as such.   (McMurtry, John, 'Education and the Market
Model', 216.)

The commodification charge is unconvincing, not because choice does
not commodify education, but because some degree of commodification
of education is both unavoidable and unobjectionable. Before I substantiate that claim, we should look at the standard kinds of reasons given for
thinking that commodification of some kind of good is objectionable.
Three reasons are commonly offered. The first is that commodification
reduces the scope for public democratic deliberation. I shall look at this
objection in the next section. The second and third focus instead on the
character of the good itself. A perfectionist argument is made that the
good in question has a certain kind of value. The second kind of objection
says that when the good is valued in the ways supported by market-
exchange a wrong is done, and the third objection makes a causal claim
that the character of the good being purchased is altered resulting in a loss
of an important source of value.

For many goods that are thought to be non-commodities both the
wrongness claim and the value-loss claim are made. Take sexual intercourse. It is often argued that making sexual intercourse available in a
legal market allows people to value sex in the wrong way—that is, shorn
of its proper connections to personal affection. It is also argued that having sex available on the market changes the character of sexual relations
for even those people who never purchase or sell it. Similar arguments are
commonly made concerning permission for commercial surrogate moth-
erhood. It is sometimes claimed that commercial surrogacy treats babies
wrongly, by treating them as things to be bought and sold on markets; and
sometimes that licensing this behaviour leads people who never engage in
it to alter the ways in which they value their own relationships toward their
own children and parents. Richard Titmuss, in his famous book *The Gift
Relationship* argues that allowing a legal market in blood discourages
blood donation because it causes people to disvalue the act of donating
blood, and thus leads to a downturn in public altruism, as well as to less
blood being available.

Whether the wrongness and value-loss claims are true of the commodification of some good depends, of course, on the specific character of
good in question. Sex and parenthood are two goods for which the argument does sound initially plausible, while the argument would be very

strange indeed if applied to standard commodities such as television sets and cans of orange juice: the moral standing of the latter goods is relatively uncomplicated, and probably unaffected by the mechanisms by which they are distributed. But even when the arguments work, they do not necessarily tell us how the state should act with respect to the goods. To show that some form of behaviour is wrong is not sufficient to demonstrate that the state should outlaw it. Furthermore, even if we were convinced that, for example, legalizing commercial surrogacy brought about a serious cultural loss, we might be willing to bear that loss if we had reason to believe that the practice would lead to more children being well cared for and more adults having the satisfaction of rearing children.

What about education? Is it the kind of good which would be wrong to commodify, or commodification of which would cause some serious value loss? Education, of course, is never bought directly. We might want to make a distinction between education and schooling parallel to the distinction between health and health care, and acknowledge that what is bought is schooling, while what the purchaser hopes to acquire through the purchase of schooling is education. Now, it does seem reasonable to fear that prevalence of market mechanisms might contribute to a common confusion between schooling and education on the part of consumers and proxy consumers. Some parents appear to believe that attendance at school should be sufficient for their children to emerge educated, whereas getting an education from schooling requires active participation which is sometimes not forthcoming.[1] But this confusion is possible under any delivery mechanism, and the way to combat it seems to be by having a clear public explanation of the character and value of education.

Like most claims concerning commodification, any causal claim that the value of education is distorted or destroyed by allowing significant weight to parental choice in the delivery mechanism is speculative, and so, therefore, is any denial. For that reason the question cannot be settled satisfactorily here, but I am sceptical. We can at least say that education does not seem to be the kind of good or service which it would be *wrong* to buy or sell, in the way that recreational or reproductive sexual services might be. An extremely complex world requires that we engage in a social division of labour such that some people devote much of the working part of their lives to acquiring the skills needed to teach well. Every adult member of society is enabled to contribute to delivering justice to children by the fact that they can pay specialists to do the job. Teaching is, of course,

---

[1] During my first experience as a teaching assistant in a university in the US I was told by a student who had failed an exam that he should have got a passing grade because he had paid $1500 to take the course.

a vocation, in the more romantic sense evoked by such cultural icons as
Mr Chips and Miss Brookes. But it is *also* a job, which should be valued,
and paid for, in monetary terms, as well as in other ways. If the service is
not paid for, at least within a monetary economy, those who are not teachers fail thereby to value the teachers properly, as well as failing properly to
value their own obligations of justice to provide education for children. It
is a matter of justice to children that society designs institutions so that
some people become good teachers and get paid to live their lives that way.
In this sense education *must* be bought, at least, and as such differs very
greatly from the kinds of services associated with prostitution and commercial surrogacy.

These considerations help us to show what is wrong with John
McMurtry's argument that education should not be commodified. His
arguments state rather crisply the objections to markets which are made,
in a rather murky way, in a great deal of literature on education; so considering them will be instructive. He analyses the goals, motivations,
methods, and standards of excellence of education and the market, and
claims that 'the aims and processes of education and the market are not
only distinct but in deep respects contradictory'.[2] Whereas the goal of the
market is to maximize profits, the goals of education are advancing and
sharing knowledge; the motivation of market actors is to satisfy wants, but
the motivation of educators is to develop understanding whether or not it
is wanted. The methods of the market are to buy from and sell to
whomever is willing to sell or buy, whereas the method in education is to
require of all who want it that they fulfil its requirements autonomously.
The standards of excellence in the market are how well a product is made
for a sale and how problem-free it is, and remains, for the buyer; but in
education, excellence is displayed in how disinterested and impartial its
representations are and how deep and broad are the problems it poses for
one who has it.[3] From the opposing logics of the two institutions,
McMurtry concludes that 'if [the application of the market model to the
public educational process] is permitted to continue, and demand becomes
compulsion, *it must end in the destruction of education itself*, though
doubtless the market model would continue to advertise some of its wares
as educational' (my emphasis).[4]

Notice that the conclusion here is a strong empirical prediction, based
on an argument which is entirely conceptual. I would quibble with some
of McMurtry's observed oppositions—market entrepreneurs have much

---

[2] McMurtry, John, 'Education and the Market Model', *Journal of Philosophy of
Education*, 25 (1991), 211.

[3] Ibid., 211–12.                                    [4] Ibid., 216.

more varied and complicated motivations and goals than McMurtry allows, as, for that matter, do educators—but for current purposes we can assume that the oppositions are basically correct. But it just does not follow from these oppositions that markets will, in fact, drive out education. Whether or not they do can only be determined by careful empirical analysis.

There is nothing strange about organizing institutions in ways that require different actors to have quite different aims and processes. Sports leagues typically involve quite precise divisions of motivational labour: players seek to win games; owners of teams seek to maximize profits; and league organizers seek to regulate the sport so as to optimize its public popularity. Health systems similarly involve opposed motives on the part of different actors. The patient wants to get, or stay, well, the physicians and nurses are motivated variously by the desires to care well for patients, fame, success, income, etc.; the administrators, whether in socialized system or an insurance-market based system, are concerned to control costs and deliver whatever services are provided as efficiently as possible. The socialization of the service does not, or at least should not, remove the opposition between the goals of the administrators and those of the patients, since the administrator acts in the service of the public which has a public interest in having the service work efficiently so that otherwise wasted resources can be freed up for other social purposes.[5]

So even where aims and procedures are in some analytical sense opposite, it is not in any sense necessary that the aims of the market dominate, still less that they drive out the value of the good being marketed. One obvious market which thrives despite clear analytical oppositions in aims and processes is the market in art. Artists themselves are motivated by a great variety of considerations: they seek fame, self-expression, or to promote revolution, in society or perhaps only in their own art-form, but a central 'analytic' aim of most artists is to produce work of aesthetic worth. Buyers have similarly varied aims, but one central aim for many institutional buyers is purely and simply investment: they seek to make money through their purchases. But the profit motive, though analytically as opposite to that of producing aesthetic worth as it is to that of advancing and sharing knowledge, does not drive out aesthetic worth. In order to succeed at investing in art, the investor has to consult with the opinions of those who are informed about the aesthetic worth of particular works. Bad art may succeed in the short term, but the investor who seeks to maximize profit over the long term needs to identify work which is not yet as well

---

[5] I'm grateful to Francis Schrag for the health service example.

valued by other investors as it will be in the long term by aestheticians, art critics, and informed private and institutional collectors. The market includes a mechanism whereby profit-seeking needs to be informed by aesthetic value.[6]

Whether markets—and in particular parental choice—in schooling will drive out education, depends on how those markets are regulated. Even the introduction of schools privately run for profit, to the range of schools among which parents may choose need not necessarily drive out education if the schools are properly regulated. Erik Wright expresses fears similar to some of McMurtry's when he predicts that:

because of parental shopping, school administrators will be under considerable pressure to compete with other schools for students. Instead of seeing education of children as a common mission requiring the exchange of ideas and best practices across schools, schools will feel threat from other schools. Advertising will become a core preoccupation of schools and, as in most commodified advertising, the goal will be to seduce rather than to inform. (Wright, Erik, 'Equality, Community and "Efficient Redistribution"', 363.)

If schools are allowed to choose among students, then there may be a serious problem here: cherry-picking, or cream-skimming, the best students will become a normal practice, and parents will clamour to get their children into the schools which are known to cherry-pick successfully. But if, as in the Milwaukee Public Choice Program, and in most left-wing proposals, school administrations are required to fill spaces by lottery when oversubscribed, the problem need not be so serious. District 'support teams' can be established, who are free to work in any schools, and whose mission is to disseminate knowledge of the most effective practices. Furthermore, it is important to note that the comparison has to be with the best possible non-choice schemes: and even in the best possible non-choice schemes members of school management teams will often be moved by the desire for prestige and future career prospects to refrain from sharing knowledge of successful practices with their colleagues. Wright's concern with the potential seductiveness of advertising would be less serious where schools had no selection powers, but it might still advantage schools to target the parents of the most attractive students with seductive advertising, by swelling the number of 'cherries' in the applicant pool. But even this concern could be met by requiring that schools publish, in accessible form, certain crucial information which would ensure that parents were able to choose schools which provided good informa-

---

[6] See Cowen, Tyler, *In Praise of Commercial Culture* (Cambridge, MA: Harvard University Press, 1998) for a subtle defence of markets in the arts.

tion. For example, schools could be forced to publish value-added tables: the average and median improvements in scores in externally administered tests for their pupils; and the ratios of their administrative expenditures to classroom expenditures to profit. Shareholders might find highly profitable schools very attractive, regardless of their educational success; but, if they are well informed, parents, who provide access to the money from which the profits come, will presumably want to see the maximum possible spent on their children, and will patronize profitable schools only if they are educationally very promising.

So it certainly does not follow from the considerations offered by McMurtry that markets in schooling drive out education, as long as we understand that markets are never the perfect markets of introductory economics textbooks, but always real institutions which are publicly regulated in some form and within which actors have a variety of motivations. Nor does the unacceptability of for-profit schooling follow from his argument, nor, crucially for our purposes, does the unacceptability of parental choice over schools.

Commodification-based arguments against markets generally presume a model on which only the market and nothing else is determining the distribution of the kind of good. But, as we have seen, in any viable voucher scheme there are *some* other determinants. Government regulation affecting both the distribution and the character of educational opportunities is not opposed by any advocate of school choice; and, as I have already indicated, even a scheme with much government regulation could properly be considered a choice scheme. Exactly how much is determined by market processes and how much by government regulation depends on the details of scheme as well as what happens in practice when they are implemented. As Friedman points out, choice has a role in allocation even in a system in which all schools are government schools and there is no formal role for school choice: some parents will decide among occupational and housing options on the basis of what schools those options would lead their children to be placed in. So the difference between that system and a voucher system is one of degree, not kind.

## THE ARGUMENT FROM DEMOCRACY

Democracy is one of the most widely accepted political values, and many theorists, especially of the left, claim that schooling should be subject to democratic control. Tim Brighouse asks of local administrative bodies 'why one would not make such a body democratic. In short, why should one mistrust the rule of the local people by the local people?'[7] Stuart Ranson similarly argues against market outcomes that they are 'literally outside anybody's control'.[8] Amy Gutmann sees democracy as the best value to ground educational policy, arguing that 'a democratic state of education' captures the rational kernel of each rival approach by recognizing 'that educational authority must be shared among parents, citizens, and professional educators'.[9]

A second objection, then, is that school choice improperly takes the governance of educational institutions out of the scope of democratic deliberation, and into a private sphere governed by market norms. Alex Molnar explicitly counterposes the ideal of democracy to markets in education: 'the debate about public education cannot be understood by thinking only about schools. It is part of a much broader struggle: whether America will move in the direction of its democratic ideals, or be further ensnared in the logic of the market.'[10] The objection does not depend on the evils of commodification for the character of the good placed on the market, though it is often conflated with the commodification objection, but says that since democracy is a crucial value, to place schooling outside democratic control is a serious wrong.

There are two ways of taking this objection, corresponding to two ways of viewing the value of democracy. It could rest on the view that democratic control of education is valuable *in principle*, and should not be relinquished even for the sake of better educational outcomes, however those are defined. Let us call this the 'intrinsic view'. Or it could rest on the view that intrinsically valuable educational goals will be better served by democratic control than by other forms of governance. Let us call this the 'instrumental view'.

Let us take the instrumental view first. Elizabeth Anderson argues that a:

principal purpose of education [at the primary and secondary level] is to prepare children for responsible citizenship, exercised in a spirit of fraternity with others of diverse class racial and ethnic backgrounds. The good of elementary and secondary education requires that its reasoned ties with such ideals be preserved.

---

[7] Brighouse, Tim, *A Question of Standards: the need for a local democratic voice* (London: Politeia 1996), 13.

[8] Ranson, Stuart, 'Markets or Democracy for Education', *British Journal of Educational Studies*, 41 (1993), 333–52 at 335.

[9] Gutmann, Amy, *Democratic Education* (Princeton, NJ: Princeton University Press, 1987), 42.

[10] Molnar, Alex, *Giving Kids The Business* (Boulder, Co.: Westview Press, 1996), 184.

People cannot see that their preferences for certain kinds of education are supported by publicly valid reasons unless they have a forum in which these reasons can be publicly evaluated. (Anderson, Elizabeth, *Value in Ethics and Economics*, 162.)

This forum is in turn provided by democratic governance, and is not present when the choices people make about their children's education are privately determined and expressed through the exercise of their option to exit from a school which is not providing what they want.

Anderson concedes that market mechanisms may have some facility for enabling parents to participate in the governance of private schools. She objects, however, that, since education provides a public good in which all have an interest, parents should not have exclusive access to the governance of the providing institutions. But the defender of choice can respond that vouchers are not incompatible with democratic governance. Whether or not they should, the citizenry can exercise democratic control over the educational infrastructure by placing conditions on the institutions which are permitted to cash in the vouchers to the state, on the model by which the US federal government places affirmative action requirements on private universities which apply for financial aid for their students. Such control is indirect, but it is control nevertheless, and there is no limit in principle to what conditions can be put in place. So appropriate public control of the providing institutions is compatible with the use of choice in allocating children to schools.

Some opponents of vouchers might say that Anderson's argument for democratic governance is insufficiently foundational, and that direct democratic control of basic social institutions is a fundamental principle of egalitarian political morality. I have conceded that vouchers do not facilitate direct political control, only indirect democratic governance. Furthermore, I agree that, generally, democratic control of social institutions is, or should be, a basic principle of egalitarianism. It is worth, then, reviewing why democratic governance of the institutions providing primary and secondary education is not intrinsically, but only instrumentally, valuable.

The intrinsic view rests on a mistaken inference from the fact that democracy is generally intrinsically valuable. Democracy is constituted by a set of procedures which confer legitimacy on decisions made about the matters which properly lie within its scope. The idea is that it is a requirement which flows from our obligation to presume an attitude of respect for others that we make available to them roughly equal opportunity to influence what happens in our shared circumstances. The legitimate scope of democracy is limited by this idea of shared circumstances: so, for example, some matters of individual privacy lie outside the reach of legitimate democratic decisions, because they lie outside the realm of our shared circumstances properly considered.[11] On this understanding of the value of democracy its intrinsic value is gained from seeing it as essentially a relationship between adults, who are obliged to treat each other as moral equals. The proper scope of democratic discretion is, furthermore, circumscribed by the other, individual, rights of citizens.

Educational institutions, however, mediate relations between adults and children. We establish, design, and pay for educational institutions to fulfil obligations which hold between us and children. There is no reason for us to treat children as our moral equals: indeed it would be thoroughly inappropriate for us to do so, because we know that they are not our equals. They have rights against us, such as the rights to protection, shelter, health-care, education and provision for other of their needs. Our obligation is to provide for them conditions and opportunities by which they are liable to become our moral equals. This is why, for example, it is appropriate for us to have stricter controls over sexual relations between adults and children than among adults. More generally, this is why both the state and parents should treat children paternalistically.

Since educational institutions are supposed to mediate our obligations to provide children with the conditions which will facilitate their becoming our moral equals as adults, then, we should select the method of governance which is most liable to achieve this end. Democracy may be this method, but it may not. It is certainly the case that the content of our obligations towards children places severe limits on democratic discretion. For example, democratic decisions which would compromise the prospective autonomy of children would be illegitimate, as, probably, would decisions which made the curriculum entirely irrelevant to future employment prospects. As I suggested in the previous section, there is no *guarantee* that democratic governance will do better with respect to these values than a choice-driven system.

A related complaint is that choice *replaces* determination of standards through the exercise of public democratic 'voice', with the exercise of the option of private 'exit': 'Exit rather than voice would become the dominant mode of affecting school policy. Education would become commodified and parents would become experts in comparison shopping for educational service.'[12] This, too, is far from decisive. One of the motiva-

---

[11] See Christiano, Thomas, *The Rule of the Many* (Boulder, Co.: Westview Press, 1995) for the view that democracy is a fundamental element of justice.

[12] Wright, Erik O., 'Equality, Community, and "Efficient Redistribution"', *Politics and Society*, 24 (1996), 363. Michael Walzer makes a similar complaint in *Spheres of Justice*,

tions of voucher proponents is that with respect to those educational goods provided by school, when the option of exit is clearly available, schools will be more responsive. Schools are relatively small institutions, and the contribution on behalf of each student is, relatively, a substantial amount of money. Any one of their several million customers, spending $3 a time, cannot have any effect on the quality of Lipton Tea by simply refraining from buying it. Nor can she have an effect by writing and telling them that she will refuse to buy it unless they improve its quality. But as one of only 1500 customers each contributing, say, $10,000 a year—as she would be in a voucher system—there would be a great incentive for the school to listen to her. In this case providing a realistic option of exit makes available better opportunities for voice. The picture of parents just withdrawing their children from a school without trying to correct the features they dislike depends on an unrealistic—one might say idealistic— picture of how markets work. Although it is made possible by a voucher scheme, exit from a school is costly for the child: mid-year exit disrupts learning, as do too many moves, and children find it disruptive having to reconstruct their social life within a new school, which distracts them from work even more than their regular social life does. Concerned parents who are likely to use the option of exit will recognize this, and may seek to improve conditions within the existing school if possible.[13] The option of exit provides the leverage which gets the voice heard. If we care about giv- ing parents the ability to affect the behaviour of the school we should not make a fetish of the means through which they are able to do that; we should be concerned just that they have what is in fact the most effective means available to them.

Brian Barry points out that Hirschman's use of the term 'voice' con- flates two quite distinct phenomena: cases where individuals pursue an entirely private good through the exercise of voice producing no benefit for others, for example the dissatisfied customer who returns faulty product; and cases where groups of individuals, by pursuing some collective good produce clear benefits for others who are not exercising voice. It might be objected that school choice enhances only the first kind of voice, and that that is not the pertinent kind. But since in the standard model of public schooling there is an option of exit already—the availability of private

218–20. See also Hirschman, Albert O., Exit, *Voice, and Loyalty* (Cambridge, Mass.: Harvard University Press, 1970).

[13] I should add a qualification here—apparently some Local Education Authorities in the UK do experience numbers of parents moving their children more than once during a year for these sorts of reasons. However they do so in the context of a national curriculum which may make such moves less disruptive than they would be in, say the US context.

schooling—and since this option is exercised by a good percentage of those parents who are, according to opponents of choice, best equipped to exercise voice for the public good, I see no reason to suppose that choice schemes will do worse than standard models of public schooling. Indeed, a universal voucher scheme may expand the barriers of government-funded and regulated schools, by making it much more attractive for parents who currently use the private option to choose schools which participate in the voucher scheme. If so, it will reincorporate those parents into the system, thus making it more likely that the latter kind of voice will be used at the level of system-wide regulation, which is the level that really matters.[14] As we saw in Chapter 2, allowing parents strong options of exit in non-ideal circumstances, furthermore, can provide more latitude for experimentation within schools.

I want to emphasize once more that neither choice nor democracy are all-or-nothing affairs. Choice schemes do not preclude considerable opportunities for governance through specifically democratic voice. Even Friedman accepts that some regulation will be necessary, and that regulation will at least be subject to democratic review. In left-wing schemes, involving more extensive regulation, the overarching regulation governing the whole school system including the curriculum will presumably be decided through some kind of democratic mechanism. This fact also mitigates the possible fear that under a choice system we shall see a general decline in lobbying on the part of parents for a general improvement in standards and conditions. There remains substantial scope for public deliberation over standards and methods. In any educational system it can be expected that parents will engage on behalf of their children at the level of the school and for general standards at higher levels of regulation. An appropriately designed choice scheme can leave plenty of scope for both.[15]

Before moving on I want to point out a possibly surprising conclusion. I have argued that democracy is not a value that should guide the design of education policy, even though it should guide many other areas of public policy. The argument I have given for that is exactly parallel to that with which I dismissed the idea invoked by 'real libertarianism' that parental choice should be a fundamental concern of education policy in Chapter 2. To regard either value as fundamental is to disregard the status of children

---

[14] Barry, Brian, *Democracy, Power and Justice* (Oxford: Oxford University Press, 1989), 203–4.

[15] For some valuable, if all too brief, comments about how a fairly radical conception of democracy might be realized in the process of governing education policy, see Whitty, Geoff, 'Social Theory and Education Policy: the legacy of Karl Mannheim', *British Journal of Sociology of Education*, 18 (1997), 149–63.

as persons in their own right, whose interests are paramount in determining how they should be treated. Our treatment of them is bound to be paternalistic and will incorporate elements both of parental choice and of democratic governance, but never because those are fundamentally important, only because the resulting institutional framework reliably promotes the proper interests of the children.

## THE ARGUMENT FROM THE COLLECTIVE OR COMMON GOOD

A final related objection to choice is that because education policy should be designed to promote the common or collective good, it should be a matter in the public rather than the private domain. Michael Strain argues that the social value of community is liable to be undermined by a policy of choice.[16] David Paris summarizes much thinking of both the founders of public education in the US and many of its twentieth-century defenders when he says that the collective good was used to justify provision: not only would public education provide basic skills of literacy and numeracy, but 'it would help forge a social bond by providing common moral and political understandings to otherwise different individuals and groups'.[17] Interestingly, one *defender* of choice invokes the notion of a common good in support of choice. David Hargreaves claims that 'paradoxically the anti-libertarian or quasi-libertarian stance of the left is unlikely to move us toward the collective good, whereas the diversity and choice advocated might . . . do so more effectively in a modern pluralistic democracy'.[18] This possibility is made available by the fact that, in a society characterized by pluralism—a persistent set of disagreements among groups of loyal citizens about how to live well—it may be that a diversity of schools in each of which there is relative homogeneity will 'enhance social cohesion within a sub-community'.[19] The social peace achieved through stabilizing the various subgroups, combined with a national civic education curriculum to which all will be subject has a good chance of serving the common good.

There are a number of difficulties with the use of the collective good to justify an education policy. The first is with the very idea of a common or

[16] Strain, Michael, 'Autonomy, Schools, and the Constitutive Role of Community: Toward a New Moral and Political Order for Education', *British Journal for Educational Studies*, 43 (1995), 4–19.

[17] Paris, David, *Ideology and Educational Reform* (Boulder Co.: Westview Press, 1995), 62

[18] Hargreaves, 'Diversity and Choice in School Education', 139.      [19] Ibid.

collective good. In a pluralistic society, in which people disagree about what counts as good, it is not clear what the common good could be. To talk about a common good in a pluralistic society requires either that we adopt an extremely 'thin' theory of the good, or that we ignore the judgements of some of the members of that society in determining the good. The latter strategy is not necessarily authoritarian: we may determine that there is some common good which some citizens fail to recognize, but that there are principled limits on what we may do to coerce the dissenters to contribute to the common good.

The second difficulty is that, whatever we claim to be the common good, it is an empirical matter, and not, as some theorists seem to think, a theoretical matter, whether the common good is advanced or impeded by any particular set of education policies. Whoever argues against markets on the basis of the common good owes a clear and defensible account of what constitutes the common good, and some clear empirical predications about the mechanisms whereby markets would undermine the common good. The argument offered by Erik Wright in the article I have already mentioned is of this kind. He identifies the common good with community, 'a belief by people that they share a common fate and to a significant extent value each other's welfare',[20] and specifies particular mechanisms that he thinks would operate within a choice scheme and would erode community. His claims are, however, as he acknowledges, empirical speculations, the truth of which cannot be determined in advance and which will depend both on the design of the particular choice scheme and the broader institutional framework within which a choice scheme is implemented. It could only be determined in advance of empirical investigation that the common good would be impeded by educational markets if it could be claimed that government schools run with the minimum of parental choice *constituted* the common good. But that makes the claim that markets impede the common good tautologous, as well as being itself deeply implausible.

The most serious difficulty, though, is the mistake of thinking that the common good, however defined, can play the primary role in justifying particular mechanisms for the delivery of education to children. Now,

---

[20] Wright, 'Equality, Community and "Efficient Redistribution"', 360. Wright is explicitly drawing on Gerald A. Cohen's conception of community, 'the anti-market principle according to which I serve you not because of what I can get out of doing so but because you need my service'. Cohen, G. A., 'Back to Socialist Basics', *New Left Review*, 207 (1994), 3–16 at 9. For Cohen's more detailed work on community, and his use of it to argue against John Rawls's difference principle, see Cohen, G. A., 'Incentives, Inequality and Community', in Darwall, Stephen (ed.), *Equal Freedom* (Ann Arbor, Mi.: University of Michigan Press, 1994).

before I substantiate the claim that this is a mistake, I want to make my position quite clear. If there is a defensible view of the common good, it may be quite appropriate for it to be used in defending, or opposing, some set of educational institutions. But this is not typically how it is used by those defenders of public education who invoke it. They typically use it as a primary consideration, one which is to be considered alongside, or even before, any other considerations. This is what is objectionable.

Think of the ways in which many socialists and conservatives have seen schooling: mainly as a means to shape the characters of future citizens so as to stabilize and legitimize the particular social order they favour. To see education in that way is to treat children, and the adults they will become, not as potentially self-determining citizens but as subjects of a pre-determined order. This violates both the liberal ideals that persons should be self-governing and that social institutions are legitimized only by the freely offered and critical consent of reasonable persons; and the individu-alist ideal that each person counts in his or her own right, and should not be treated merely as a means to some collective end.

Consider a principle which most participants in the debate over choice find acceptable: the principle enshrined in the *Universal Declaration of Human Rights* that 'education shall be free, at least in the elementary and fundamental stages'.[21] What is it that justifies this principle? I take it that the central reason this principle is correct is a child-centred, and not a soci-ety-centred, reason. We do not think that any child should be deprived of access to education simply because they had the misfortune of being born to a parent who cannot afford to pay for it. This, in turn, is because we think that every adult in a given society has an obligation as a matter of justice to contribute to each child's development both as a citizen capable of participating in a democratic polity, and as an independent adult cap-able of earning a living within the society into which she was born. To put it simply, if slightly misleadingly, each child has an individual right to an education.[22]

---

[21] By 'free' the principle means something like 'free to the parent of the child': I take it that any reasonable reading of this principle is compatible with the introduction of vouch-ers, as long as the voucher covers an adequate level of schooling at an accessible school.

[22] I am very uneasy about the language of children's rights, and avoid it wherever pos-sible. The language of rights makes most sense to me where the bearers of rights are beings who are capable of some substantial degree of autonomy, capable of making choices that ought to be respected about how to use and whether to waive their rights, and are not per-missibly treated paternalistically in a wide range of contexts. None of these descriptions apply well to children. See O'Neill, Onora, *Constructions of Reason* (Cambridge: Cambridge University Press, 1990), chapter 8. In this context, however, I think the lan-guage of rights is illuminating in that it uncomplicatedly designates education for children as a matter of justice.

I cannot provide the argument that a child has an individual right to an education independently of the arguments for what kind of education children have a right to; and I provide these arguments in the next four chapters. But if we do regard education as an individual right then that right must be one of the primary determinants of education policy, and the common or collective good must be taken as a secondary consideration at best. To use Ronald Dworkin's famous metaphor, rights are trumps: their exercise must be protected even at the expense of the common good, and can only be curtailed when they come into conflict with the rights of others. The obligation each adult has to contribute to providing an education to all children is akin to the obligation each adult has to each other adult to contribute to their right to a fair trial: which involves both financial contributions to the court system and refraining from interfering with the fair working of that system. The right to a fair trial is not justifiable by its contribution to the common good, but by its contribution to the good of each individual person. That a particular fair trial might damage the common good, for example by enabling a criminal to evade conviction, does not count against it.

Similarly, that the education of a particular child does not contribute to the common good would not count against it. Education is something we owe to each individual child regardless of what that child goes on to do with that education, and regardless of the opportunity cost of providing the education—other than the opportunity costs for the security of other, more or equally fundamental, rights, and subject to the constraint that conditions in which that education is useful must not be undermined by the expense of providing the education.

Of course, real social benefits do arise from providing both the right to a fair trial and fair trials, and also from providing the education which justice requires of us to each individual child. But these benefits play no role in justifying either policy. The point here is that all adults have an obligation as a matter of justice to contribute to the provision of education to each individual child. Different theorists will give different content to this obligation, and the content of the education to be provided will vary across theories. But on all viable views the content of the obligation to the child, whatever it is, is the primary consideration when designing the mechanism of delivery. We must design educational institutions to ensure that they deliver properly on our obligation to each individual child to educate it. The common good is, at best, a secondary consideration, which might guide our choice only between systems which deliver equally well on our obligations to individual children.

Of course, a child's right to an education is not the only right that the child has, and, of course, other people have rights too. My claim has only been that considerations of the common good must be secondary to considerations of rights, not that the rights of children must always take precedence over the rights of adults or that even that the educational rights of children must always take precedence over other rights of children. Consider the following choice:

Educational Scheme A perfectly implements a child's right to an education. But implementing scheme A will demonstrably erode the kind of public order required for security of people's rights to free expression, religion and association, and for the kinds of material redistribution required by justice. Scheme B implements a child's right to an education imperfectly, though not badly. But scheme B poses no threat to the kind of public order required to secure freedoms of expression, religion and association and material redistribution. Which should we choose?[23]

Faced with the choice described in this scenario, nothing I have said implies that we should choose scheme A, and my intuition, though I do not have an argument for this, is that we should choose scheme B. Such a choice would not violate the stricture that the common good must be of only secondary importance in the determination of education policy because although public order of the relevant kind is a common good, it is its contribution to the security of justice that makes it legitimate to invoke it. And children's interests and rights are not neglected in this choice because they are future bearers of the full array of rights guaranteed by justice. Their educational rights are important, as we shall see, partly because education will prepare them to be effective users of the rights of adults: to place their rights as adults in jeopardy for the sake of an incremental benefit for their educational rights would be irrational.

But, although it seems clear to me that in the scenario described scheme B should be preferred to scheme A, it needs to be kept in mind that children have a special place when we think about trade-offs that need to be made between rights. It is true that the rights of adults and of children are both the rights of the same people: childhood and adulthood are just different stages in a single life. But children are uniquely vulnerable: they are the proper objects of paternalism, whose interests have to be guarded entirely by other people. The trade-offs we make between rights, and the rules we adopt for making those trade-offs, must respect this fact.

---

[23] This choice is modelled on one posed to me by Eamonn Callan in a lengthy criticism of a previous draft. In that draft I had, wrongly, claimed that the common good was completely irrelevant to education policy and, even more wrongly, implied, though not claimed, that a child's right to education trumps the rights of adults. This section owes a great deal to Callan's criticisms: I am fully responsible for whatever remains wrong with it.

## CONCLUDING COMMENTS

We have seen, then, that the three values commonly invoked to make a principled case against school choice, are either not relevant to the design of educational institutions or, to the extent that they are relevant, whether they are better realized under a choice system than a nationalized system cannot be determined a priori. In the following four chapters I shall argue for the two principles that are primarily relevant to the design of educational institutions: the principle that all children should have a real opportunity to become autonomous, and the principle that all children should have an equal education.

# 4

# The Case for Autonomy-Facilitating Education

We have seen why invocation of the values of non-commodification, democracy, and the common good, all fail as arguments against school choice. It is not clear how education could fail to be a commodity in some sense, and it *is* clear that however commodified, it is does not matter if its institutional structure serves the interests of children adequately. Again, while all adults are indeed owed democratic rights as a matter of justice, these rights do not include rights to discretion over the design of educational institutions, which regulate the development of people who can have no reciprocal power: children. The common good may well be served by providing a good education for children, but it would be incumbent on us to provide a good education to them even if that did not serve the common good. Providing education is properly seen as a matter of justice, not of democracy or of public good.

The upshot of the last chapter, then, is that the interests of children should be paramount in guiding our decisions as to how to design educational institutions. In particular, their developmental interests should guide us. What are these interests? My focus in most of the rest of this book will be on two: the interest in becoming an autonomous adult; and the interest in equal opportunity. Both these interests are often invoked in arguments against school choice. The burden of this and the next three chapters is to explain why the invocation is appropriate: that is, why these two values do appropriately guide the design of educational institutions. I do not claim that only they should guide us, and only in Chapter 7 will I take up the question of whether school choice really does violate these values.

The first fundamental value that should guide the design of educational policy is the ideal that all children should have a realistic opportunity to become autonomous adults. Autonomy is, of course, used in many different ways by different theorists. On Kant's view, for example, one is autonomous only when one wills in accordance with the Categorical Imperative. On some other views, one is autonomous when one's actions accord with one's values, whatever they are.[1] The conception I am using is less theoretically loaded, because it draws on features that most conceptions of autonomy have in common, but it nevertheless has significant practical implications.

To see what is meant by autonomy, it will help to give some examples of types of belief and preference formation which are typically impugned by most conceptions of autonomy. Four familiar non-autonomous processes are worth discerning. First, preferences are usually considered to be non-autonomous when coercive practices have illegitimately restricted the options available to the agent. For example, it is true of the highwayman's victim that she genuinely wants to give up her worldly wealth when presented with the options 'your money or your life'. But her preference, while genuine, is not fully autonomous: it is, in an important sense, coerced. Second, some preferences and beliefs formed are non-autonomous where someone deliberately manipulates an agent by providing false information about the options available or costs and benefits attached to the options. Suppose, for example, that a stockbroker persuades her client to purchase shares in a company which she knows is about to post unexpected losses, by intimating that she has inside information that it will post unexpected gains. The choice is genuine, but not autonomous. Third is the familiar process, captured in the fable about the fox who dismisses as sour, grapes that he cannot reach, whereby people adapt their preferences or beliefs subconsciously to apparently unchangeable circumstances. Finally is the process whereby people *consciously and deliberately* accommodate their preferences to unjust background conditions: this process is captured by the stories of stoic slaves, or repressed housewives, who come to embrace their unchangeable lot as a way of making their lives more bearable.

Some of the above types of non-autonomy are present in each of our lives. However, teachable skills can enable us to avoid or overcome many instances of non-autonomy. Broadly speaking, the capacities involved in critical reflection help us to live autonomously. We can be taught methods for evaluating the truth and falsehood, or relative probability, of various claims about the world. We can be taught, for example, the difference between anecdotal and statistical evidence and the differences in reliabil-

---

[1]  See Kant, Immanuel, *Groundwork to a Metaphysics of Morals* (New York, NY: Harper and Row, 1964). For alternative versions of autonomy and why it matters see Frankfurt, Harry, *The Importance of What We Care About* (Cambridge: Cambridge University Press, 1988); Dworkin, Gerald, *The Theory and Practice of Autonomy* (Cambridge: Cambridge University Press, 1988); Raz, Joseph, *The Morality of Freedom* (Oxford: Oxford University Press, 1986); Hill, Thomas Jr., *Autonomy and Self-Respect* (Cambridge: Cambridge University Press, 1990).

ity with respect to the truth. Manipulation can be avoided, to some extent, by ensuring that we have the developed ability to investigate truth claims with somewhat reliable tools, on our own. We can be taught that adaptive and accommodationist preference-formation are features of human behaviour, and people, to some extent, can avoid these by 'stepping back' from their commitments and reflecting on how they were formed.

My focus so far has been on the processes of preference and belief *formation*. Someone might object that many of our commitments *must* be formed non-autonomously. Many of our most deeply held beliefs were not selected through careful and rational weighing of the reasons for holding one belief or another, but by internalizing impressions, by trusting the testimony of others, or by trusting our hunches. A theory of autonomy which impugned all such commitments would make autonomy an almost unattainable condition.

But whether a belief or preference is held autonomously is not just a function of its genesis. Commitments can be autonomous in a second way. Commitments generated by non-autonomous processes become autonomous when the agent reflects upon them with an appropriate degree of critical attention. The person whose commitment to socialism originated in childhood stories told by her much adored grandmother, is not forced to choose between non-autonomously remaining a socialist, or becoming an autonomous renegade: she can subject her socialist beliefs to rational criticism in the light of contending ideologies. If the socialist commitments survive, they are now held autonomously. The same holds for many commitments.

Finally, of course, some beliefs and preferences are never subjected to scrutiny. Even agents thoroughly committed to autonomy, and who should count as autonomous by any reasonable standard, will have beliefs and preferences that are not autonomous on any reasonable standard. Our musical tastes, our preferences among table condiments, our tastes in clothing and decor, to mention a few examples, are often formed by processes about which we are unaware and on which we never reflect. These examples are morally trivial, which ensures that they do not affect the claim to autonomy of the person who has them.

What then, is the argument for having the state impose an autonomy-facilitating education on all children? One way of arguing for an autonomy-facilitating education appeals to the Socratic ideal that the unexamined life is not worth living. Critical reflection on one's own goals and values, on this view, is an essential part of living well. Since everyone should have an opportunity to live well, everyone should be taught to be autonomous.

This suggestion is often cited by opponents of teaching autonomy, and is properly dismissed. Think of Hattie and Eric, both of whom live, quite strictly, by exactly the same genuinely worthy values. The difference is that Hattie has reflected on those values and continues, throughout her life, to reflect on them, while Eric simply received them from his parents. There is certainly a difference in the internal lives of Hattie and Eric, and there may even be a moral difference between them, but it is surely implausible to say that Hattie's life had worth, but Eric's had none at all. It may be plausible to say that autonomy adds worth to a life lived according to good values, but quite implausible to say that it is a precondition of that life having worth.

A different argument for teaching autonomy is suggested by Amy Gutmann. She argues that the state has an interest in teaching children how to be good democratic citizens, inclined to join in collective deliberation about the public good. In order to do this it has to expose them to a range of political views, and to equip them with the skills needed to reflect on them rationally. But, as she says, 'The skills of political reflection cannot be neatly differentiated from the skills of evaluating one's own way of life.' Furthermore, teaching children to think about social justice 'is threatening to the moral convictions of many parents (and teachers and other authorities) and to their way of life, often no less threatening than teaching children about less politically relevant matters'.[2]

There is a great deal to Gutmann's argument, but it will not do as it stands, because she deploys a conception of justice that places too much weight on the value of democratic participation. It privileges democratic participation as something which should be regarded not only as a fundamental right of all citizens but as a political duty. This is controversial and, in my view false, though this is not the place to elaborate the reasons why. If we want an argument for autonomy-facilitation capable of achieving wide acceptance, it will not come from the civic republicanism Gutmann presupposes.

There is, fortunately, an argument which neither appeals to the intrinsic value of autonomy, nor to any connection it may have with a specifically civic education. I shall call this the instrumental argument, which shows that we have a direct obligation to provide autonomy facilitating-education to all children.[3] The instrumental argument starts by asserting that justice requires that each individual have significant opportunities to

[2] Gutmann, Amy, 'Civic Education and Social Diversity', *Ethics*, 105 (1995), 557–79 at 578.
[3] A similar argument is made in Shapiro, Ian, *Democracy's Place* (Ithaca, NY: Cornell University Press, 1996), 167–71 (in a chapter co-authored with Richard Arneson).

live a life which is good for them. Liberals are properly reluctant to have the state comment on the substantive ends of citizens. But if someone has all the resources and liberties that justice requires, but has, as an avoidable result of the design of social institutions, hardly any opportunity to live well, she has not been treated justly. One purpose of delivering the resources and liberties that justice requires is that they enable people to live well, and to live well by their own judgement. But to live well one needs more: one needs also some sense of what constitutes living well.

Were learning how to live well an entirely mysterious matter, or if equipping people with the skills associated with learning how to live well conflicted with other elements of justice, it might be conceded that justice requires only the delivery of external resources and conditions. But the basic methods of rational evaluation are reliable aids to uncovering how to live well. This is especially important in modern conditions, with 'fast changing technologies and free movement of labour [which calls for] an ability to cope with changing technological, economic and social conditions, for an ability to adjust, to acquire new skills, to move from one sub-culture to another, to come to terms with new scientific and moral views'.[4] Without autonomy-related skills we are easily lost in the moral and economic complexity of modernity. This does not imply that no-one will hit upon, or at least approach, good ways of life without their aid, nor that rational deliberation is infallible. As in other areas of knowledge, inspired guesses, trusting the reliable communication of another, and manipulation by reliable others can help us find out how to live well. Rational deliberation confronts barriers, but in the absence of fortunate guesses and well-informed parents, children will be better able to live well if they are able rationally to compare different ways of life.[5]

Some clarification is needed of the notion of living well. Living well has two aspects, one concerning the content of the way of life and the other concerning the way the agent relates to it. The way of life must be good; and the person living it must endorse it 'from the inside', as it were.[6] Some ways of life are not good, and children whose parents pass them down cannot live them well even if they endorse them: those children have no opportunity to live well unless they are able to find good ways of life. Other ways of life are, of course, good. But some whose parents try to pass those ways of life down cannot endorse them from the inside: although the ways of life are good, these people cannot live them well. They have opportunities

---

[4] Raz, *The Morality of Freedom*, 369–70.
[5] See the valuable discussion in Raz, *The Morality of Freedom*, 370–8.
[6] See Kymlicka, Will, *Multicultural Citizenship* (Oxford: Oxford University Press, 1995), 80–4 for an elaboration of the idea of living a life from the inside.

to live well only if they can exit into other good ways of life. How able they are to exit into a good way of life depends, partly, on whether they possess epistemically reliable ways of evaluating different ways of life.

It might be objected that the notion of living well I am deploying unacceptably demotes unchosen commitments, such as commitments to the welfare of our parents or other relatives. I think that is wrong: whether one lives well in carrying out such commitments, depends not on rationally choosing the commitment, but on whether the obligations flowing from it are accepted 'from the inside'. The obligations are undertaken from the inside if the agent identifies with them. She does not live well if she undertakes them with deep resentment and anger, even if what she is doing is good. But she can live well, consistent with undertaking these obligations, without choosing them or the commitments from which they flow.

These facts support a strong presumption that children should have the opportunity to learn the skills associated with autonomy and that parental preference is not sufficient reason to deny them that opportunity. In waiving the opportunity, parents would be depriving their children of skills which are of great value in working out how to live well. Does the argument, though, support intervention in the school curriculum? It is important to see that the primary question here concerns the institutional distribution of authority over children. The instrumental argument suggests that the state, as an agent on behalf of society, has the authority to provide children the opportunity to be autonomous. Whether this requires intervention in schooling, and what form that intervention should take, will depend on the character of non-educational institutions and facts about developmental psychology.

If, for example, a robust public culture provided abundant opportunities to develop the relevant skills, and parents could not shield their children from those aspects of the public culture, then perhaps no intervention would be needed. I assume that this is false in most liberal democracies; many parents who would exempt their children from autonomy-facilitating education at school also refrain from teaching them the relevant skills at home.[7] In the US, parents who waive autonomy- facilitating education for their children typically live in tight-knit communities which limit

---

[7] See Bates, Stephen, *Battleground: One Mother's Crusade, The Religious Right, And The Struggle For Control Of Our Classrooms* (New York, NY: Simon and Schuster, 1993) for an account of *Mozert vs. Hawkins*, in which parents demanded that textbooks teaching, among other things, that a central ideal of the Renaissance was a belief in the equal worth of all human beings, be removed from the school. The Mozert parents, like the Amish parents in *Wisconsin vs. Yoder*, took the prospective autonomy of their children as a threat to their continued adherence to their religion.

opportunities for exposure to other ways of life and for the development of critical faculties.

Assumptions about developmental psychology underlie all discussions of the educational curriculum. If children were hard-wired to be rational rebels, perhaps a repressive and religiously sectarian education would be autonomy-facilitating.[8] I am assuming, in common with most other theorists, that to hold one's moral commitments autonomously requires the use of skills and knowledge which, for most people, must be explicitly taught. If this is false, then, while the claim about the distribution of authority stands, the recommendations concerning autonomy-facilitating education may be undermined.

The conception of autonomy I have invoked looks rather abstract. Rational reflection does not suffice to weigh different alternatives of how to live, or different immediate choices about what to do, in the way that propositional logic suffices when evaluating the validity of arguments. However, no other known device is so reliable in this area of human understanding. Rational reflection can help us to detect inconsistencies and fallacious argumentation, and to uncover misuse of evidence. It helps us to see whether a choice coheres with our given preferences, including our higher-order preferences. It helps us, therefore, in determining the relative plausibility of different positions both on the grounds of evidence and coherence.

Notice that the instrumental argument is structured differently from standard arguments for a specifically *civic* education. Civic education aims to teach children the beliefs and habits which will help to stabilize the, presumably just, state. Those arguments often start with the need to maintain the state in some prescribed form, and then prescribe education of a certain kind to cultivate in children the characters likely to stabilize that state.[9] The instrumentalist argument for teaching autonomy, by contrast, starts with the obligation which adults have towards prospective adults, to provide them with certain kinds of opportunity to live well. The state is charged neither with maintaining its own stability, nor with promoting the attitudes and abilities which will make the institutions of the state healthy and just, but with providing prospective citizens with the substantive means to select pursuit of a better, rather than worse, conception of the good. The fundamental interest each person has in living well yields an

---

[8] I owe this example to Laura Osinski, who helped me identify the different levels of abstraction relevant to my argument.

[9] Gutmann and Galston both offer arguments, which are similar in structure, though quite different in the content of the civic education they recommend. See my 'Civic Education and Liberal Legitimacy', *Ethics*, 108 (1998), 719–45 for criticisms of their views.

obligation on all to provide prospective adults with an instrument for selecting well among ways of life. Confidence that others have a real opportunity to live lives that are good for them is only possible if we provide the means to select one.

Some may be unpersuaded that *justice* requires that all children have the opportunity to become autonomous. It might be a very good thing for children to learn the relevant skills, but that does not suffice to show that justice requires it. The connection with justice can be shown by considering an argument *against* requiring autonomy-facilitating education recently offered by Francis Schrag. Considering Schrag's argument is particularly helpful because it shares some of my own argument's key premises.

Schrag takes it for granted that what matters fundamentally is that children have real opportunities for living well, and he posits the Berlinian claim that there are plural and conflicting good values. There are, in other words, many diverse ways of life which human beings are capable of living well. He claims furthermore—consistently with the claims I have made—that some deeply religious ways of life are good, or, as he puts it 'choice-worthy', quoting the articulate and well-considered testimony of an Orthodox Jewish woman, Lisa Aiken, who was brought up in mainstream secular America, but converted as an adult to Orthodox Judaism. We know the following about her:

1. She was not brought up in the Orthodox community and hence her socialization did not confine her to the Orthodox world-view.
2. Her conversion was—at least according to her testimony—neither a coerced nor a sudden transformation that bypassed her rational processes.
3. She is able to articulate the features of the life she's chosen that make it fulfilling.[10]

Her testimony is thus powerful evidence that this deeply religious way of life can be chosen autonomously and is hence capable of being lived well. But, as I have suggested earlier, it would be implausible to think that the goodness of her way of life depends on its being chosen autonomously. Her testimony is ultimately evidence that the way of life can be lived well even when it is not chosen autonomously: that is, even when it is lived by someone who was brought up in the faith without ever being taught about other options. Surely, then, we do not need to teach children the skills

---

[10] Schrag, Francis, 'Diversity, Schooling and the Liberal State', *Studies in Philosophy and Education*, 17 (1998), 29–46 at 43.

needed to make comparative evaluations between their parents' and other ways of life in order to give them a real opportunity to live well.

Notice that Schrag's argument does not rely on any claim about parental rights, or obligations to respect parental authority. His central moral premises are just the same as those of the instrumental argument: that there are plural and conflicting ways of life and that children are owed real opportunities to live well.

However, there is a problem with his argument, which highlights the connection between justice and autonomy-facilitating education. I have already accepted value pluralism, and that lives can be lived well without being autonomously chosen. But there is another facet of pluralism that Schrag, like others who seek to accommodate the demands of religious parents, neglects. This is the recognition that people have different personalities, characters, or internal constitutions, that suit them differently well to different ways of life; and these differences do not correlate perfectly with the demands of their parents' or their communities' religious commitments. To give a stark example, assume that homosexuality is substantially an unchosen trait, and take a homosexual boy who grows up in a community in which the religious norms prohibit any avenues for living well as a homosexual. This boy has far less opportunity to live well—in a way that he can endorse from the inside—than others growing up in his community. In fact it is quite plausible that he has no such opportunity at all. This is not to say that there is anything bad or wrong about living heterosexual lives, just that this boy cannot live life well as a heterosexual.[11]

If what we might call constitution pluralism is true, and religious parents are permitted to exempt their children from autonomy-facilitation, then some children will have few or no opportunities for living well. Those children in mainstream communities, however, who get autonomy-facilitating education, and those growing up in religious communities whose constitutions suit them to the given ways of life, will have great opportunities. This constitutes a strong prima facie injustice.

Defenders of accommodation are not unaware of this problem, and they typically place considerable emphasis on the fact that in modern societies there are many exit options available to children who grow up in deeply religious families. They typically can, and do, enter mainstream

---

[11] In fact, recognizing the plurality of internal constitutions and that such plurality implies that some good ways of life cannot be lived well by some people is compatible with a certain kind of moderate perfectionism: it is possible to hold that heterosexuality is morally superior to homosexuality, while recognizing that most homosexuals can live better as homosexuals than as heterosexuals. I mention this only to clarify the content of the conceptual claim, not because this particular perfectionist claim is plausible.

society in significant numbers. I shall have more to say about this later in Chapter 5. But it is important here to note that the fact that children can exit their parents' way of life is not sufficient to undermine the injustice claim. Children who leave their parent's religious way of life are predictably worse off than those who stay, and those they join in mainstream society, in two important respects. They are not educationally prepared for the social milieu they will have to negotiate as adults, unlike those who stay and those whom they join; and they have, in a predictably large proportion of cases, fractured the relationship with their parents which is not only valuable in itself but also underwrites a good deal of risk-taking by their peers. They are doubly disadvantaged *vis-à-vis* their peers. Justice, it appears, requires that they be educationally prepared for mainstream society: since they cannot be identified before the fact, this suggests that justice requires that all children receive some sort of autonomy-facilitating education.

The key to seeing why justice is involved here, then, is to think about the requirement of equal opportunity. Equality of opportunity impugns unequal life-prospects when they arise from unequal circumstances, but not when they arise from conscious choices. But unequal prospects are faced by children who learn the skills associated with autonomy and those who do not, and those inequalities are the result of their circumstances rather than their choices; although, in the case of children, it is not clear that the principle of equal opportunity even permits inequalities arising from choices. In my argument I have used the even weaker notion that we owe others merely some significant—rather than strictly equal—opportunity to live a good life.

What are the curricular consequences of autonomy-facilitation? It is difficult to be precise about this, for the reasons given above. But we can identify four important curricular elements which are likely to be crucial for facilitating autonomy in modern societies. Children would learn:

1. The traditional academic content-based curriculum. Proponents of teaching critical thinking skills and autonomy in the curriculum often sound as if they are opposing the traditional emphasis on teaching 'facts' and 'content' in the curriculum. But there is no real conflict here: an autonomous life cannot be led without the information about the world in which it is led, and the critical thinking skills involved in autonomy can neither be developed nor exercised without the ease of access to a considerable amount of information which is provided only by having learned and internalized it. It is true that there is far more information available than any child can expect to learn, and that it is crucial that children learn how to get access to information, but the idea that they might develop the

more complex skills of reasoning about information without having a good deal of it instantly available is silly.

2. How to identify various sorts of fallacious arguments, and how to distinguish among them, as well as between them and non-fallacious arguments. The autonomous person needs to be able to distinguish between appeals to authority and appeals to evidence, between inductive and deductive arguments, as well as to identify *ad hominem* arguments and other misleading rhetorical devices.

3. About a range of religious, non-religious, and anti-religious ethical views in some detail; about the kinds of reasoning deployed within those views; and the attitudes of proponents toward non-believers, heretics, and the secular world.

4. About the diverse ways, including non-reason-based ways, in which secular and religious thinkers have dealt with moral conflict and religious disagreements, and with tensions in their own views; and how individuals have described, and to the extent possible how they have experienced, conversion experiences, losses of faith, and reasoned abandonment of ethical positions.

These last two elements are particularly important, since autonomy with respect to one's religious and moral commitments requires exposure to alternative views. It also requires that this exposure be done in a controlled and non-pressured way, but also in a way that reflects the reality of the lives lived according to these commitments. Exposure to moral views would be done best by allowing proponents of views to address children in the controlled environment of the classroom. While the instrumental argument is connected to the liberal humanism which is anathema to many religious sectarians, the implementation of autonomy-facilitating education would probably require a nuanced attitude to the exposure of children to religion in schools. A child cannot be autonomous either in her acceptance or rejection of a religious view unless she experiences serious advocacy. As John Stuart Mill argues, concerning the exposure of adults to free speech:

Nor is it enough that he should hear the arguments of adversaries from his own teachers, presented as they state them, and accompanied by what they offer as refutations. That is not the way to do justice to the arguments, or bring them into real contact with his own mind. He must be able to hear them from persons who actually believe them; who defend them in earnest and do their very utmost for them.   (Mill, John Stuart, *On Liberty*, 36.)

Neutral, antiseptic textbooks describing each view and serially explaining its advantages and defects may contribute little to autonomy-facilitation—

they certainly would not suffice. Autonomy, though susceptible of an abstract description, cannot be practised outside the specific situation of individual lives; education should reflect this.

There is a second argument for autonomy-facilitating education which is worth explaining here, because if it is correct it suggests that other elements should be added to the curriculum. Unlike the instrumental argument, the second argument appeals to the connection between auto-nomy-facilitating education and liberal legitimacy as it is usually con-ceived. While in political practice, legitimacy and justice are rarely separated, in ideal liberal theory they are quite distinct. While a theory of justice will specify how the state ought to distribute benefits such as rights, opportunities and resources among its citizens, a theory of legitimacy specifies what stance citizens must have toward a state in order for it to have distinctive authorization to use coercive power. One commonly accepted criterion of legitimacy is captured in the phrase 'Justice must not only be done: it must also be seen to be done'. Another is captured in the phrase that a 'government must have the consent of the governed'.

It is this second criterion which concerns us in the supplemental argu-ment for autonomy-facilitating education. While accounts of liberal legit-imacy differ significantly, three common features can be identified. First, to be legitimate, a state must seek the consent of the governed. Since unan-imous consent is unlikely to be forthcoming, and since some citizens are not expected to give their consent, for example lunatics and the congen-itally bloody-minded, a weaker condition is that the state should be susceptible of hypothetical consent: it must be true that citizens would give their consent if they were reasonable, informed, and not overly self-interested.

Backing off to the more realistic demand for merely hypothetical con-sent forces us to strengthen other requirements, lest legitimacy become too easy. A state to which no-one consents even though all *could* consent should not congratulate itself on its legitimacy. So some concern that the state aspire for the actual consent of at least a majority, and preferably a vast majority, is usually added to the hypothetical conditions.

Finally, liberals are not satisfied with actual consent achieved by coer-cion or manipulation. The state cannot demonstrate legitimacy by merely showing that citizens could reasonably have consented to the arrange-ments under certain hypothetical conditions and that most do actually consent; it must also show that the actual consent is free and authentic. Consent should not simply be caused by the state itself, through mecha-nisms which have nothing to do with the appropriateness of the arrange-ments: for example through the persecution of dissenters—which is prohibited by the substantive principles of liberalism—or a programme of indoctrination, or the placing of a 'loyalty drug' in the water supply—neither of which is straightforwardly prohibited by the substantive principles. Standard accounts of liberal legitimacy require that, in some sense, all citizens be able to consent freely to the state.

The problem with legitimacy is that even the most conscientiously self-limiting state is unlikely to refrain entirely from encouraging consent in ways that bypass or pre-empt their rational scrutiny. The state has a monopoly on the legitimate use of coercive power: some of the just uses will be likely to encourage consent. The state quite properly sets the rules which establish the background to the institutions of civil society. In setting these rules it is liable to produce an atmosphere in which consent develops other than through the scrutiny of individuals. The state issues official reports and official histories, sets national holidays and operates within traditions which it thereby maintains. It also, unavoidably, pronounces on its own legitimacy through the mechanisms for protecting the fundamental rights liberalism guarantees. Even publicly guaranteeing rights encourages citizens to view themselves as rights-bearers, thus conditioning support. Weak conditioning of consent is, in other words, a predictable consequence of many proper activities of the liberal state. But in conditioning the citizens' consent the state may appear to be violating this condition of legitimacy.

What does this have to do with autonomy-facilitating education? The idea is that by providing for an autonomy-facilitating education and, in particular, by directing the critical attention of future citizens to the justifications of the state itself, the state can mitigate the extent to which it conditions the consent on which its legitimacy depends, by ensuring that all citizens have the opportunity to become the kind of people whose consent counts towards the state's legitimacy.[12]

While autonomy-facilitating education helps ensure that children have the real opportunity to become the kind of people whose consent matters for legitimacy, it does not *suffice*. Autonomy-facilitating education equips children to reflect on alternative ways of life, but does not encourage critical reflection on the design of social institutions. Autonomy-facilitating education *partially equips* children for such reflection: many of the skills involved are the same as those involved in reflecting on how to live one's own life. By equipping prospective citizens to review social arrangements rationally, as well as the values that have been inculcated in them, the policy diminishes room for reasonable suspicion on their part that reason

---

[12] I make the legitimacy argument in more detail in 'Civic Education and Liberal Legitimacy'.

does not support their acceptance of those arrangements. It does this even if they choose not to reflect critically: knowing that the state has enhanced my ability rationally to criticize its structure and policies may diminish my suspicion of its motives in inculcating the virtues.

However, autonomy-facilitating education does not *fully* equip children for the reflection which underpins legitimacy: in particular my description of autonomy-facilitating education includes neither the knowledge base concerning the actual design of institutions, nor the appreciation of the complexities involved in assessing historical feasibility essential to the evaluation of institutions.

How could autonomy-facilitating education be supplemented to support legitimacy? Again, any recommendations are, of necessity, both speculative and underspecific. But three elements, likely to be common among known democratic societies, can be discerned:

1. *History as a social science*: To give reasoned consent to the status quo citizens need an accurate sense of how the institutions work and of how they were designed and reformed over time. The history citizens are taught must meet reasonable standards of completeness, and must be critical, displaying the difficulties with establishing what the facts are and of assessing the motives of historical agents and the effects of their actions.

2. *Alternative Ideologies*: Citizens need an appreciation of the range of alternative ideologies concerning political and economic institutions. The consent of citizens of socialist countries cannot be fully reasoned unless they are aware of the moral and pragmatic critiques of socialism provided by defenders of capitalism; similarly, fully reasoned consent to capitalism is possible only if informed by socialist critiques of inequality and property relations, and critiques of high-growth 'consumer society'. It is not essential, or possible, for *all* competing ideologies to be presented fully: but a range should be presented such that the student can develop the facility to grasp and think through new ideologies as she uncovers them. At least some of the ideologies presented must be non-liberal.

3. *Disagreement and conflict*: The different ways political thinkers and actors have dealt with disagreement, both within and among ideological traditions, should also be taught. This need not be prescriptive: the aim is to give students an accurate sense of how political actors have perceived and dealt with conflict.

These elements may not exhaust the requirements for a legitimizing education, and institutions of civil society may be sufficiently powerful in fostering careful critical thinking about social institutions in some liberal regimes that some of these recommendations may be omitted from the curriculum. But citizens lacking the knowledge and skills aimed for in these recommendations are ill-placed to consent to institutions in the way liberal legitimacy needs.

A contrast with the recommendations made by Amy Gutmann concerning civic education will be instructive. Gutmann's civic education includes education for autonomy, but also substantive teaching of values. She suggests that the need for a common civic education flows from the 'democratic ideal of sharing political sovereignty as citizens'.[13] The ideal of sharing political sovereignty requires both behaviour which is in accordance with political authority and critical thinking about authority. Democratic civic education aims at inculcating in children the habits and values which the good democratic citizen will possess.

Deliberative citizens are committed, at least partly through the inculcation of habit, to living up to the routine demands of democratic life, at the same time as they are committed to questioning those demands whenever they appear to threaten the foundational ideals of democratic sovereignty, such as respect for persons. (Gutmann, Amy, *Democratic Education*, 52.)

In order to produce such citizens the state should educate children in a way that predisposes 'children to accept ways of life that are consistent with sharing the rights and responsibilities in a democratic society'[14] as well as foundational democratic values.

As I mentioned earlier Gutmann claims that civic education requires teaching the skills associated with autonomy. She appeals to the requirements for effective participation in political debate. Gutmann argues that *mutual civic respect* must be taught to secure the 'minimal conditions of reasonable public judgment'.[15] Mutual civic respect is contrasted with mere tolerance: when we are merely tolerant we refrain from coercing those with whom we disagree, but when we accord them civic respect we take them, and their ideas, seriously. The idea is that, in order to take adherents of other beliefs—and their beliefs—seriously, children must learn skills such as how rationally to evaluate different moral claims. The basic idea is that unless citizens know what other citizens believe and are able to evaluate their arguments, their abilities to press their own interests effectively in democratic processes, and to assess the arguments pressed by others, are both hampered.

[13] Gutmann, Amy, *Democratic Education* (Princeton, NJ: Princeton University Press, 1987), 51.

[14] Ibid., 42.         [15] Gutmann, 'Civic Education and Social Diversity', 578.

But the skills involved in

political reflection cannot be neatly differentiated from the skills involved in evaluating one's own way of life.

Most (if not all) of the same skills and virtues that are necessary and sufficient for educating children for citizenship in a liberal democracy are those that are necessary and sufficient for educating children to deliberate about their own ways of life, more generally (and less politically) speaking'. (Gutmann, Amy, 'Civic Education and Social Diversity', 578, 573.)

Education for autonomy is, then, a by-product of what is needed to teach civic respect, which in turn is an element of civic education.

There is obvious similarity between my proposals and Gutmann's, but also interesting divergences. Under my recommendations children are taught that diversity is a fact, but they are not taught that it is desirable. Correlatively they are not taught sympathetically to address views about the good life other than their own; only about such views, and how to engage them seriously. They are taught neither Gutmann's virtue of civic respect nor Galston's of tolerance.[16] Though not value-free, my recommendations favour knowledge and skills over virtue.[17] This is because the recommendation is for autonomy-facilitating rather than autonomy-promoting education. The argument claims that equipping people with the skills needed rationally to reflect on alternative choices about how to live is a crucial component of providing them with substantive freedom and real opportunities, by enabling them to make better rather than worse choices about how to live their lives. The education does not try to ensure that students employ autonomy in their lives, any more than Latin classes are aimed at ensuring that students employ Latin in their lives. Rather it aims to enable them to live autonomously should they wish to, rather as we aim to enable them to criticize poetry, do algebra, etc. without trying to ensure that they do so. The argument suggests that, other things being equal, people's lives go better when they deploy the skills associated with autonomy, but does not yield any obligation to persuade them to deploy them: autonomy must be facilitated, not necessarily promoted.

On my account autonomy-facilitating education differs from autonomy-promoting education on two dimensions. The justificatory strategy is different: the argument for autonomy-facilitating education does not

[16] There may be reasons that children should be taught these virtues. The instrumental argument does not provide them.

[17] Although I have focused on the 'skills associated with autonomy' I am sceptical that any cognitive skills can be taught independent of teaching knowledge. See Hirsch, Eric D. Jr., *The Schools We Need and Why We Don't Have Them* (New York, NY: Doubleday, 1996), chapter 2.

appeal to the civic responsibilities of future citizens or to the intrinsically superior value of autonomous living over non-autonomous living. The content is also at least somewhat different, in a way that fits with the justificatory strategy: the education is purportedly 'character-neutral', in that it seeks to provide certain critical skills without aiming to inculcate the inclination to use them.

Two criticisms can be made of the purported character-neutrality of autonomy-facilitating education. The first is that, although the methods recommended will be more sombre than evangelizing, it may still be hard to distinguish autonomy-facilitating from autonomy-promoting education in practice. Compare this with teaching some sports: it is hard to teach the skills without also communicating that the sport is worth playing. As Erik Wright suggests, 'the rewards and punishments that inherently accompany the instruction and practical activities may have the character of causally encouraging the expression of the potential, not just the capacity to choose'.[18]

The second criticism is that character-neutral autonomy-facilitating education is not just difficult, but incoherent. It seems wrong to say of anyone that they have had a real opportunity to become autonomous if, though having learned the critical skills associated with autonomy, they have failed to develop the habits of character that go along with those skills. Think of Mill's earlier recommendations that people encounter new ideas through contact with actual believers of those ideas. Unless a child has developed the open-mindedness and self-restraint of the autonomous person, they cannot truly make contact with new ideas, and so cannot truly exercise the acquired critical skills.[19]

I concede the first criticism unconditionally. While that criticism will make it more difficult to win and maintain widespread political support for a policy of autonomy-facilitating education, it does not impugn the very real differences in the justificatory strategies. I am less certain about the second criticism. It seems right to me that the full benefits of autonomy—and of the education I have recommended earlier—are not enjoyed by the person who lacks the relevant character or habits. But the instrumental argument appeals only to the benefit for the opportunity to live well, and this benefit may well be gained by the person with the skills but not the habits, for two reasons. First, again recognizing the plurality of internal constitutions, I suspect that some people may simply be unable to learn the relevant habits or gain the relevant character. Second, there

[18] Erik Wright, personal communication with author (March 1996).
[19] Eamonn Callan presented this objection to me in his comments, and has developed them in his 'Liberal Legitimacy, Justice and Civic Education' (unpublished manuscript).

are other, more affective, facets of personality which are relevant to learning how to live well, which may be undermined by trying to alter the characters of those whose constitutions are such that they cannot become fully, or habitually, autonomous.

Whether or not the second criticism is right, I should emphasize that I have not shown that autonomy-facilitation is *all* that is owed to children, and am open to the possibility that autonomy should be actively promoted. While the considerations I have invoked concerning legitimacy suggest that critical reflection on the values underlying social institutions should be actively encouraged, they also appear to work against the *promotion* of autonomy, since they suggest that a state which actively encourages its citizens to live autonomously undermines their ability to give unconditioned consent, since it actively conditions their preferred way of life. Callan has also argued powerfully against this consequence, claiming that, despite appearances to the contrary, education for legitimacy in fact *requires* the promotion of autonomy. To count as legitimating, consent has to be offered by citizens who have an effective sense of justice: this, he thinks, is the principle underlying my qualification that non-consent from overly self-interested persons is no barrier to legitimacy.[20] If Callan is right, this does not undermine the distinction between autonomy-facilitating and autonomy-promoting education, but it does undermine its significance, in that it would show that children are owed, on the basis of the legitimacy argument, an autonomy-promoting education. This difference may seem unimportant to many readers, and indeed in *this* context I do not think a great deal hinges on it. But it is worth pointing out that in both this chapter and the next I occasionally claim that deeply religious parents may be more amenable to a neutrally-justified autonomy facilitating education than the more loaded civic education—including an autonomy-promoting education—favoured by theorists like Gutmann and Callan. If Callan's argument is correct, this pragmatic advantage of my position would have to sacrificed.

[20] Callan, 'Liberal Legitimacy, Justice and Civic Education'. Manuscript in progress, available from author.

# 5

# Objections to Autonomy-Facilitating Education

The argument of Chapter 4 succeeds in showing that all children have a strong interest in becoming autonomous, and suggests that institutions external to the family have a crucial role to play in fulfilling that interest. Nevertheless, it does not establish that it is permissible for the state to protect that interest by designing educational institutions to facilitate autonomy against the wishes of the parents. Justice requires that, only if there are no other considerations of justice that prohibit it. So we have to take on a series of arguments asserting that whatever interest children have in becoming autonomous, it is the business of the family, rather than the state, to protect that interest, or neglect it, as it sees fit. If any of these arguments is successful, then, although autonomy is valuable, it is not a value that may guide the design of educational institutions, and so may not be invoked in opposition to school choice.

## THE STRONG RIGHT TO FORM ONE'S CHILDREN'S VALUES

Conservative libertarians are generally uncomfortable with the idea that the state should play any deliberate role in affecting the relationship between children and parents. In public life they often appeal to the 'right to freedom of association', or the 'right to raise one's own children' to block government interference. But, as we saw in Chapter 1, these rights are underspecific.

Consider the right to freedom of association. This is an important right, but it is one which most naturally holds among consenting adults. The right to free association does not support claims to associate with those who wish to avoid your company. It does, standardly, protect consensual sexual relations, but only among adults, not between adults and children or among children. The right to raise a family, similarly, does not permit parents to do whatever they might want to do to their children. We usually think that they lack the rights to have sex with their children—even though they have the right to have sex with their spouses—to beat them senseless, or to starve them. The government may clearly protect children from some of their parents' behaviour: the question is *what* it may legitimately protect them from. This question can only be resolved by *theorizing* the right to raise a family, not by merely asserting it.

One theorist who has attempted to fill out the right is Charles Fried. He makes the argument that parents should have the right to form their child's values, one consequence of which would be that they would have the right to block efforts to provide their children with autonomy-facilitating education. Fried's argument starts by claiming that:

The right to form one's child's values, one's child's life plan and the right to lavish attention on that child are extensions of the basic right not to be interfered with in doing these things for oneself. (Fried, Charles, *Right and Wrong*, 152.)

What would be implied by the suggestion that parents have no special title to determine their children's values? 'Surely such a view implies that parents' reproductive functions are only adventitiously their own: . . . they have no special relationship to the product of that reproduction'.[1] But this would be a mistake, because one's sexual, and hence reproductive, functions are central to one's identity: 'sexuality is part of one's basic equipment and resources as a person'.[2] This centrality justifies the conclusion that we must not only respect the person as an abstract entity, but that we must concretely respect their bodily natures: 'it shows that the sense of possession of oneself . . . extends to possession of one's function. And this extends naturally to reproduction'.[3] Children are, of course, independent persons, but 'this independent status is sufficiently recognized by obliging the parents to care for and educate the child in the child's best interests'.[4] To demand that parents share authority over the formation of their children's values would, therefore, amount to disrespect for the parents as persons.

Fried uses the considerations he offers to justify extensive authority over children's upbringings. But in fact the considerations, while well founded, justify much less than that: they simply justify the idea that there is a right to raise one's children, not that such a right includes extensive authority over their education. 'Special' title to form one's child's values can be recognized without granting *exclusive* title. That other agencies are

---

[1] Fried, Charles, *Right and Wrong* (Cambridge, Mass.: Harvard University Press, 1978), 153.

[2] Ibid., 154.      [3] Ibid.      [4] Ibid.

granted *some* influence, and discretion concerning the use of that influence over the formation of a child's values, neither implies that parents have no rights over their children nor that their rights are not special. So a mandatory autonomy-facilitating education does not threaten special title since it is quite consistent with permitting parental influence in the home. Parents may have an exclusive right to determine which church, if any, their children attend at the weekend; whether their children attend Sunday school or Hebrew school; whether their children will be allowed to watch commercial television: none of these rights are threatened by a policy of autonomy-facilitating education in the school curriculum.[5]

Furthermore, even if there were a conflict, Fried is wrong to think that denying that parents have a fundamental right to the power to determine the course of their children's lives implies that they have no special relationship to their children. Parents may indeed have a special relationship to their children, which derives from their having brought the children into the world. But what is special about that relationship is probably best specified in terms of the *obligations* they have toward their children; and toward their fellow citizens who will now have to share their world with, and have new and unchosen obligations towards, the children. It is not clear why we should think that the parents have special *rights* over their children. They may indeed have the right against society that they not be prevented from fulfilling their obligations toward their children, but this does not extend to the right that the rest of society refrain from stepping in when the parents fail to fulfil their obligations. The right to be allowed to fulfil an obligation is precisely that. It does not imply the right to refrain from fulfilling that obligation, nor the right to prevent others from fulfilling their obligations to the same persons. It is wise, for the reasons we reviewed in Chapter 1, to establish a presumption in favour of a rough social division of moral labour which grants parents some conditional and limited power over their children. If so, that is primarily because this is the best available mechanism for delivering our obligations to children, and only in a very limited way because the parents are properly thought to have rights. But if ensuring that future citizens have the opportunity to become autonomous persons is an obligation that we all share, and that we share with parents of children, mandating autonomy-facilitating education is acceptable, even given the claim that parents have a special relationship with their children, which society is obliged to respect.

It is worth noting that, even on a libertarian or conservative view, other people are bound to have an interest in the outcome of their fellow

---

[5] Amy Gutmann makes this point in 'Children, Paternalism and Education: A Liberal Argument', *Philosophy and Public Affairs*, 9 (1980), 338–58.

citizens' reproductive activities. The decision to have children unavoidably creates new moral burdens for other members of society. It does this obviously by introducing new competitors for fixed social benefits. It does so less obviously and more importantly by creating new substantive moral obligations for other people. I am arguing that these obligations are extensive, but even conservatives and libertarians must view the obligations as non-trivial. The new person has numerous rights against interference in his or her life which must be observed, and substantive rights on becoming an adult, such as the right to vote and the right to a fair trial, which fellow citizens must grant and pay for. To use a metaphor which is familiar—if rather distasteful in this context—children 'take up space' which is now off-limits for the free activities of other adults. The decision to have children alters the moral circumstances of all one's fellows. This does not mean that it is something that must be justified to them, but it does mean that one cannot say, simply, that it is none of their business.

## THE WEAK RIGHT TO FORM ONE'S CHILDREN'S VALUES

As we have seen, there are two quite distinct versions of the parents' rights thesis. One is that parents have fundamental rights over their children, rights which are intrinsic to the concept of justice. This is Fried's position. Loren Lomasky argues that parents' rights have a different status. On his view parents' rights, although they have content similar to what Fried grants, have a different *status*: they exist because the most efficient way of organizing society with respect to the important interests of all members is to vest primary responsibility for the care of the child in its parents and the extended family.

Lomasky advances three considerations which support this allocation of authority. First, 'it is the progenitive act of the parents that is causally responsible for the existence of the child and so for any weal or woe that befalls it',[6] and so 'Producing children makes them one's own. That is so whether or not conception of the child was desired and intended. No other individuals stand in the same causal relation as the parents'.[7] Second, parents as project pursuers have an overwhelming interest in being able to raise their own children: the fact that 'having children is often an integral component of persons' projects', and that this fact is 'remarkably constant over

---

[6] Lomasky, Loren, *Persons, Rights, and the Moral Community* (Oxford: Oxford University Press, 1987), 165
[7] Ibid., 166–7.

times and places of human activity' is a powerful reason for vesting primary responsibility for the care of a child in its parents. Finally, 'regard for someone as a rights-holder is grounded in the recognition of that being as a distinct individual' and since parents immediately recognize their children as distinct individuals they are likely to foster in children the sense of self crucial to being a project pursuer. Hence we are obliged to grant parents immense latitude in forming their children's conceptions of how to live.[8]

Despite the tenor of his comments, it is important to see that Lomasky is not claiming that parents have fundamental rights over their children. Like Friedman he recognizes that children have an independent standing as potential persons, so that an individualist theory cannot consistently subsume their interests under those of their parents. He goes on to say that:

Families do not enjoy some mystical status that renders them untouchable: it is in the first instance, concern for the child's good and who is best situated to act to attain it that underlies the privileged status of the family. Parents no more than anyone else are at liberty to inflict harms on the child. Political institutions are certainly entitled to prohibit flatly abusive treatment and to enforce vigorously those laws protecting children. (Lomasky, Loren, *Persons, Rights and the Moral Community*, 172.)

Given this stipulation, how can it be that Lomasky's touchable parental rights include the right to shield their children from an autonomy-facilitating education? The answer is that he denies that individuals have an interest in becoming autonomous, and so the state, in guarding children's welfare interests, has no business trying to provide them with a real opportunity to become autonomous. As potential project pursuers, says Lomasky, children only have an interest in becoming non-servile. The servile man is one 'who takes on the ends of others because he has none of his own', and who thus treats himself as 'an instrument for the ends of others and not an end in and for himself'.[9] But non-servility can be achieved without autonomy. It is quite possible to come to have ends which are genuinely one's own without either having exercised critical reflection over them or even having had the opportunity to do so. Adopting ends simply as a result of environmental influence may, if one lacks the skills associated with autonomy, be non-autonomous, but it is not servile, and that is all that matters. 'If the child comes to subscribe almost entirely to the ends held by the parents but does so through taking on those ends as projects of his or her own which now shape a life that is recognizably coherent in its own terms, then the child's rightful claim to live as a project pursuer has been satisfied'.[10]

[8] Ibid., 167.     [9] Ibid., 184.     [10] Ibid., 185.

The family, then, though it does not have a mystical status, does have a *privileged* status, and Lomasky accuses anti-family theorists 'from Plato to Mao to the Reverend Moon' of attempting 'to relocate primary loyalties from the home to the collective enterprise'[11] and of giving undue weight in their theorizing to impersonal value: 'For impersonal value to be enthroned, personal value must go—and with it the family as a fount of distinctive attachment to particular others'.[12]

Lomasky's history is probably right: the opponents of the family probably *have* pursued an agenda of impersonal value and collectivism at levels higher than, and to the detriment of, the family. But his comments about opponents of the family are revealing: like Fried, he seems to have in mind that what he is doing is justifying the family against its opponents, and I suspect that this argument is successful in doing that. But to justify the institution of the family is one thing: to justify extensive authority over children's upbringings is quite another. The main arguments for *limiting* parental authority, while retaining the family, are the argument that there is a fundamental interest in autonomy, and that there should be equality of opportunity among all citizens. Neither of these arguments appeal to impersonal value, or to the need for fealty to some collective enterprise. The claim regarding autonomy is that it enhances dramatically the ability of individuals to identify and live lives that are worth living. The principle of equality of opportunity identifies various goods which are valuable whatever one's goals and says that each individual should have equal chances to get use of those resources: it is an individualist, not a collectivist principle, and one which appeals to the personal, not impersonal, interests of individuals.

The key to Lomasky's defence of extensive parental authority is his claim that while individuals have an interest in non-servility, they have no interest in autonomy. I have already argued in detail that we *do* have an interest in autonomy, and do not want to reiterate it here. But it is worth revisiting one point which is relevant to Lomasky's limitation of his concern to non-servility. If children are brought up to be non-servile but not autonomous, many will find themselves unable to live well within the constraints they effectively face, and will thus be deprived of the opportunity to live well. Furthermore, unlike the other liberal theorists we shall consider who are hostile to teaching autonomy, like Galston and Burtt, Lomasky does not even make the qualification that in modern societies there will unavoidably be opportunities for contact with ways of life other

---

[11] Lomasky, Loren, *Persons, Rights, and the Moral Community* (Oxford: Oxford University Press, 1987), 169.
[12] Ibid.

than those of one's parents. It is quite consistent with his view that a child be brought up in an entirely closed society with but a single way of life, and that they be inducted, non-servilely but non-autonomously into that way of life, and that no wrong is done. In such circumstances many will be deprived of the ability to live lives with which they can identify from the inside: they will, then, be alienated from their projects. The interest in being a project pursuer seems to justify more than Lomasky allows.

Lomasky's rejection of the other principle which justifies limiting parental authority, equality of opportunity, is also worth commenting on. He says that 'Liberal rights theory denies that there is one Grand Racetrack on which we are all bidden to run . . . rather, individuals assume from themselves the course that they are bidden to run and take charge of providing for themselves the resources they require'.[13] But of course, inspiring as it sounds, this is extremely misleading. A government, such as that recommended by Lomasky, which enforces free market-based property rights, and unconstrained rights to inheritance, imposes on the children of the poor particularly, a great burden of providing for themselves the resources they require; and frees those children of the rich who can retain their parents' affection from that burden completely. It is true that the success of some does not necessarily imply the failure of others, and many pursuits are such that the level of one's own success depends upon the level of success of others.[14] But there are resources which can be expected to assist us whatever our project, and which are readily distributable: money, nutrition, shelter, and education. If, as Lomasky recommends, the government makes education exclusively a parental responsibility, then even the ability to assume for oneself the course one should run, which depends on knowledge of oneself and the realistic options, will be contingent on the success of one's parents. Support for principles of equality of opportunity, as we shall see, does not assume that all social activity is strictly competitive: it just assumes that, to the extent that it is predictably competitive, we want access to the means to compete to be fair.

## THE RIGHT TO RELIGIOUS LIBERTY

Like Fried, Brenda Almond premises extensive authority over the formation of children's values on a fundamental right of parents, but she

[13] Ibid., 180–1.
[14] For example, my book is better than it would have been had Lomasky not written such a good one.

grounds the authority simply on their own right to religious liberty. She argues that the religious liberty of parents would be effaced by measures which interfered with their authority over their children's education. She advances this argument as follows:

It is clear . . . that there are persisting cultural disagreements as to the extent and limits of parental authority, and that some of these disagreements are based on strongly held religious views . . . once some necessary exceptions have been made there is a strong prima facie case for the principle that cultural and religious freedom for people of mature years should carry with it freedom for those same adult people to bring up their children according to their own beliefs . . . Freedom of religion, then, together with freedom to maintain and perpetuate one's culture, provides one kind of independent argument . . . for assigning ultimate authority in educational matters to parents. (Almond, Brenda, 'Education and Liberty: Public Provision and Private Choice' 199–200.)

She claims that this commitment supports three sorts of measure:

(1) 'permitting individual families to opt out of the education system altogether';
(2) 'permitting the existence of independent schools (though not providing them with special subsidies)'; and
(3) 'permitting individuals to perpetuate their own ideals and beliefs, particularly religious beliefs, through the family structure by retaining in their own hands ultimate control of the shape and direction of their children's education'.[15]

There are several problems with Almond's position. First, as I suggested earlier, even admitting parental power over religious upbringings does not commit us to allowing withdrawal or private schooling. The state could establish and sponsor a wide variety of religious schools, spending roughly the same on all children, and require that all parents send their children to one of those schools. State support for religious diversity is not inherently more incredible than state toleration of religious diversity.

However, the above response does concede the parental rights. The real question is whether Almond given us any reason to do that, and the answer seems to be no. She asserts that there is 'a strong prima facie case for the principle that cultural and religious freedom for people of mature years should carry with it freedom for those same adult people to bring up their children according to their own beliefs',[16] but she never actually says what that prima facie case is. The argument I gave in Chapter 4 constitutes

---

[15] Almond, Brenda, 'Education and Liberty: Public Provision and Private Choice', *Journal of Philosophy of Education*, 25 (1991), 193–202 at 200–1.
[16] Ibid., 200.

a strong prima facie case *against* this principle. Is there a similarly strong case for the principle?

To see why there is not, think of the general case for religious tolerance. We think that individuals should be permitted to live their lives according to their own religious values because we think that to do otherwise is unacceptably paternalistic. Paternalism is usually unacceptable because it presumes that the patient of the action is a less competent judge of their own good than the agent is. It thereby displays disrespect for the moral agency of the patient. If an obligation to presume respect for our fellow citizens grounds our obligations of justice to them, then justice contains a strong presumption against paternalism.

But the presumption against paternalism assumes that it is appropriate for us to respect the moral agency of our fellows. Under what conditions is this assumption correct? On the standard view it is defeasible by certain conditions of the agent. Addiction, brainwashing, hypnotism, and insanity all put the agent in a situation in which the assumption fails. Children, especially young children, whose moral capacities have not yet been developed, are exempt from the presumption.

What makes the assumption correct is that our fellows have had a realistic opportunity to become autonomous persons, and have the internal resources to take advantage of that opportunity. The insane and the addicted lack those internal resources; in the hypnotized and the brainwashed those resources have been bypassed; and in children the opportunity has not yet been presented. Unless we have good reason to believe that children have been presented with realistic opportunities to become autonomous, we have no reason to believe that they will become the kind of people to whom the presumption against paternalism applies. Yet if we abandon children to the religious fates chosen for them by their parents we have no reason to believe they will have the realistic opportunity to become autonomous. Contra Almond, then, the case for religious tolerance is far more compelling when parents are not regarded as having ultimate authority over their child's education than when they are.

I should, at this point, clarify the position elaborated in Chapter 4. In denying that parents have ultimate authority I do not deny that they have *any* authority. It is entirely compatible with my argument that parents have an *exclusive* right to take their children to church, the mosque, or Communist party meetings, and subject them to Sunday School, Hebrew school, or Bolshevik school. The point is only that there is a significant part of their educational experience, autonomy-facilitating education, which will involve exposure to a variety of religious and non-religious views, and secular as well as sectarian moral thinking, as well as provision of knowledge and skills, from which their parents should not be allowed to exempt them, regardless of their own religious inclinations. Second, it is worth noting that I have not relied on anything as strong as the premise that the case for tolerance requires autonomy facilitating education in my argument for autonomy-facilitating education. I have invoked that here, only to show that the case for religious toleration does not naturally extend to permitting ultimate parental authority over education.

## THE RIGHT NOT TO BE AUTONOMOUS

Another strategy for opposing mandatory autonomy-facilitating education is to argue that it illegitimately elevates the ideal of the autonomous life to one for which all must strive. William Galston argues that, while the state should promote certain civic virtues through the education system, it may not mandate autonomy-facilitating education. He specifically rejects the idea that students should be taught to respect other ways of life than their own, and that they should be exposed to a wide range of ways of life and conceptions of the good, and educated in how to evaluate them critically.

Galston's argument can be best understood in the context of an ongoing debate between him and Amy Gutmann concerning the content and permissibility of civic education. As we saw in the previous chapter, Gutmann argues for an educational curriculum designed to produce democratic citizens replete with the civic virtues of deliberative citizenship. In learning to be respectful of their fellow citizens children would learn how to take seriously and think through moral commitments other than their own and those of their parents. In learning effective public deliberation, furthermore, they would learn how rationally to evaluate evidence and argument presented in favour of proposals concerning the public good. The exercise of these virtues require skills that, once they are acquired, almost inevitably lead morally honest people to critical reflection on their own values, commitments, and ways of life. Civic education, then, for Gutmann, unavoidably leads to autonomy.

Galston's argument has two elements. First is the fact that the argument for promoting civic virtues through compulsory schools simply does not support the further measures needed for autonomy-facilitating education. Galston objects both to Gutmann's conception of the just polity as a deliberative democracy, and consequently to the content of her proposed civic education. Galston emphasizes, instead, the individual liberty to pursue one's life as one sees fit. The argument for imposing a specifically civic education proceeds from the need to preserve the preconditions for effective exercise of this liberty. As he points out, even Locke, though he thought that the state could not legitimately command adherence to any religious or moral doctrine, could quite properly use its educative and persuasive powers to encourage citizens voluntarily to behave in accordance with the requirements of civic order. Locke's view was that the benefits of civil government required social peace for their security, and hence it was reasonable to persuade any who selected to enjoy those benefits to behave in ways likely to promote social peace.

Galston endorses a special case of this argument, saying that guaranteeing freedom of conscience requires the background of a stable civil society. Furthermore,

If citizenship means anything, it means a package of benefits and burdens shared, and accepted, by all. To be a citizen of a liberal polity is to be required to surrender so much of your own private conscience as is necessary for the secure enjoyment of what remains. To refuse this surrender is in effect to breach the agreement under which you are entitled to full membership in your community. (Galston, William, *Liberal Purposes*, 250.)

Acceptance of the right of the state to educate us and our children in the specific virtues which serve the stability of the liberal democratic state, is grounded in the requirement to share the burdens of social co-operation fairly. Galston describes the liberal virtues programmatically. A liberal civic education should 'engender not only the full range of public excellences but also the widest possible acceptance of the need for such excellences in the conduct of our public life'.[17] The public excellences are tied to offices and positions which are not held by all: judges should have fair judgment, elected representatives should be attentive to those they represent, etc. Although, as we shall see, Galston mentions a good number of civic virtues, he only explicitly talks about inculcating two broad virtues: 'a willingness to coexist peacefully with ways of life other than ones own', and 'the minimal conditions of reasonable public judgment'.[18]

However, living by those virtues is compatible, both in theory and in practice, with a quite determined and unreflective commitment to a sectarian conception of the good. As he says, 'tolerance of deep differences is perfectly compatible with unswerving belief in the correctness of one's own way of life', and civic deliberation, which only requires that 'each

[17] William Galston, *Liberal Purposes* (Cambridge: Cambridge University Press, 1991), 248.
[18] Ibid., 253.

citizen accept the minimal civic commitments without which the liberal polity cannot long endure' is compatible with 'unshakable personal commitments'.[19] The argument for promoting civic virtues, then, does not suffice to generate permission for autonomy-facilitation.

The second element of his argument is that autonomy-facilitating education gets its appeal from the unacceptable premise that 'the unexamined life is an unworthy life'.[20] This claim is unacceptable, he thinks, because a liberal state could not build it in to the system of public education without

> throwing its weight behind a conception of the human good unrelated to the functional needs of its sociopolitical institutions and at odds with the deep beliefs of many of its loyal citizens. As a political matter, liberal freedom entails the right to live unexamined as well as examined lives—a right the effective exercise of which may require parental bulwarks against the corrosive influence of modernist skepticism.   (Galston, William, *Liberal Purposes*, 254.)

Notice that for Galston the problem is *not* that the policy is non-neutral. When a policy is required for the self-reproduction of liberal institutions, such as the promotion of the civic virtues; or for overcoming barriers to the normal development of children, such as the enforcement of laws against incestual rape, that it is non-neutral is no objection to it, on Galston's view. But intrusions into the upbringing of children which are not required for either of these purposes are unjustifiable. And requiring autonomy-facilitation is therefore impermissible.

However, Galston's arguments fail for three reasons. First, autonomy is compatible with a wide variety of ways of life including those which involve traditional values. One can autonomously choose to live unreflectively, and so autonomy as a value does not conflict with many traditional values. Second, there are solid justifications for requiring autonomy-facilitating education which do not rest on the premise that the unexamined life is an unworthy one, and which do not therefore require that the weight of the state be put behind autonomy. The argument of Chapter 3 is exactly such a justification. Nothing is claimed about the specifically *moral* importance of living autonomously: it is only claimed that effective autonomous reflection is a great aid to moral learning. Furthermore, on the argument I have provided, although the skills associated with autonomy are taught, children are not encouraged by the state to live

---

[19] William Galston, *Liberal Purposes* (Cambridge: Cambridge University Press, 1991), 253.

[20] Ibid., 253. Gutmann does say quite explicitly that 'a good life must be one that people live from the inside, by accepting and identifying it as their own'. 'Democracy and Democratic Education', *Studies in Philosophy and Education*, 12 (1993), 1–9 at 8. It is not clear to me that she ever goes as far as to say that the unexamined life is unworthy.

autonomous lives: any more than children taught how to speak French are encouraged to live French-speaking lives. Finally, even accepting Galston's restriction that the state should only coerce in ways that are necessary to reproduce stable liberal institutions, it is arguable that the liberal state has an obligation to ensure that all children have an opportunity to become the kind of person whose consent to coercive institutions matters. If it does have such an obligation—or, to put it another way, if adult citizens have this obligation toward children who will become citizens of the state those adults have maintained—then requiring autonomy-facilitation appears to be a consequence.[21]

Before leaving Galston I want to address a related objection which he raises only briefly. At one point he says that 'The greatest threat to children in modern liberal societies is not that they will believe in something too deeply, but that they will believe in nothing very deeply at all. Even to achieve the kind of free self-reflection that many liberals prize, it is better to begin by believing something'.[22] Autonomy-facilitating education, it might be said, misleads children into a crude moral relativism, or toward a nihilism, by encouraging in them 'skeptical reflection on the ways of life inherited from their parents or local communities'.[23] This would, of course, be bad for the sceptics because they would not only have a false belief about the nature of moral truth, but would also lack the ability self-confidently to organize their own lives according to moral norms.

Relativism is indeed a real danger. But why think that it is peculiarly supported by the practice of autonomy-facilitating education? Autonomy-facilitation gets its point, in fact, from the falsity of relativism and, like other kinds of education at the high school level, this can be explained fairly clearly to students. Some students may not get the point, but even this is no more likely to generate relativism than another feature of civic education which most liberals including Galston and, it seems, Rawls, find acceptable: the teaching of tolerance as a virtue. Proponents of a minimal civic education, teaching only the virtues which support stability of the liberal state, accept that civic tolerance—'the willingness to coexist peacefully with ways of life very different from one's own . . . rest[ing] on the

[21] I argue in 'Liberal Legitimacy and Civic Education', 721–5 against the restriction Galston imposes. See also Callan, Eamonn, *Creating Citizens* (Oxford: Oxford University Press, 1996), chapter 5 for a fine and detailed rebuttal of Galston's views.

[22] Galston, William, *Liberal Purposes*, 255. This quote, in context, does not purport to provide an argument against autonomy-facilitating education, only a warning against restricting the authority of parents over their children. The argument which I consider here is worked up from comments not of philosophers, but of political proponents of parental discretion.

[23] Galston, *Liberal Purposes*, 253.

conviction that the pursuit of the better course should (and in many cases must) result from persuasion rather than coercion'[24]—should be taught. But it is *this*, I think, that leads to relativism, by a route that should be familiar to teachers of college-level beginning philosophy courses. Those in whom civic tolerance is inculcated, but who are not led to reflect critically about tolerance, are often deeply confused about why they should be tolerant, inferring that it has to do with the equal status of the beliefs of those whom they tolerate, rather than the equal status of the persons whose beliefs they are expected to tolerate. Since their own views are true and their fellows' views have equal status, they conclude that their fellows' views are true. Since their views and their fellows' views conflict, they conclude that truth can apply equally to conflicting views, and hence that some form of relativism must be true. This sometimes leads toward the superficial belief that Galston fears, though it sometimes does not, since people rarely think this process through as explicitly as it has been represented here.

Autonomy-facilitating education might actually help to avoid the confusion described above, and hence tend away from relativism and superficiality. By teaching students rational methods for evaluating the truth-value of moral claims, autonomy-facilitating education conveys the idea that moral claims have a truth value, and that this truth value is susceptible of rational inquiry. Teaching Gutmann's stronger value of 'mutual respect among persons', far from leading toward relativism, might actually lead away from it, by clarifying that our reason for taking seriously the beliefs of others is our respect for those others, not the epistemological status of their beliefs. Including as it does the idea that we should take seriously their views, civic respect does not support, though it does permit, the abstention from comment on others' beliefs suggested by mere tolerance: it supports us evaluating those views, and acknowledging falsehood when we find it, while also accepting that mere falsehood of somebody's view does not justify disregarding it in our actions affecting that person. So in fact, civic respect is, like civic tolerance, 'perfectly compatible with unswerving belief in the correctness of one's own way of life',[25] although again, like tolerance, that compatibility depends on the content of the way of life in question and, unlike mere tolerance, it is not compatible with an unwillingness to subject one's own way of life to rational scrutiny.

---

[24] Galston, *Liberal Purposes*, 253.        [25] Ibid.

## THE RIGHT TO ONE'S OWN CULTURE

The traditional liberal attitude to culture is that, however important it may be to people subjectively, and however valuable it may be in explaining their behaviour, it occupies no special moral status in considering the obligations of the state. People have a right to culture only in the very weak sense that the state may not deliberately coerce them into cultures to which they object. The individual rights to freedom of expression, freedom of religion, and freedom of association describe the proper state stance towards culture, and no more is required than that the state leave individuals alone to their own pursuits.

But in recent years a number of political philosophers have challenged this standard liberal position which is dubbed by one opponent, Will Kymlicka, as 'benign neglect'. Benign neglect is an erroneous attitude, according to its critics, because culture does indeed occupy a morally central place in people's lives which the state has an obligation to respect, and because some cultures suffer systematic disadvantages with respect to others in multicultural societies. These disadvantages, for which they cannot reasonably be held responsible, redound to the disadvantage of the adherents of those cultures. Since liberalism, especially in its egalitarian forms, places great weight on the distinction between choices, for which individuals can be held responsible, and circumstances, for which they cannot, and since culture appears as a circumstance, it seems that liberals ought to require that the state take proactive measures in defence of cultures which go beyond the benign neglect described above.[26]

Liberal advocates of proactive government action towards culture typically say that certain group rights must be implemented to protect cultures, but they are also typically non-committal about the relationship between these rights and individual rights, especially individual rights to education. Kymlicka himself is circumspect about group rights over education, claiming only that it is probably appropriate to allow Quebec to require that all children be educated in French, but expressing reservations about the content of the Yoder decision.

A different version of the right to culture, which does appear to prohibit making autonomy-facilitating education mandatory, is offered by Avishai

---

[26] The previous paragraph is a very brief description of the central argument in Kymlicka, Will, *Liberalism, Community and Culture* (Oxford: Oxford University Press, 1990), chapter 7. I discuss Kymlicka's argument critically and in much more detail in 'Against Nationalism', *Canadian Journal of Philosophy*, Supplementary Volume 22 (1996), 365–405.

Margalit and Moshe Halbertal. I should emphasize that they give little explicit discussion to education policy, so I hesitate to attribute to them the view that this policy may not be mandated. However, that position does seem to implied by their assertion that the right to culture implies that 'both the Ultra-Orthodox and the Arab minorities should be assisted in maintaining their educational institutions and their judicial autonomy in marital and family matters as long as their courts do not impose their norms on other Israeli citizens.'[27] I shall argue that if their view does prohibit the mandating of autonomy-facilitating education then it is robbed of much of its apparent appeal. Certainly, their theory is a sophisticated theorization of considerations which are often advanced by other theorists against autonomy-facilitating education and other similar policies.

Margalit and Halbertal start with the importance of what they call personality identity, which captures what is important in the concept of the anthropological individual:

The same person can undergo a radical change in personality yet remain the same person, whereas the converse is not the case. Culture plays a crucial role in shaping the personalities of individuals, especially in those aspects that they and their environment consider central for constituting their personality identity. (Margalit, Avishai, and Halbertal, Moshe, 'Liberalism and the Right to Culture', 501–2.)

Individuals thus have a morally powerful interest in preserving the conditions which make for security of their personality identity. But cultural environment plays a crucial role in making for such stability. Were the culture to change dramatically, or were individuals deprived of the cultural context in which they were accustomed to operating, their personality identity would be threatened, made insecure. So, according to Margalit and Halbertal, individuals have a right to their own culture.

It should be obvious that this right to one's own culture can support claims to more extensive government action than the mere benign neglect liberalism traditionally requires. Margalit and Halbertal identify two levels of the right to culture, and say that their main aim is to vindicate a third. The first level is the 'right to maintain a comprehensive way of life within the larger society without interference'—the traditional benign neglect. The second level adds 'the right to recognition of the community's way of life by the general society'.[28] The third adds 'the right to support for the way of life by the state's institutions so that the culture can flour-

[27] Margalit, Avishai, and Halbertal, Moshe, 'Liberalism and the Right to Culture', *Social Research*, 61 (1994), 491–510 at 507.
[28] Ibid., 498.

ish'.[29] This third level of support involves the redistribution of resources from members of secure cultures to support the underlying sources of stability for less secure cultures: 'In our example of the Ultra-Orthodox culture this means financial support for Torah institutions and Torah scholars, which is a crucial condition for the culture's flourishing'.[30]

There are two ways of responding to Margalit and Halbertal in this context. We could deny that there is a right to one's own culture, at least if that involves redistributing resources to support cultures in the way they suggest; and we could deny that a right to one's own culture supports giving communities such extensive control over their childrens' educations that they can deny them autonomy-facilitating education. I shall briefly explain why I think both these responses are correct.

The central problems with Margalit and Halbertal's argument for the right to one's own culture are that cultures evolve and people are adaptable. Cultures evolve often as a result of the unintended consequences of practices that take place within the culture, and changes in material conditions over which nobody has any real control. British culture is different in 1998 from how it was in 1958, and only partly because of the introduction of members of different cultures to British life. Yet nobody could have foreseen the cultural changes, at least in any detail. But government aid to a culture, if it is to be effective, has to be guided by some picture of how the culture is or should be. If government aid is forthcoming to some minority culture it will inevitably affect the development of the culture. Usually the effects will be conservative: the aim, after all, on Margalit and Halbertal's view, is to preserve the culture, and since the natural direction of the culture is so hard to gauge, the government will be guided by the current content of the culture. But this action takes the direction of the culture, to some extent, out of the hands of the members of the culture. Furthermore, within any culture, there are disagreements about the true content of the culture. In aiding the culture with a particular vision of it in mind, the government must of necessity take sides on these disagreements. It will thus be strengthening a particular vision of the culture against the wishes of some of the members of that very culture.

It is worth commenting here that material and regulatory support for a particular culture is always coercive, and is often coercive of members of that culture. Margalit and Halbertal suggest apparently harmless measures such as funding Torah scholarship, but the funding has to come from somewhere, and it will typically come from coercive taxation, which will often have been imposed on Orthodox Jews themselves, among others.

---

[29] Ibid., 499.    [30] Ibid.

Along similar lines David Miller advocates support for a national culture, arguing that 'very often this [protection of the national culture] can be done by inducements rather than by coercion: farmers can be given incentives to preserve their hedgerows; the domestic film industry can be subsidized out of cinema revenues; important works of art can be purchased for national collections; and so forth'.[31] But the mechanisms he describes *are* coercive. Certainly, they do not coerce the farmer and the broadcast company owner; instead they coerce the cinema-goer and the taxpayer. Even regulation which does not directly redistribute resources can restrict the freedom of members of the protected culture to live their lives by their own lights, and thus both coerces them and constrains the free development of the culture itself. A famous example is Quebec's Bill 101 of 1977, which required, among other things, that all companies which employ more than 50 people must function in French, that all commercial and road signs must be in French only, and limited the access to Anglophone schooling for all children. These measures do, of course, immediately affect the behaviour primarily of anglophone citizens, but francophone citizens are not exempt: they, too, have to send their children to francophone schools, whether they want to or not, and to use French in their business operations whether they want to or not.

People are, furthermore, quite adaptable. Because cultures evolve and change, they have to be, if their personality identities are to be secure. There are many changes in circumstances, some tragic, such as loss of spouses, parents, children, or friends; others less so, such as loss of jobs, changes in working conditions, changes in job shifts, or relocations, which people regularly bear with fortitude. The *gradual* change of, or even disappearance of, a minority culture, which is the worst we would expect to occur if the standard liberal stance toward culture were maintained by the state, may be a hurdle for someone to overcome but it seems extravagant to claim that people will lose their personalities as a result of it. The case of sudden catastrophic disappearance of a culture may, of course, be different. But, in the rare cases where this will happen within liberal democracies—I cannot think of a single actual example—there seems to be as strong a case that the government should provide resources to smooth the transition for the individuals involved, as there does for the government to try to maintain the culture artificially.

As I pointed out, while Margalit and Halbertal do not explicitly use their argument to defend community-controlled education from the requirement that children receive an autonomy-facilitating education,

---

[31] Miller, David, *On Nationality* (Oxford: Oxford University Press, 1995), 88.

their examples of what would be implied by a right to one's own culture do point in that direction. Now I want to resist that implication directly. Even if we think that individuals can properly be said to have a right to their own culture, this should not be taken to imply that children should be raised exclusively in the culture of their parents. There are good reasons, which we have already surveyed, for giving parents a good deal of authority over the cultural environment of their children. But fundamentally, children do not have a culture. Ensuring that children are being raised exclusively in the culture of their parents is not granting them their right to their own culture because they do not have their own culture. To suggest that they do is to suggest that they are the kinds of beings that can evaluate and assess the options available to them, which they are not.

There are two possible responses to this. Neither is successful. The first is to say that, while it is right that children do not have their own culture, we have an obligation to ensure that they are able to function effectively in whatever culture turns out to be theirs when they reach adulthood. I accept this, but it does not imply that they may be raised exclusively in their parent's culture for two reasons. As I pointed out in the previous chapter, even if they are raised in their parents' culture there is no guarantee that that will be their culture in adulthood, so for those children who quit we shall have failed to prepare them if we allow them to be raised exclusively in their parents' culture. More tellingly, perhaps, the kind of education we provide for children will have effects on which culture they end up in, as well as on the character of the options available to them, so we cannot read anything off from the obligation to provide them with the resources to function effectively in the culture which will be theirs.

The second response is suggested by some comments made by Joseph Raz in an important essay on multiculturalism. Raz says, rightly, that cultural membership has powerful effects on the kinds of relationships available to us. As Raz says:

A common culture facilitates social relations and is a condition of rich and comprehensive personal relationships. One particular relationship is especially sensitive to this point . . . in one's relations with one's children and with one's parents a common culture is an essential condition for the tight bonding we expect and desire. A policy that forcibly detaches children from the culture of their parents not only undermines the stability of society by undermining people's ability to sustain long-term intimate relations, it also threatens one of the deepest desires of most parents, the desire to understand their children, share their world, and remain close to them. (Raz, Joseph, 'Multiculturalism: A Liberal Perspective', 71.)

There are two distinct fears here: one is that the exit of children from the culture of their parents will deprive their parents of fulfilment of one of their deepest desires; the other is that it will undermine the capacity of the children for meaningful relationships. Raz emphasizes these as bad consequences of a policy of 'forcible' detachment, but a policy such as autonomy-facilitating education, which does not even seek to get children to exit their parents' cultures could have similar consequences: at least the problem of non-fulfillment of the parents' desires comes from the fact that the children cease to share the culture of their parents rather than the process by which they leave it.

As I have indicated, I do not think that the possible costs to parents of the exit of their children should play a large role in constraining educational policy, for reasons I shall elaborate on further in the final section of this chapter. But Raz's second point is more troubling—if sharing a common culture with one's parents is a precondition of being able to participate in lasting intimate relationships, then it is a tremendously important good. Again, Raz emphasizes the malign effects of forcible detachment, and in this case it seems right that the manner of detachment is more significant than the fact of detachment itself. Sharp ruptures of the relationships between children and parents which inhibit the ability of the children to reflect on the relationship, the reasons for its end, and other features are disruptive of their ability to develop and maintain healthy relationships.

But the cessation of the relationship itself need not be disruptive. If the conditions supporting cool reflection are maintained, and if cultural barriers are permeable or vague, then children can experiment 'outside' their culture without leaving it. They can test the barriers, and test their parents, and if rupture occurs it is less likely to be traumatic or permanent than if it occurs either forcibly or in the face of force. So, again, while Raz's observation weighs heavily against policies which aim at detaching children from their parents' cultures by force, I do not think that it rules out autonomy-facilitating education.

## NEUTRALITY

A further argument appeals to the value of neutrality I described in Chapter 1: it claims that a state imposing autonomy-facilitating education is unacceptably non-neutral in that it presumes the falsehood of moral commitments of some reasonable citizens. This objection might also claim that the non-neutrality constitutes a failure of legitimacy: how can the state be said to be seeking the consent of people against whose wishes it imposes autonomy-facilitating education on their children?

I doubt that religious parents will object to the recommendations I have made in Chapter 4 as strongly as they would to the more morally-laden recommendations of theorists like Gutmann. But, anyway, neutrality is an inappropriate constraint on the state regarding policies concerning children. In Chapter 1 I argued that if neutrality should constrain government policies concerning adult citizens, it is for one or both of the following reasons. First, it might help in securing the free consent of its citizens which is, in turn, a condition of legitimacy. So neutrality might facilitate, though it may not be a prerequisite of, legitimacy. Second, and more importantly, justice requires that citizens be equal in the sight of the government, and it may be that non-neutral justification of policy treats citizens with unequal respect. People's ideas about the good and their views of themselves are known to be intimately connected, and therefore they might reasonably feel that when coercive force is used on them for reasons they morally reject, the government, acting on behalf of their fellow citizens, not only discounts their views, but, in doing so, fails to respect them equally as persons.

It is controversial whether these are sufficient reasons to license a neutrality constraint on policy. But even if they are, neither supports neutrality concerning children. Children are not yet intimately tied to conceptions of the good, and we do not think that respecting the ties they do have is either a condition of legitimacy of the state or of treating them with respect. Liberals are so impressed with the intimate connection between persons and their conceptions of the good because persons are presumed properly to regard them as their own. But we should not regard children's conceptions as their own, because they are unequipped to make them genuinely their own.

Furthermore, it is not clear to me that the instrumental argument for autonomy-facilitating education is non-neutral in the relevant way. It invokes not a moral value, but a true epistemological claim: that rational evaluation is more reliable than other methods for discovering the good. This is controversial, but the controversy concerns epistemology, not morality. Admittedly, since the epistemological efficacy of autonomous reflection is part of the case for its moral significance,[32] those who deny its moral importance often deny its epistemological efficacy. But neutrality does not prohibit sincere appeal to controversial empirical premises: it prohibits only appeal to controversial moral claims.

---

[32] Though not the whole of it. An autonomous life may be valuable in a distinctive way even when its content is, other things being equal, less worthy than an alternative non-autonomous life, because it is in some sense the more authentic life, the one which more truly belongs to its author.

Should neutrality prohibit justificatory appeal to some controversial empirical claims? Such a constraint would probably paralyse governments if neutrality were taken seriously as a constraint. But that may not be a sufficient argument against it. A more important argument is that the sources of appeal for neutrality do not support expanding its scope. Neutrality's appeal rests partly on the intimate connection between persons and their conceptions of the good. This intimacy, partly consequent on the view that individuals are morally responsible for working out and living by a set of true moral precepts, supports a person's feelings that they are being shown disrespect when justifications of coercive action, undertaken either against them or on their behalf, presume their moral views false. The same intimacy is not present in the case of empirical beliefs. While significant revision of our moral beliefs supports revision of our identities, this is not true of our empirical beliefs, especially abstract beliefs such as epistemological beliefs.

That the instrumental argument is neutral, whatever its theoretical interest, may have little practical significance. It shows only that even if neutrality were an appropriate constraint on government action regarding children, any justified complaint religious parents could advance against autonomy-facilitating education could not be on the grounds of non-neutrality. This need not mean that opponents will press their case less strongly, even if they acknowledge neutrality is fulfilled.[33]

So where does this leave the concern with legitimacy? If legitimacy is the more basic value, then showing that neutrality is fulfilled should not satisfy us. This is the point, then, at which liberals have to take a stand. Eamonn Callan, criticizing Rawls's claim that political liberalism supports only a minimal civic education, and not an autonomy-facilitating education, says that parents who object to their children becoming autonomous must be regarded as unreasonable to some degree.[34] To that degree, then, their consent does not legitimate, and their objections do not delegitimate. Callan's response preserves the possibility of maintaining the conventional view that legitimacy could be an all-or-nothing affair. An alternative response, which gives up that possibility, and accepts the suggestion I

---

[33] I discuss the possibility that neutrality must be seen to be done in Brighouse, Harry, 'Neutrality, Publicity, and State Funding of the Arts', *Philosophy and Public Affairs*, 24 (1995), 36–63.

[34] Callan, Eamonn, 'Political Liberalism and Political Education', *Review of Politics*, 58 (1996), 5–33, especially 22–3. Callan's more general argument is that political liberalism is in fact 'a kind of closet ethical liberalism' (22), and that the distinction between political liberalism and ethical, or comprehensive, liberalisms is thus of limited interest. I make a similar argument in 'Is There Any Such Thing As Political Liberalism?', *Pacific Philosophical Quarterly*, 75 (1994), 318–22.

made earlier that liberal legitimacy may be achieved to greater or lesser degrees, would say that when the legitimacy-related interests of children clash with the demands of reasonable adults, the interests of children should take precedence, even at the cost of losing the legitimizing consent of those adults. Both these responses have some appeal to me: but the important point is that to refrain from making either response would be to neglect the separate and vulnerable status of children and thus, again, abandon liberalism's claim as an individualistic doctrine. The legitimacy objection can be sustained only at the cost of disregarding the way in which children ought to count in a liberal polity.

## THE LIBERAL CASE AGAINST AUTONOMY-FACILITATING EDUCATION

However, autonomy-facilitating education is not yet out of the woods. I now turn to a final argument, which claims that children's interests are best served if parents are guaranteed a preponderance of authority over children, allowing them to exempt children from autonomy-facilitating education.

Two clarifications are in order. First, any argument of this form must be somewhat speculative, and to that extent will be inconclusive. Second, it is important to see why the argument needs to appeal to the arrangement's benefits for children's interests, and not just to overall social benefits. The expected *general* bad consequences of a policy—say for the general culture—do not suffice for its rejection if justice requires the policy. If justice requires a measure, then it must be shown that the expected consequences are sufficiently bad to undermine the tendency of the policy to generate the goods the provision of which is required. This is because, to use Ronald Dworkin's metaphor, justice trumps mere social benefit.

Shelley Burtt has recently provided a partial defence of the view that mandating autonomy-facilitating education violates a general policy of parental deference which is grounded in concern for the interests of children. She responds to common fears that a policy of parental deference will undermine a tolerant social order by claiming that liberals generally misunderstand the aims of deeply religious parents. Far from aiming to inculcate intolerance, or to impose a religious education on other children, religious parents have two central purposes: they seek to 'provide and preserve a sense of the transcendent in the face of an aggressively materialist culture', and 'to supply their children with the resources necessary to live a righteous life, to prevent . . . the corruption . . . from too early or over-whelming a temptation to sin'.[35]

Burtt then argues that children 'need an upbringing that enables them to pursue and live a good life as they come to understand it'.[36] Providing a consistent moral and religious upbringing is one important way 'of building the psychological and cognitive resources the child will need' for this task.[37] But if the home environment provides such an upbringing, efforts to facilitate autonomy in the school curriculum will send conflict-ing messages, thus undermining the capacity of parents to deliver the goods in the home. The authorities governing public schools would, she says, 'do better to encourage parental efforts to create a moral environ-ment filled with consistent, not conflicting, messages'.[38]

Finally, the policy of parental deference is supported by the character of some deeply religious ways of life. Burtt invokes the importance of auto-nomy to support her proposal, by arguing that in materialist secular soci-eties 'certain of these [religious] lives may depend for their possibility on not being exposed too early or too insistently to secular alternatives'[39] so that 'if children are truly to have the choice of a strong religious faith, their early contact with the pluralistic and secular values of a modern society must be guarded and carefully supervised'.[40]

Two possible criticisms of Burtt should be avoided. Why not object that if the messages from home and school conflict, that is as much the fault of the parents as the school? This is true, but irrelevant, because the family is already assumed as the basic unit of organization for child-rearing, by advocates and opponents of autonomy-facilitating education alike. They accept that relationships between parents and children, even when they are not good, are important for the development of a child's moral capacities, including their capacity for autonomy. Most advocates of autonomy-facilitating education will accept that even when a child's parents will do a worse job of raising them than some other set of people, there should be no transfers unless the parents abilities fall below some low threshold. In ceding a great deal of influence to parents, advocates of autonomy-

---

[35] Burtt, Shelley, 'Religious Parents, Secular Schools', *Review of Politics*, 56 (1994), 51–70 at 63.

[36] Burtt, Shelley, 'In Defense of <u>Yoder</u>: Parental Authority and the Public Schools', in Shapiro, Ian, and Hardin, Russell (eds.), *NOMOS 38: Political Order* (New York, NY: New York University Press, 1996), 412–37 at 425.

[37] Ibid. See also 428: 'Children need a moral and sentimental education: we owe them an upbringing that provides the material and psychological resources that allow for a full and flourishing human life'.

[38] Ibid., 426.        [39] 'Religious Parents, Secular Schools', 66.        [40] Ibid., 67.

facilitating education make schools *de facto* secondary authorities with respect to upbringing.

Note that the problem, for Burtt, is *not* that parents strategically withdraw loving attention from their children in order to put the state in the position where the best it can do for the children is exempt them from autonomy-facilitating education. Parents willing to make that move probably have, antecedently, sufficiently bad relationships with their children not to warrant deference.[41] The problem is that, in doing the best that they know how to—in many cases a good best—parents put the state into this position.

A second objection might deny that liberals should be concerned that the opportunity to choose deeply religious ways of life is made less real for children. These options are still available: children will learn about them, and will not be prevented from adopting them. Why should liberals be concerned with the substantive ability of children to choose ways of life, rather than their formal freedom to choose among them?

The response is that a concern with substantive opportunity underlies the interest in autonomy-facilitating education. Autonomy-facilitating education makes substantive the formal freedom to form, revise, and pursue conceptions of the good. An advocate of autonomy-facilitating education cannot consistently resort to formalism with respect to the ways of life for which autonomy causes difficulty.

Burtt's position is genuinely liberal because it accepts that children have a powerful interest in becoming autonomous persons, and takes the interests of children as paramount in determining the institutional distribution of authority over their upbringings. Her view is thus unlike those of Galston, Fried, and even Gutmann, who, though she conceives of children's interests similarly, gives more weight to the interests of society. Any liberal position that accepts the institution of the family, must concede some degree of deference to parents, since it accepts that the family provides goods which children are owed as a matter of justice. The question is not *whether* to defer to parents, but *how much* to defer, and over what aspects of upbringing.

---

[41] Conscious strategic withdrawal is, presumably, rare. But there are two more common cases where relationships may be damaged indirectly by autonomy-facilitating education: where parents are angry at the children who leave the way of life; and where they are resentful at the school authorities for exposing their children to other ways of life, and this resentment colours their relationship with the child. It may be that these responses are both fuelled by a socially sanctioned but mistaken view that they have strong rights to determine their children's ways of life, which would, presumably, diminish over time if autonomy-facilitating education were successfully carried out. But both cases reveal worrying features of the parent-child relationship involved.

The policy of autonomy-facilitating education I have described may trouble Burtt's deeply religious parents less than Gutmann's policy. Gutmann's policy inculcates a substantive value, civic respect, which requires that we take the conflicting ways of life of others seriously, and this genuinely conflicts with the teachings of many religious parents. Autonomy-facilitating education merely aims to enable children to take different ways of life seriously if they wish. Similarly, it does not inculcate an inclination to participate in public life, but only equips them to do so rationally. The recommendations I have made with respect to legitimacy, unlike Gutmann's, seek to enable children to think critically about the justification of the status quo, which may even buttress some of their parents' anti-materialist values.[42]

Deeply religious parents are still likely to object. Those who do, however, must point to the conflict between autonomy and their ways of life, not to a conflict with the values taught at home. If they object to autonomy, *per se*, their position is much weaker, on Burtt's argument. Burtt places great emphasis on the fact that autonomy is displayed in many religious, even deeply religious ways of life. Canons of rationality govern argument concerning scripture in many Protestant churches; knowledge of scripture and non-deference to authoritative interpretation are emphasized in some churches, which liberals typically find troubling.

Burtt also stresses the availability of exit: she says that the defection rate from the Amish community, for example, shows that parents do not disenable a child's ultimate choice,[43] and that her argument

assumes that, despite the best intentions of American parents they will not be able to shield their children completely from the country's largely secular, highly commercialized mass culture. If the evidence were to suggest the contrary ... the state's responsibility to provide an alternative ... would be correspondingly stronger.   (Burtt, Shelley, 'In Defense of <u>Yoder</u>: Parental Authority and the Public Schools', 433.)

Galston similarly mitigates his opposition to teaching autonomy, because even a minimalist civic education would lead children to quit their parents' ways of life:[44]

---

[42] Gutmann's recommendations would, in my view, be likely to have similar effects, but that is not part of her aim.

[43] Burtt, Shelley, 'In Defense of <u>Yoder</u>', 432.

[44] Rawls makes a similar point: 'It may be objected that requiring children to understand the political conception in these ways is, in effect, though not in intention, to educate them in a comprehensive liberal conception. Doing the one may lead to the other, if only because once we know the one we may of our on accord go on to the other. It must be granted that this may indeed happen in the case of some'. Rawls, John, *Political Liberalism* (New York, NY: Columbia University Press, 1993), 199–200.

From a very early age, every child will see that he or she is answerable to institutions other than the family—institutions whose substantive wishes may well cut
across the grain of parental wishes and beliefs . . . the basic features of a liberal
society make it virtually impossible for parents to seal their children off from
knowledge of other ways of life. And as every parent knows, possibilities that are
known but forbidden take on an allure out of all proportion to their intrinsic merits.   (Galston, William, *Liberal Purposes*, 255.)

This seems right: it is difficult for parents to hold their children to the
religious and moral commitments in which they were raised, because most
religious communities in liberal societies are penetrated by the secular
materialist culture that surrounds them. So even quite tight-knit illiberal
subcultures will usually experience substantial defections.

But liberals have no interest in counting the likely departures from religious subcultures. This may indicate how easy it is to exit a faith, but tells
us nothing about the process by which people decide to exit or remain; and
it is the character of the *process*, rather than the numbers involved, that
interests liberals. Galston and Burtt ignore the circumstances and direction of the defections. The mainstream culture, as they both emphasize,
does not always exert its appeal through rationality-respecting mechanisms. If children are exposed to that appeal it seems unfair not to equip
them to scrutinize both the way of life they would be leaving and that
which exerts such a powerful, non-rational, appeal. If children encounter
displays of alternative ways of life, they are better able to deal with these
displays, *and* to have a sympathetic understanding of the creed from which
they may defect, if they have the skills associated with autonomy.
Autonomy-facilitating education might *mitigate* the tendency of former
believers to bitterness, so that when people abandon their parents' way of
life for another they do so not irrationally and with resentment, but with
a cool appreciation of the good and bad aspects of both. It may help salvage aspects of the relationships between the defectors and their parents,
the good of which relationship motivates some scepticism about autonomy-facilitating education.

Additionally, as we saw in the previous chapter, a powerful ideal of
equality of opportunity counts in favour of ensuring that those children
who do enter mainstream society have been educated not 'to certain minimum standards',[45] but to standards equal to those who already inhabit
the mainstream. Such children are doubly disadvantaged, having been less
well prepared for the complex demands of modern economies than other
children; and having lost, in many cases, the security which comes from

---

[45]  Burtt, Shelley, 'In Defense of <u>Yoder</u>', 428.

good relationships with parents continuing into adulthood, and the sense that short-term failures will be mitigated by parental support.

Still, the worry remains that deeply religious ways of life will be made, in effect, *unavailable* by autonomy-facilitating education, which thus restricts autonomy. But many adults from mainstream liberal society become life-long adherents to religious ways of life, despite the low popular regard for such ways of life. The ways of life are thus available to people raised in mainstream secular society, and so may be available to children raised within them but exposed to autonomy-facilitating education. The fact of conversion is not *sufficient* proof of availability for these children, since all converts may be non-autonomous. But if it were impossible to enter these ways of life from the outside autonomously, that would be evidence against their being compatible with autonomy.

## CONCLUDING COMMENTS

I have shown that a series of possible objections to mandating autonomy-facilitating education fail. But, although I believe it to be wrong, I do not have a decisive refutation of Burtt's recommendation of parental deference. However, I hope I have shown that the children of deeply religious parents have interests which support less rather than more deference. Furthermore, Burtt's argument does not prohibit that public policy regarding children should be guided, in part, by the goal of a social settlement favourable to autonomy-facilitating education. It may be that the hostility of deeply religious parents to secular education is less well explained by any conflict between autonomy and their considered moral views, than by their cultural marginalization from mainstream society: a marginalization which might be lessened, over time, by a nuanced policy of partial deference combined with willingness to allow adherents to represent their views in public schools.

We can see how intricately institutional the issue between Burtt and myself is by observing that the latter policy would not be a compromise of principle: it is recommended for its own merits. The former policy—partial deference—is indeed a compromise, but may be worth making, for the sake of the children, in order to erode their hostility to autonomy-facilitating education. A policy of demarginalization might have a further benefit, of making more permeable the boundaries between ways of life within a pluralistic society, thus making it easier to maintain, across those boundaries, the affective bonds of kinship which are so important to healthy living. The important point is that children should have a real opportunity to become autonomous. This requires that we arrange institutions so that, other things being equal, we optimize the likelihood of them having that opportunity. I believe that in most circumstances, including those faced by the countries contemplating choice reforms, this requires mandating autonomy-facilitating education, but I cannot prove it, and there certainly could be circumstances in which it did not.

# 6

# The Case for Educational Equality

A second value often invoked by opponents of school choice, as well as by critics of schooling as it is traditionally carried out in capitalist democracy, is the value of educational equality. As we shall see, the precise content of educational equality is difficult to elaborate, but those who invoke it generally have two concerns in mind. The first is that children should not have significantly better access to education simply because they have wealthier parents, or live in wealthier communities, than others. Jonathan Kozol has documented the 'savage inequalities' within the US public school system, whereby twice as much per pupil is spent on schooling in wealthy suburban school districts as in poorer inner-city districts.[1] In the UK the argument is often made that the elite private schools such as Eton and Winchester not only perpetuate the sharply divisive class character of British public culture, but also confer better educational and other opportunities on pupils for no reason other than that their parents have great wealth.

The second concern of advocates of educational equality is that some children get a better education simply because they are tagged as brighter, smarter, or more intellectually able than other children. The main moral source of opposition to the Grammar Schools in Britain, and to tracking in the US, has been the perception that the children who go to secondary moderns, or languish in the bottom track, receive an inferior education solely because they are marked out as less able. Notice that this objection to tracking does not invoke the view that children cannot be accurately identified as more or less able; nor the equally current view that all talents are of equal value so that it does not make sense to talk of some children as more talented than others. The proponent of educational equality says that even if it does make sense to talk of children as unequally able, and even if those inequalities can be accurately identified early on, it is wrong

---

[1] Kozol, Jonathan, *Savage Inequalities* (New York, NY: Harper Perennial, 1992).

to devote more educational resources to the more able, because to do so violates an ideal of equality.

A third concern, which has arisen since the introduction of choice schemes in some educational systems, such as in Australia and the UK, is that the quality of a child's education should not reflect the quality of her parents' ability to choose schools or classes for her. As we shall see in Chapter 8, recent research carried out in several Local Education Authorities in the UK shows that parents differ widely in their ability to choose well on behalf of their children.[2] Much of this difference correlates with social class, or household wealth, but not all: two children in the same social class may differ considerably in the quality of their schooling if one has attentive and savvy parents, and the other has parents who know little about educational processes or simply do not care very much about their child's education.

It is easy to see how educational inequality may be facilitated by school choice. If a 'top-up' is permitted then wealthier parents, often those who, in a system which allows private education, already purchase private education for their children as well as paying through taxation for the public education their child is not taking up, can send their children to more expensive schools. These schools can then provide more opportunities by purchasing better equipment, reducing pupil/teacher ratios, offering better salaries for teachers, and other obvious mechanisms. Parents who are better educated themselves, and better informed about which schools perform better are likely to be more effective consumers and hence able to purchase more opportunities for each unit of expenditure. Children of these two kinds of parents are likely to be more attractive to schools, and therefore there will be a tendency for different schools to stratify along class lines, with only the most promising poorer children brought into the wealthier schools. Finally, there is a fear concerning children with disabilities, and especially educational disabilities, that since they are more expensive to educate schools will shun them, thus ensuring they will have fewer opportunities than ordinarily-abled children.

We cannot draw any conclusions about the validity of the educational inequality objection to school choice until we have established that it is a legitimate concern in the design of educational institutions. This is the burden of this and the next chapter. In the course of the argument I shall try to elucidate how best to conceive of educational equality. The partial conception I elaborate and defend suffices for many public policy purposes, though it falls short of the complete account that philosophers

---

[2] Gewirtz, Sharon, Ball, Stephen, and Bowe, Richard, *Markets and Equity in Education* (Buckingham: Open University Press, 1995).

should ultimately seek and that would be necessary for determining some other purposes which I shall identify.

It is tempting to bring the first three concerns together and to characterize the ideal of educational equality as the view that children should have equal resources spent on their education, regardless of the wealth or choice-making quality of their parents and regardless of their level of ability. In practice, for most children, this is probably the policy that an egalitarian government will attempt to pursue.[3] But it is not an accurate rendering of the ideal, as we can see by thinking of the case of children with disabilities, especially disabilities related to their ability to learn. For example, a deaf child may well need to have an interpreter in order to make the same use of her education as hearing children. A pure policy of equal resources would deny her that additional resource: but it is implausible to think that educational equality is fulfilled without such provision. Similarly children with cognitive or emotional disabilities need more resources and attention devoted to them before they can make as much use of the education offered to all other children.

Before looking at the argument for educational equality, it is worth deflecting a concern which might lead some readers to ignore this chapter. Egalitarianism as a political movement has suffered serious setbacks in recent years, and is regarded by many as dead. How, it is asked, can we expect to take seriously substantive claims in favour of equality, when the only governments that have tried to advance that ideal have turned out to be either repressive, or incompetent, or both?

I would take a less pessimistic attitude to the prospects for equality. There have been relatively successful and competent attempts to limit the extent of material inequality in capitalist societies, which have been no more repressive than the attempts in those societies to increase inequality. There are no reasonable standards, for example, by which it could be claimed that the British Conservative government of the 1980s was less repressive than the Social Democratic governments which ruled Sweden for most of the past fifty years. There are certainly practical difficulties with achieving greater material equality in the face of the increasing globalization of capital markets, and the antagonism of capital markets to redistributive measures; but these difficulties, while they should inform the design of egalitarian policies, do not impugn egalitarian goals.

Anyway, the desirability of equal outcomes is largely beside the point because the ideal of educational equality is significantly independent of more general ideals of equality. How can this be true? Equality, more gen-

---

[3] For an argument to this effect see Jencks, Christopher, 'Whom Must We Treat Equally for Educational Opportunity to Be Equal?,' *Ethics*, 98 (1988), 518–33.

erally conceived, attempts to ensure that different people have roughly equal resources available to them over the course of their full lives, with inequalities permissible only when they reflect the greater effort of the beneficiaries. So, for example, if one person earns twice the income of another because she works twice as many hours, or works the same number of hours at an occupation which required many more years of training, egalitarians will not find the resultant inequality *prima facie* objectionable. They will, however, object if one person earns, say, fifteen times the income of another, at a job which is only slightly more time-consuming, and carries with it many intrinsic rewards which the less well-paid job lacks. Egalitarians also do not, contrary to the accusations of their enemies, usually require that people be paid an income independently of whether they seek useful employment. They do think, however, that when, as in most capitalist economies, there exists a significant level of involuntary unemployment, those who are effectively excluded from the workforce should be compensated with a reasonable income.[4]

But in itself the claim that people should be equally educated, or have equal opportunity in education, does not have any bearing on how much they should be paid after the point at which they leave full-time education. It states, instead, a condition on how they must be prepared for the quite possibly unequal material prospects which they will face in the world after the age of majority. In fact, what I shall call the basic argument for educational equality *assumes* that material rewards in the labour markets will be significantly unequal, and takes that as one of the central reasons for making education equal. Although most egalitarians are also educational egalitarians, there is no need for an educational egalitarian to be an egalitarian *simpliciter*.[5]

[4] There is a large literature on egalitarianism, and two basic camps can be distinguished. Some, so called 'luck' egalitarians, say that it is morally required to treat people as responsible for their voluntary choices, and that this requires that those who choose not to work, or to work less hard than others, should be given fewer resources, or holdings, than those who choose to work, or to work harder. Other theorists support an unconditional basic income arguing that in some cases it is not correct to hold people fully responsible for their voluntary choices, and in other cases that holding people responsible simply does not imply that they should be rewarded materially in proportion to their work. Examples of the former include Arneson, Richard, 'Equality and Equal Opportunity for Welfare', *Philosophical Studies*, 56 (1989), 77–93; and Dworkin, Ronald, 'What is Equality? Part 2: Equality of Resources', *Philosophy and Public Affairs*, 10 (1981), 283–345. Examples of the latter include Fluerbaey, Marc, 'Equal Opportunity or Equal Social Outcome?', *Economics and Philosophy*, 11 (1995), 25–55; Van Parijs, Phillippe, *What, if Anything, Justifies Capitalism?* (Oxford: Oxford University Press, 1996); and Levine, Andrew, *Rethinking Liberal Equality: From a 'Utopian' Point of View* (Ithaca, NY: Cornell University Press, 1998).

[5] John White makes a case that the indefensibility of egalitarianism *per se* implies the indefensibility of egalitarianism in education. See 'The Dishwasher's Child: education and the end of egalitarianism', *Journal of Philosophy of Education*, 28 (1994), 173–82.

I shall pursue the precise content of the ideal of educational equality later in this chapter. In fact, I think that the ideal can only be unpacked in the light of the argument for it. One of the problems with the debate over educational equality is that proponents tend to take it for granted, without argument, that educational equality is a central value, prior to other political values governing education; while opponents simply assume, again without argument, that other values, such as parental freedom to lavish resources on their children, are more important. Why, then, is educational equality so important a value?

## THE BASIC ARGUMENT AND A SECONDARY ARGUMENT

The argument for educational equality rests on a fundamental value, shared among many political theories which otherwise differ significantly, and many of which would not be counted as egalitarian—the idea that social and political institutions should be designed or reformed to realize equal respect for the value of all individual persons.[6] We shall see in the next chapter that there may be limits on what the state may do to implement educational equality, but those are limits to be placed after we have elaborated the ideal, rather than limits which rule out educational equality as an ideal. In other words, while the argument supports the value of educational equality, it supports it only as a *prima facie* value. However, the burden of the next chapter will be to argue that the limits to be imposed on measures aimed at achieving equality are much less than supposed by equality's enemies.

The full argument for educational equality has two facets, corresponding to the two functions of education for the individual which we have observed in our discussion of Friedman. Education yields two distinct kinds of good. It provides competitive advantages in economies which distribute benefits and burdens unequally: being better educated enhances your prospective lifetime income and job satisfaction. It also provides non-competitive opportunities for fulfilling life experiences: not only the reward of executing excellently those tasks which demand the skills one

---

6 See Dworkin, Ronald, *A Matter of Principle* (Cambridge, MA: Harvard University Press, 1985), chapter 11 who uses this principle as the basis for his theory of liberal equality. Amartya Sen argues that all political theories endorse equality in something like the sense I am using, and that the real differences between them rest in their *interpretation* of equal respect in *Inequality Re-examined* (Cambridge, MA: Harvard University Press, 1992).

has learned—reading great literature, solving equations, bowling a yorker, pitching a curve ball—but also the rewards which come from entertaining, executing, and reflecting on those tasks in a social context. I shall refer to the competitive benefits as 'instrumental benefits' and to the non-competitive benefits as 'intrinsic benefits', though these designations should be treated as a stylistic convenience rather than as implying some normative comment on their value.[7] In both cases, the benefit consists not in the education itself, but in what the education does for the person who receives it. The principle of educational equality will focus not on what educational opportunities are available to children, but on the benefits that education provides opportunities for.[8] Finally, before presenting the argument, I would remind the reader that the case for educational equality is an 'other things being equal' rather than an 'all things considered' case. The argument establishes that the principle is a valid principle, but not that it is the only valid one: there may be, and in my view there are, other values that properly may inhibit the full realization of educational equality. I shall discuss these qualifications later.

What exactly, then, is the case that we should try to provide children with roughly equal opportunities for both the competitive economic advantages conferred by education and the intrinsic rewards it yields?

First let's look at what I call the basic argument, which supports equalizing the competitive economic advantages. I shall state the argument formally, then comment on the premises:

1. Where social institutions license unequal rewards, the competition for them must be designed to ensure that the individuals who benefit from the rewards, *deserve* to in some sense.
2. Unequal rewards are only *deserved* if the candidates can reasonably be held responsible for their level of success in the competition for them.
3. Where someone's level of success in the labour market is due *to some extent* to their family background circumstances, or their family's choices, it is unreasonable to hold the competitor responsible for that level of success *to that extent*.

---

[7] I especially would not want to be committed to the idea that all the benefits of education which happen to yield no competitive advantages in the labour market are intrinsically good. The following argument has some plausibility, for example. There is no intrinsic value to trashy pot-boiler novels. Learning to enjoy such novels has no benefits in the labour market. But low-achieving children get a real, though intuitively instrumental, benefit from learning to enjoy them—the novels bring them pleasure. On my designation learning this enthusiasm is an intrinsic benefit of education, though it is not intrinsically valuable.

[8] I owe this enlightening formulation to Dan Hausman.

4. Education significantly affects labour market outcomes, that is, level of success in competition for higher levels of income, and the quality of educational inputs affect the quality of educational outputs.
5. If unequal inputs to a child's education are affected by family background circumstances, and/or family choices, then labour market outcomes cannot reasonably be considered the responsibility of the competitors. This follows from 3, and 4.
6. For inequalities of income to be deserved, educational inequalities must not be due to family background circumstances or family choices. This follows from 2 and 5.
7. Conclusion: Educational inequalities due to family background circumstances or family choices are unacceptable. This follows from 1 and 6.

This argument proceeds against a background assumption that there will be unequal rewards to labour. There are many arguments for the acceptability of inequality of income, and I do not want to tie myself to any of them: one does not even have to accept the propriety of unequal incomes in order to accept that in the foreseeable future it is likely to be a fact of life. It is widely assumed that economic agents require material incentives in order to work hard and produce the technical innovations on which economic growth depends. Even if this is false—and it is probably far less significant a feature of economic motivation than many people assume—economists have identified another reason for needing economic inequalities: the need to signal to economic agents what are the most productive uses of their talents. Even assuming that there are altruistic economic agents who want to put their talents to the best use for the sake of society, they need to know what occupation to take up and where: inequalities can function to tell them where to deploy their efforts. The need for inequalities is almost universally accepted, even by most people on the left. If they are unnecessary, or if equality of outcome is more morally important than the need for a dynamic equality, then the basic argument for educational equality will not get off the ground, though, as I shall explain later, there is a different argument that does not depend on this premise.[9]

Premise 1 relies on the idea that social institutions are constructs of human agency, and thus embody moral relations between people.

_____

[9] In 'Rewarding Effort', *Journal of Political Philosophy* (forthcoming), Andrew Levine makes a powerful argument that inequalities of material reward cannot be justified on the basis of differentials of effort. In the current argument I therefore steer clear of any such justification. The basic argument does not premise the desirability of inequality of reward on the notion of desert: instead it premises the desirability of educational equality on the notion of desert, given the *fact* of inequality of reward.

Institutions such as the market, then, are not given, natural institutions, but institutions which we can establish and alter to some extent depending on our will.

I take premise 2 to be relatively uncontroversial. There may be other reasons for thinking that people should, in some circumstances, keep benefits that they do not deserve, but it is part of the idea of desert that people deserve what they are responsible for, and do not deserve what they are not responsible for.

Premise 3 seems reasonable. None of us is responsible for having been born to the parents we have, or for ending up in the adoptive family we ended up in. If that piece of fortune leads to benefits in the labour market, it is unreasonable to hold us responsible for having gained those benefits.

Premise 4 is, I take it, a true empirical generalization. But it is worth noting that its truth is dependent on the economy being structured a certain way. We can imagine the economy being structured to reward only hours of work—'to each according to their work'—or even so that education did not correlate with reward to labour— garbage-collectors get paid more than brain surgeons. No educator will want to deny the second part of premise 4: it is widely assumed in most industrial societies, but I should say that if it is false then most of the political and moral debates about schooling are robbed of their interest.

From the straightforward conclusions of premises 5 and 6 we can derive the principle of educational equality as we have described it so far, that educational inequalities due to family background circumstances, or family choices are *prima-facie* unacceptable.

Some will find this conclusion intolerable. I answer them in the next chapter, by countering arguments which claim that educational equality is undesirable, or that other more fundamental values prohibit all efforts to remove particular barriers to educational equality. Those who find this conclusion intolerable may, furthermore, find even more troubling a conclusion which I have not stated but which seems to be implied by a parallel argument, which is that if they are to be deserved, educational inequalities must not be due to inequalities of natural ability or talent. After all, we do not deserve our natural endowments or talents, any more than we deserve our parents or the benefits they confer on us: we did not choose our talents, and there is no sense in which we can be considered responsible for them. I shall postpone discussion of this implication, which raises difficulties for any conception of educational equality or equality of opportunity, to the section, 'Understanding Educational Equality' later in this chapter.

It is, however, worth deflecting a couple of possible misunderstandings at this point. The argument does not aim to abolish or reform the institution of the family—rather it accepts the family as a legitimate unit of social organization and specifies a *prima facie* limit on its permissible effects: educational inequalities must be insulated from the family. Of course, inequalities cannot be completely insulated from the family. As James Tooley points out, even if 'all schools were comprehensively the same, with none recognized to be better than others . . . to some families it would matter very much to provide their children with extra educational opportunities outside of schooling. Children of these families would presumably have the edge when applying for positional goods'.[10]

But that state intervention in schooling cannot completely *eliminate* educational inequalities does not mean that it cannot *reduce* them significantly. Compulsory equal state schooling can designate around 15,000 hours of each child's life in which their parents could not be conferring on them opportunities superior to those which others will enjoy. Under such a system the beneficiaries of socially-sanctioned inequalities can have some confidence that at least some part of their benefit is deserved. The fact that some problem cannot be eliminated never justifies abandoning attempts to mitigate it. The issue, which we shall deal with in detail in the next chapter, is why we should maintain the institution of the family, and what measures we can take to reduce educational inequalities consistent with respecting the family.

This clarification also helps us to understand what may seem the puzzling focus of educational egalitarians on schooling. Schooling is, of course, not identical with education: much education goes on outside schools, and there are schools in which very little education goes on. But what goes on outside the school is extremely hard to monitor in a public way, and even harder for public authorities to influence consistent with maintaining a stance of non-interference in the private lives of people, and in particular of non-interference in functional families. Equal schooling, whatever that is, will not amount to equal education, but equal schooling is something that the government may and can aim at.

A second clarification leads us to a secondary argument for educational equality. I want to emphasize again, that the basic argument does not challenge the propriety of material inequality. It offers, instead, a condition which needs to be met in order for us to be able to claim that material inequalities are distributed on the basis of desert. This feature should reassure readers who are sceptical of the more global egalitarianism that

---

[10]  Tooley, James, *Disestablishing the School* (Aldershot: Avebury Press, 1995), 20.

defenders of educational equality often also espouse. But it also raises the question of whether there would be any case for educational equality *in the absence of* material inequality. The focus of the basic argument is on the *instrumental* benefits of education: those benefits which contribute to the effectiveness of recipients in the labour market. If education yielded no benefits for effectiveness in the labour market what would be the case for educational equality.[11]

The secondary argument for educational equality is concerned not with the instrumental benefits of education, but with what I characterized as the intrinsic benefits: the benefits which, whether directly or indirectly, make our lives more fulfilling, regardless of whether they help bring us more material wealth. Again, the argument rests on the general ideal that the government should treat its citizens, and potential citizens, with equal concern and respect. The idea is that to devote more resources to one person's education than another's is to provide more opportunity for them to get the intrinsic rewards: this will appear to confer more value on their life than on the life of those to whose education less is devoted. If, knowingly, we distribute goods to the advantage of some so that they can be expected to have richer and more fulfilling lives than others, it will appear that more value is being placed on the lives of those so favoured, and thus that unequal respect is being accorded. This appearance can be defeated when there are reasons, grounded in equal respect for persons, for allowing resources to be distributed to the advantage of some. But the baseline against which inequalities have to be justified is equality.[12]

Because the intrinsic and instrumental benefits of education cannot be insulated from one another in practice—we cannot teach people to read job application forms without teaching them skills they can use to read *Emma*—this secondary argument would probably vindicate educational equality in an inegalitarian economy, but it is also unnecessary since we have the basic argument. However, in an egalitarian economy, where there are no instrumental benefits, or, to put it more awkwardly, where the instrumental benefits have little or no impact on lifetime income expectations, it may not vindicate educational equality *per se*. The intrinsic benefits of education differ crucially from the instrumental benefits in their structure. While the instrumental benefits are competitive, in that whether they yield material advantages depends on whether they give you an edge

[11] In other words, the focus is on education as a *positional* good. For the idea of positionality, see Hirsch, Fred, *The Limits to Social Growth* (Cambridge, Mass.: Harvard University Press, 1976).

[12] I'm grateful to both Peter Vallentyne and Adam Swift for challenging earlier versions of this argument.

in the competition for high-income occupations, the intrinsic benefits often have a positive sum structure. Reading *Emma* is more rewarding if there are other educated people with whom you can discuss it: I get a positive intrinsic benefit from being able to discuss philosophy with other well-educated philosophers, even while I compete with them for access to the limited financial rewards of the profession. If there were reasons for thinking that dividing education unequally would lead ultimately to the least well-educated being better educated, for example by producing better educated and more effective teachers, then there would be a case for carefully designed inequalities. However, the one standard invoked in the basic argument, that educational provision should be insulated from the quality of choice-making and background wealth of parents, would still probably stand, because it is hard to imagine how schemes of unequal input, designed to track positively unequal prudence and wealth of parents, would benefit the educationally least advantaged.[13]

Furthermore, not all access to rewarding and valuable experiences is determined by education, unless education is understood so broadly as to include almost every experience a child has. Some people, by virtue of their personalities, geographical locations and simple fortune in life, will have more real access than others to rewarding experiences. Others can, in principle at least, be compensated for a lack of access to the experiences requiring education by providing greater access to other experiences. If our aim is to ensure that people have roughly equal access to rewarding experiences then these other factors could offset the demand for educational equality. Again, though, educational provision would be devised to be insulated from parental choices and parental wealth.

### EDUCATIONAL EQUALITY AND EQUALITY OF OPPORTUNITY

So far I have avoided the terminology of opportunity in my description of, and arguments for, educational equality. But the basic case I have made for educational equality depends on its role in the ideal of equality of opportunity. Equality of opportunity, in this context, means equality of opportunity among all citizens for the packages of burdens and benefits distributed by the labour market. Educational equality means at minimum, that the resources devoted to a child's education should not depend

---

[13] For an excellent and entertaining discussion of the structure of education as a good, see Hollis, Martin, 'Education as a Positional Good', *Journal of Philosophy of Education*, 16 (1982), 235–44.

on the ability of their parents to pay for, or choose well among educational experiences, on the assumption that educational experiences will yield opportunities for the rewards distributed by the labour market. The connection I have relied on between the two ideals, however, is normative and practical, rather than logical. There are two ways we could avoid educational equality playing a major role in equality of opportunity, but neither has much appeal. First, we could achieve equal opportunity by limiting everybody's opportunities greatly. Such a strategy might not require us to focus much on education, since we could ensure that everyone has less opportunity than they would have if they had an education. The proponent of equal opportunity will not be satisfied with mere equality, but seeks equality at the highest level compatible with the observance of other fundamental values.

Second, strictly speaking equal opportunity is attained when some have many opportunities early in life and others have many much later in life. If public policy aims at equal opportunity in this way, then the provision of education might not be an important focus of egalitarians. But this is unattractive. As with health, concentration on the development of children is a more efficient and reliable method of delivering opportunities than trying to provide balancing opportunities late in life. Furthermore, if equality should not only be achieved but should also be seen to be achieved, a method of delivery that can be monitored publicly with relative ease is preferable. Focusing on what can be delivered to everyone at the same stage of their lives will make this condition much easier to fulfil.[14]

The concept of equality of opportunity I am using here is controversially strong, so stands in some need of defence. In public life, though not in political philosophy, proponents of equality of opportunity generally mean something much weaker than equality of opportunity to attain the benefits distributed by the labour market. They usually mean just that employers should not be allowed to discriminate against people on bases which are irrelevant to their job performance, such as sex, race, religious or political affiliation. Of course, equality of opportunity *does* require that there be no discrimination on irrelevant bases. But such a standard is problematic in a number of ways. An anti-discrimination principle clearly does not amount to equality of opportunity on any reasonable understanding of what 'equality' and 'opportunity' mean. If Julian and Sandy both have identical natural talents and inclination to exert effort, but Julian is educated only to age 10, while Sandy is put on a route which lets

---

[14] There are other reasons for rejecting this suggestion. I develop the idea of manifestness and its importance in 'Neutrality, Publicity, and State Funding of the Arts', *Philosophy and Public Affairs*, 24 (1995), 36–63.

him pass through Harvard Law School, we would place a much higher probability on Sandy's getting a job in a high powered law firm than on Julian's getting it, even though there is no discrimination on irrelevant bases at the point of hiring. Anti-discrimination at the point of hiring is necessary but not sufficient for equal opportunity, because the principle of equal opportunity requires that we compare people's whole lives, not just discrete interactions. And achieving equality of opportunity over complete lives requires attention to the entire institutional framework within which those lives are lived, not just one particular point of competition. Unless equality has been maintained in equipping the competitors for jobs for acquiring them, what happens at the point of hiring cannot tell us anything.[15] Most importantly, though, the moral basis of equality of opportunity, grounded as it is in the concept of desert, supports the strong conception I am using.

Some readers friendly to the strong notion of equality of opportunity and educational equality I am deploying will nevertheless be concerned that the focus of the basic argument on the instrumental benefits of education and on labour market competitiveness, supports a certain kind of conservatism with respect both to the curriculum and to the structure of the economy itself. It seems to support privileging those elements of the curriculum which are focused on the labour market over those that are not: art, music, physical education, and religious education will take their traditional back seat to both the more standardly academic subjects and so-called vocational education. Should we not, though, aim to educate the whole child, aiming to get children to value their own artistic or musical skills over their ability to do well in the labour market? The line I am taking also seems to take the economy as it currently is, or as we can reasonably predict it will be, structured, as the framework for which we are preparing children. Should we not be envisioning and preparing children for a more egalitarian, co-operative and less alienated economy, and thereby, perhaps, help to give birth to it?

The replies to both these charges have the same foundation. Principles of equal opportunity are, in general, insensitive to the structure of the packages of burdens and benefits for which equality of opportunity is sought. What we aim for is that, whatever the structure of the packages

---

[15] I want to be clear that I do not think that either the principles of non-discrimination or of equality of opportunity rule out the permissibility of affirmative action in the real world. In a society like the US which is characterized by dramatic inequalities of opportunity which track race, affirmative action is a messy and desperately inadequate tool for partially rectifying those inequalities, but as long as it pushes us in the direction of equal opportunity and does not stand in the way of other more promising programmes for correcting inequality, it is acceptable.

and patterns of likely outcomes, the competitors for those outcomes do not unfairly face unsimilar outcomes. This is not a problem with principles of equality of opportunity, but with the idea that they are the only principles of justice. It may well be that the final correct theory of justice comments a great deal on the patterns of outcomes, and requires that they are much more egalitarian than we currently have or than principles of equal opportunity alone would demand. But when we are considering how to design educational institutions in the world that we actually live in, one in which the most important goods distributed by social institutions are distributed very unequally, we have a duty to children to prepare them for that world, the one that they will actually inhabit, rather than for some other world which they will not inhabit. Of course, children who face certain poor material prospects may have their lives greatly improved by the discovery of skills and capacities which, though economically useless, are intrinsically rewarding to exercise. But it is no kindness to develop their artistic capacities if that is obviously *at the expense of* developing capacities which would be a great deal more instrumental for them in the labour market.

Assume that a much more egalitarian economic order would be more just than the one that we expect to inhabit. Shouldn't we use the education of children as one of the means to achieving that order? The problem here is three-fold. First, it is not at all clear how to use education as a harbinger of the new and just order. Educating the 'whole child' may help, but it may not; even teaching children how important material equality is, as a value of justice, may have little effect. The second problem is that, unless we have good reason to think that we shall succeed in reforming the economic order; if in pursuing justice our educational practices have failed to prepare some children for the economic order; then those children have, it would seem, a complaint of injustice against us. We will have failed to implement equality of opportunity, they have been the losers in this failure, and they therefore live in an inegalitarian economy which is doubly unjust. Third, though, assume that we succeed in transforming the economy. No children now have a complaint of injustice: they live in a just economy, which they would not otherwise have done. But they may have a different kind of complaint: a complaint of legitimacy. There is something deeply suspect about using the education of children as the means to achieve goals the legitimacy of which depends on their being endorsable by informed and critical citizens. This legitimacy consideration is serious, but not, I admit, decisive. Legitimacy and justice considerations are often in tension, at least in an imperfectly just or unjust world, and I cannot offer a theory of which should trump which and when. Furthermore, it should be clear that even though legitimacy considerations give weak support to a certain kind of conservatism here, they count strongly against an uncritical conservatism. While we should prepare children to compete effectively in an inegalitarian economy, the legitimacy considerations I elaborated in Chapter 4 direct us to enable children to give critical attention to the structures they face. We need to prepare them to challenge the injustice in the world they face even as we prepare them to live successfully within it and, as I indicated in Chapter 4, we need to do this even if we think that the world they face is just.

I should note, finally in this section, that while it is my focus in this book, education is of course not the only good, access to which is important for children to have a full range of opportunities, and equal access to which serves equal opportunity. Another rather obvious good is health care. Unequal access to health care for children leads to unequal opportunities for success in the labour market—even for life itself! In the United States, where health care for poor children is limited, the infant mortality rate among the poorest 10 per cent is *four times* that among the richest 10 per cent. Simply put, children in the wealthiest decile have more opportunity to become adults than children of poor people. Additionally, of course, how we respond to other people, how we respond to education, and how much we enjoy our childhoods are all affected by how healthy we are, which, in turn, is affected by how much access we have to health care. In focusing on education I do not mean to downplay the significance of health care: it simply does not play a direct role in this investigation. That said, policies aimed at educational equality in, say, the US, which neglect the inadequate health care received by the poorest children, can only be expected to fail: health and dental problems in children which go unaddressed will often affect adversely their ability to learn.


## UNDERSTANDING EDUCATIONAL EQUALITY

We have seen the basic argument for educational equality, and the connection between that ideal and the principle of equality of opportunity. We now have the task of understanding educational equality: working out exactly what the argument is an argument for. As we shall see in the next chapter, one of the objections to educational equality is that it is incoherent—it does not express a genuine value, let alone a true and binding one. I shall run through three understandings of educational equality, the first two of which are clearly flawed, and the third of which is insufficient.

First we might understand educational equality in terms of equal resources being expended on each individual's schooling. But equal resources expended is at best a poor proxy for the deeper notion of educational equality. Consider, as before, children with disabilities. Some of them have no prospect of achieving an educational output which would be equal on any reasonable standard to the outputs achievable by exceptionally talented students, regardless of how much money is spent on their education. It seems wrong to say of them that equal money spent on them gives them equal opportunity.

In response to this problem some have tried to describe educational equality in terms of equal outcomes. There is an obvious objection to this, which is that, in general, educational outcomes are a poor measure of how much education was provided, since individuals make different choices with respect to what is provided, some making better and some making worse decisions, and hence equality of input is liable to produce inequality of outcome. They are certainly conceptually distinct.

One response to this objection is to say that children cannot be held responsible for the quality of the choices they make with respect to the education provided to them. They are, after all, children, and it is therefore not proper to hold them responsible for their choices in the way that we would hold adults responsible for choices.[16] Furthermore, their preferences, especially their preferences for expending effort specifically on education, may well be adaptive: many children may not want to work hard because they have come to believe, rightly or wrongly, that education will not yield long term benefits for them specifically.[17] But while the basis of this objection seems to be correct, it does not establish the conclusion that educational outcomes are a good measure of educational quality. Rather it seems to suggest that educational inputs are at best a second-best equalandum for the purposes of social policy. Furthermore the fact of disability, which was so devastating for a principle of equal educational resources, is also a problem for an equal-outcome account of educational equality. Some of the disabled, who certainly should be granted more resources than the ordinarily abled, other things being equal, could never

---

[16] Howe, Kenneth R., 'In Defense of Outcome-Based Conceptions of Equal Educational Opportunity', *Educational Theory*, 39 (1989), 317–36; 'Equal Opportunity is Equal Education', *Educational Theory*, 40 (1990), 227–30; 'Equality of Educational Opportunity and the Criterion of Equal Educational Worth', *Studies in Philosophy and Education*, 11 (1993), 329–37. See also Burbules, Nicholas C., 'Equal Opportunity or Equal Education?', *Educational Theory*, 40 (1990), 221–6; and O'Neill, Onora, 'Opportunities, Equalities and Education', *Theory and Decision*, 7 (1976), 275–95.

[17] Marshall, Gordon, Swift, Adam, and Roberts, Stephen, *Against The Odds* (Oxford: Oxford University Press, 1997).

be expected to reach the level of educational attainment that some of the ordinarily abled could.

For a third account of educational equality we might modify John Rawls's principle of fair equality of opportunity. For Rawls, fair equality of opportunity obtains when 'those who are at the same level of talent and ability, and have the same willingness to use them, should have the same prospects of success regardless of their initial place in the social system, that is, irrespective of the income class into which they are born'.[18] The parallel account of educational equality might say that: Children with the same level of natural ability and the same level of willingness to learn should have the same prospects for educational attainment regardless of their initial place in the social system.

Notice that this interpretation of educational equality would require a considerable departure from a policy of equal educational resources: it is quite likely that more resources would have to be directed to the children of less wealthy parents than to the equally talented children of wealthier parents.[19] This seems to be an intuitively acceptable result, and consistent with the spirit of the general principle of equality of opportunity. But it seems too weak a principle to capture the idea of educational equality, because it fails to comment on the relationship between the prospects for attainment of children with *different* levels of talent. It is compatible with this interpretation of the criterion that we devote almost all our educational resources to a small elite with a very high level of talent and willingness to learn, and hardly any resources to the vast majority who range from the extremely lazy and untalented to the very but not extremely talented and willing. Intuitively, this violates any ideal of equality of opportunity.[20]

We could modify the above account by requiring that it comment on the distribution of resources among students of the same social class and different levels of natural ability and inclination to exert effort: that is by filling the gap we have identified. The problem is this: *how* are we to fill the gap? A requirement that children receive the same resources regardless of their abilities is intuitively inadequate since those with least ability, and especially those with disabilities, will be shortchanged by this: they will face much worse prospects for attaining the instrumental and intrinsic

[18]  Rawls, John, *A Theory of Justice* (Cambridge, MA: Harvard University Press, 1971), 73.

[19]  It is worth noting that many teachers of young children say that they find children who are used to being given attention far more demanding of their time and energy—which are educational resources—than children who are used to being given less attention.

[20]  I should say that I do not think that Rawls's fair equality of opportunity proviso is vulnerable to the parallel of this objection given the role it plays in his theory.

benefits of education than other students because of facts for which they cannot reasonably be held responsible—their lack of ability or disabilities. But a modification of the principle so that it requires that all students face similar prospects regardless of their level of ability, willingness to exert effort, or social background, collapses back into conceiving of equality in terms of equal outcomes.

We could avoid this problem by claiming that society should attempt to overcome the educational effects of children's social backgrounds, but not those of their genetic disadvantages. Christopher Jencks has suggested that there is a great deal of support in society for this idea. His diagnosis of the different attitudes to social and genetic disadvantages is that we think of society as being responsible for social disadvantage but not for genetic disadvantage. As he points out, if we do think this we are mistaken: in, quite properly, allowing the genetically weak to procreate with one another society incurs some responsibility for the resultant genetic disadvantages.[21]

Other diagnoses of the tendency to hold society responsible for correcting social but not genetic disadvantages are possible. David Miller is reported to have speculated that differences of natural ability are integral to personality, whereas differences in developmental conditions, that is, social disadvantages, are not. As Marshall *et al.* report Miller's comment:[22]

It makes sense to think about what a particular child might have achieved if he or she had had more encouraging home background or better schooling, whereas if we think abut someone with different natural abilities we are thinking about a different person. (Marshall, Gordon, *et al.*, *Against the Odds*, 185–6.)

I think this view does explain why some people worry more about correcting social than genetic disadvantages, but that it does not justify their doing so. If what is meant by person is what we usually mean by personality, then it is clearly affected both by genetic and developmental

---

[21] Jencks, 'Whom Must we Treat Equally for Educational Opportunity to be Equal?', 522–3. In fact I would dispute his claim that correcting for social disadvantages is more popular than correcting for genetic disadvantages: in the US at least there is significant legislation supporting extra resources being devoted to the education of disabled students, and very little supporting extra resources going to socially disadvantaged children. In fact, expenditure on such Federal programmes as Head Start, which are directed at low income children, much less than compensates for the extra money spent by school districts on children from wealthy families.

[22] Miller's comments were on a draft of Marshall, Swift and Roberts, *Against the Odds* and are reported in the note 20 of chapter 8, 185–6. I do not mean what follows to be critical of Miller, only of what he would have been committed to if he had said what he is reported to have said in a more committal context.

conditions, such as being raised atheist, having abusive parents, or charming or brutal siblings. If what is meant by person is something more like what philosophers mean when they discuss the problem of personal identity then this seems an implausibly demanding criterion: it has the consequence that pre-natal gene therapy would always and inevitably result in the birth of a different person. Furthermore, it is a criterion that does not suitably ground the different attitudes to society's responsibility. Consider Dougal, who has a genetic disorder resulting in incurable blindness, and Florence, who was incurably blinded by an error in the delivery room. It will cost exactly the same amount to teach each of them Braille. Should society be responsible for ensuring that Florence but not that Dougal learns Braille? While the view about personal identity may, but only may, rule out gene therapy it is not clear why it should rule out assistance to the genetically disadvantaged.

In fact, it should not rule out assistance. The idea that society is only responsible for attending to those disadvantages which it played some role in bringing about rests on a mistaken view about the moral relationships between persons. Allen Buchanan has contrasted two different stances toward justice: subject-centred justice and justice as reciprocity.[23] Whereas justice as reciprocity considers the proper subjects of justice as those with the capacity to engage productively in social co-operation, subject-centred justice focuses on the needs and interests of subjects as the features which justify their being considered participants in a scheme of justice. Justice as reciprocity is, according to Buchanan, a deeply flawed model, since, among other things, an individual's capacity to co-operate productively can depend on the particular conditions and terms of co-operation selected: for example, in a literate economy dyslexia is a co-operative disadvantage, whereas in a pre-literate economy, or one with extremely advanced computers, it is not. Justice as reciprocity also has great difficulties accounting for the obligations which adults have to children, none of whom are, and some of whom may never become, productive citizens. Yet only if we held the view that justice was purely a matter of reciprocity could we regard the causal role of society in producing disadvantages as determining its obligations to attend to those disadvantages. Subject-centred justice, while it is the less dominant paradigm in our tradition of thinking about justice, accounts better for our fundamental intuitions about the role of justice in our moral lives, and, in particular, with the intuition that we can have obligations of justice to people who are in no position, and will never be in a position, to reciprocate. Yet on subject-centred

---

[23] Buchanan, Allen, 'Justice as Reciprocity versus Subject-Centered Justice', *Philosophy and Public Affairs*, 19 (1990), 227–52.

justice it is not legitimate to assume that society's obligations are limited to those disadvantages it has played a role in causing.[24]

So, we cannot dismiss learning-related disabilities as irrelevant to the problem of educational equality. The problem we now face can be stated simply. For children of the same level of natural talent it seems right to say that roughly equal resources should be devoted to their education. This suggests that, as long as the socially disadvantaged are not systematically less talented than the advantaged, it is legitimate for the state to expend more educational resources on the children of socially disadvantaged children so that they face similar prospects for material and educational success to those of children from wealthier backgrounds. It also seems that children at different levels of natural talent are not treated educationally equally when equal resources are devoted to their education. Yet in the case of natural disadvantages, while unequal educational resources seem appropriate, equal prospects for material and educational success do not seem to be the appropriate goal. Aiming at equal prospects would have the consequence that we may completely neglect the education of the extremely talented, devoting all educational resources to the least talented who may never reach the level of achievement that the most talented can reach with very little input. Since achievement is inevitably used as one measure of talent, furthermore, such a policy would have extremely perverse incentive effects on both the more and the less talented: if low achievers are rewarded, everyone has an incentive not to exert effort. Even more counter-intuitively, if the least talented are sufficiently untalented, even the averagely and below averagely talented will be neglected educationally. But what other rule governing the distribution of educational resources could there possibly be?

Before discussing answers to this question I should warn the reader that I do not have a solution to the problem: both the solutions I consider seem to me to be flawed, and I do not have an alternative. Given the power of the argument for educational equality, I do not think that the absence of a solution to the problem I've identified constitutes an objection to the principle of educational equality, just as I do not think that the existence of bottomless pit problems in medical contexts constitutes an objection to principles of equality in health care. It simply means that we cannot yet give a full description of that principle. Furthermore, given the practical problem this book aims to address, this lacuna is not objectionable, since we can just use those aspects of the principle that we do understand to evaluate choice and non-choice schemes. In the final section I shall briefly

---

[24] See also Barry, Brian, *Justice as Impartiality* (Oxford: Oxford University Press, 1995), especially chapters 1–4.

explain what criteria we must use, in practice, to evaluate policy alternatives, given the understanding we do have of the principle. With that said, I shall explore further the problems with attempts to solve the problem.

Amy Gutmann has presented an influential proposal through which she attempts to evade the bottomless pit problem we have identified. The following intuitions must be respected by any account of educational equality: it must focus on outcomes, since children cannot ultimately be held responsible for their degree of uptake of educational opportunities; it must demand that more resources be accorded to the disabled than to the ordinarily abled, and it must have something plausible to say about the bottomless pit problems. Gutmann proposes an interpretation of equal educational opportunity which meets all three of these criteria—she calls it the *democratic threshold principle*. Under the democratic threshold principle, 'inequalities in the distribution of educational goods can be justified if, but only if, they do not deprive any child of the ability to participate effectively in the democratic process (which determines, among other things, the priority of education relative to other social goods)'.[25] Since the standard proposes a threshold, it is immune to the worst bottomless pit problems. Inequalities of educational achievement above the threshold are entirely acceptable, as long as every child reaches the threshold. Those inequalities might reflect differences of ability—or even, though I think Gutmann would reject this for other reasons, differences in parental wealth—and so as long as more than enough resources are devoted to education to ensure that all reach the threshold, there is no bottomless pit.

There are some minor problems with Gutmann's proposal. Randall Curren has pointed out that it is not clear what is meant by 'the ability to participate effectively in the democratic process'.[26] In most areas of activity, effectiveness is elucidated in terms of success. But this is, by definition, not possible in the area of democratic participation. Outliers in political debates might be highly effective without having any prospects of success in achieving their aims. Their lack of success is a function, not of ineffectiveness, but of the marginality of their views. I think, however, that Gutmann can overcome this problem relatively easily. Borrowing from Ronald Dworkin, we could define effectiveness in the following terms:

Imagine that we know nothing of the distribution of citizens' views on some issue. Imagine that we discover what Pertwee's view is on the matter. Pertwee is an effective participant in the democratic process if, having discovered that he

[25] Gutmann, Amy, *Democratic Education* (Princeton, NJ: Princeton University Press, 1987), 136.

[26] Curren, Randall R., 'Justice and the Threshold of Educational Equality', *Philosophy of Education*, 50 (1995), 239–48. See 245.

intends to make efforts to get his view implemented, we should assign a higher probability than before that his view will be adopted. (see Dworkin, Ronald, 'What is Equality? Part 4: Political Equality'.)

This definition allows that effectiveness is non-trivial, while also ensuring that it does not depend on success.

However there are further problems with Gutmann's standard. A lesser bottomless pit problem re-emerges since there may be children who can be brought up to the threshold, but only with the devotion of extensive resources which might be thought to be better spent on others or even on enhancing other more intuitively central aspects of their own welfare. Furthermore, as Curren points out, Gutmann's standard does not identify a fixed baseline: it may be that as the best educated individuals get more education, the least well educated need to get more in order to be able to participate effectively.[27] This threatens to generate another bottomless pit problem.

Curren offers an alternative threshold proposal which he thinks succeeds in avoiding bottomless pit problems: what he calls the *threshold of social inclusion*. He argues that lacking a certain level of education puts citizens at serious risk of being unemployed or of very low social status, both of which conditions are significant predictors of criminality. Punishment of criminality involves the denial of otherwise inalienable rights, so a state which fails to educate all its citizens up to the level required to avoid unemployment and low status puts them at serious risk of having their rights withdrawn. This is *prima facie* unjust.[28] This criterion demands less than Gutmann's democratic threshold, specifies a baseline which is unlikely to rise much with the level of education given to the most educated, and thus faces less pressure from potential bottomless pit problems.

I accept that both Gutmann's and Curren's thresholds must be met, of course. And, in practice, I find Gutmann's proposal an appealingly egalitarian goal.[29] But neither threshold proposal constitutes a philosophical solution to the problem of educational equality. Both proposals allow

[27] Curren, 'Justice and The Threshold of Educational Opportunity', 243.
[28] Ibid., 246–7.
[29] In Chapter 4 I expressed scepticism about Gutmann's strongly republican conception of democracy. Although I maintain that scepticism, and disagree about the precise content of democratic education, I think that more defensible egalitarian conceptions of democracy probably have similar implications for the level of educational resources to be expended on children. I also agree with her that democratic rights are fundamental to justice, and so am inclined to think that the level of educational resources required for democratic education should be protected even if we think that other powerful values of justice inhibit the implementation of educational equality overall. See my 'Egalitarianism and Equal Availability of Political Influence', *Journal of Political Philosophy*, 4 (1996), 118–41.

people to face radically unequal prospects both for the attainment of jobs which are rewarding and status-conferring, and for the acquisition of resources for consumption and enjoyment, due to factors for which it is unreasonable to hold them responsible. Accidents of birth will continue, to a significant extent, to determine people's life prospects, and this violates a fundamental intuition about responsibility and desert.

Now, I should add that any complete theory of justice will probably allow prospects to be determined partly by factors for which individuals cannot reasonably be held responsible. But the problem with Gutmann's and Curren's theories is that they make that concession within the theory of educational equality offered, rather than seeing it as a result of the propriety of constraints imposed by values other than educational equality on what may be done to achieve educational equality. It may turn out that there are reasons connected to the value of the family, the importance of religious freedom, and the value to everyone of economic growth, that suggest we should place limits on what we do to achieve educational equality. But these limits are, in my view, imposed by other values, rather than internal to the value of educational equality itself.

I do not have a solution to the problem that differences in natural ability present to conceiving of educational equality. Two things can, I think, be said. The first is that there may be a principled limit, motivated precisely by considering the interests of the disabled, on what resources should be devoted to them. If it is true that various incentives, and especially substantial education, must be provided to more talented persons in order to sustain a reasonable degree of economic growth, and to get them to turn their attentions to medical, educational, and technological innovations which will yield educational benefits to the less-able and disabled, then the prospect of a long term benefit for the disabled yields support for limiting the resources expended on their education right now.

Some egalitarians would go even further, and say that inequalities of education can be justified when they can be expected to yield superior overall material well-being to the disabled over the long term. Richard Arneson has recently challenged the priority that Rawls gives to fair equality of opportunity over the so-called difference principle, which requires that resources be distributed to the greatest benefit of the least advantaged.[30] Rawls grants lexical priority to fair equality of opportunity, meaning, among other things, that even if equality of opportunity created inefficiencies which left everyone worse off in material terms, it should be upheld. This scenario—that equality of opportunity conflicts with the

[30] Arneson, Richard, 'Against Rawlsian Equality of Opportunity', *Philosophical Studies* (forthcoming).

material well-being of the worst off—is precisely that which we have reason to suspect, if equality of opportunity requires that massive resources be devoted to the education of the disabled.

Arneson's response to the problem is that where there is such a conflict, our concern should be with the overall condition of the worst-off persons, and not equality of opportunity. The reasoning which best supports this response is to look at the situation from the perspective of the worst-off persons: from *their* perspective what matters is how well off they are overall, not how good their opportunities are relative to those of others. In the context we are discussing, Arneson's view would support allowing whatever inequalities of educational opportunity gave us the best chance of benefiting the disabled overall. The difference between Arneson's suggestion and mine, then, is that whereas mine allows inequalities of educational opportunity only when they can be expected to enhance the educational opportunities of the disabled, his allows inequalities of educational opportunity whenever they can be expected to yield a net overall benefit to the disabled.

There is insufficient space here to deal with Arneson's powerful arguments in detail. I refrain from endorsing his position because I fear that it has the counter-intuitive consequence that equality of opportunity has no privileged status in a theory of justice: this, I should note, is a consequence that Arneson appears to accept. I refrain from *rejecting* Arneson's suggestion, however, because I am confident that in the context we are concerned with—the evaluation of school choice proposals against the defensible ideals of educational equality—the differences between his and my suggestions will not show up. The fortunate egalitarian planner who designs a scheme from scratch would have to be concerned with the difference between my view and Arneson's, and it is a significant philosophical gap in my account that I do not respond to Arneson; but for the practical purposes at hand our accounts have similar enough implications.

The second thing to be said in the face of the difficulties with conceptualizing educational equality is to note that many disabilities, especially learning-related disabilities, *can* be addressed, and that there are more and less cost-effective ways of addressing them. The *Americans With Disabilities Act 1990* suggests a standard for accommodation of disabled people in public life which is objective and could readily be modified for use in our context: 'this standard calls for projecting how objective social practice would be transformed were unimpaired functioning so atypical as to be of merely marginal importance for social policy'.[31] As Elizabeth

---

[31] Silvers, Anita, 'Reconciling Equality to Difference: Caring (f)or Justice for People with Disabilities', *Hypatia*, 10 (1995), 30–55 at 49, quoted in Anderson, Elizabeth, 'What is the Point of Equality?', *Ethics*, 109 (1999), 287–337 at 334.

Anderson explains, 'The act asks us to imagine how communications in civil society would be arranged if nearly everyone were deaf, and then try to offer the deaf arrangements approximating this'.[32] We can readily modify this standard for application in an inclusive classroom setting when dealing with many physical disabilities, and specific impairments such as deafness and blindness, as follows: that disabled children should be accorded the resources that make their classroom experience as much as possible like the one that would be deemed appropriate if they were being educated among others with their disability. So, for example, hearing impaired students are provided with a signer, since were the classroom full of hearing-impaired students the teacher would be a signer. Whether children should be educated in inclusive classrooms is beyond the scope of my inquiry, but if they should then it is clear that this principle should be applied.

## MULTICULTURALISM AS EQUALITY?

A final clarification of the conception of educational equality we are deploying is worth making. In contemporary debates in the English-speaking world, the ideal of educational equality has become associated with the movement for multicultural education. Educational equality, as I understand it here, is connected only very tenuously with multiculturalism.

How is the conception connected with multiculturalism? It does not require, as do some radical versions of multiculturalism, that all cultures be treated equally in the curriculum, or that students have a right to have the cultures of their ancestors fully or equally considered in the design of the curriculum. It takes an interest in the cultures of the students' homes only in so far as that serves the aim of having the student take full advantage of the academic opportunities presented. To give an uncontroversial example where culture is relevant, it would be difficult for a monolingual French-speaking student to learn as well in an exclusively English-speaking classroom as it would for an English-speaking student. More controversially, but still plausibly, it may also be hard for students to learn from texts which implicitly make, what are to them, foreign cultural assumptions. For example, it may be difficult for children recently arrived in the US from Mexico to learn to read from a text concerned with chil-

[32] Anderson, 'What is the Point of Equality', 334.

dren playing baseball together. It may even be more difficult for inner city children to learn about literature by reading Shakespeare than by reading more contemporary authors who write about contexts more familiar to those children. In a society where students come to the same classroom from many different cultural backgrounds it is important that the curriculum be designed with the understanding that the cultural assumptions of texts and teachers should be explained and made transparent. But beyond that, educational equality is insensitive to cultural backgrounds. There would be no case, for example, based on the value of educational equality, for ensuring that Welsh children are taught in Welsh, and there may even be an egalitarian case against that policy. Educational equality, as I conceive of it, is friendly to the concrete curricular demands of many Latinos and African-Americans in contemporary debates, but it is hostile to more radical versions of multiculturalism which treat cultures rather than children as fundamental objects of moral consideration.

We have to design educational institutions so that a child from a poor Latino family faces similar prospects with respect to expected lifetime income as a similarly talented child from a white American family. In the US, unless she becomes a proficient English speaker and learns how to function in an English-speaking job market it is unlikely, though not out of the question, that we can achieve that goal. In the debate about bilingual education versus English-immersion programmes, the conception does not take a principled stand: it requires that we find out which kinds of policy best prepare children from non-English speaking homes to participate effectively in anglophone labour markets. Educational equality may, then, require the weakening of cultural barriers; if that is the price of equality then so be it.

Does this mean that educational equality contains within itself an assimilationist bias? To respond to this charge we need to distinguish between *assimilationism* and *cosmopolitanism*. Whereas assimilationism requires that measures be taken to make it more likely that members of a minority culture join a fixed majority culture, cosmopolitanism requires only that measures be taken to make it more likely that all citizens can move more easily between cultures within the society. Educational equality certainly supports cosmopolitan policies, but it places no intrinsic importance on the maintenance of particular cultures.[33]

---

[33] See Olneck, Michael R., 'Terms of Inclusion: Has Multiculturalism Redefined Equality in American Education?', *American Journal of Education*, 101 (1993), 234–60, for a fine discussion of multiculturalism as equality.

## WHAT EDUCATIONAL EQUALITY REQUIRES

The discussion in the section 'Understanding Educational Equality' shows that it is hard to elaborate a conception of educational equality, though it certainly does not show that it is impossible. A full and principled account of educational equality would say something about how much more must be devoted to children with disabilities than to ordinarily-abled children. Even among students without disabilities there is a range of ability levels, such that, assuming that the same level of resources is devoted to each, those in the top ability levels simply have more prospects for the rewards of the labour market than those in the bottom ability levels. So the account must also be able to guide the distribution of resources among more and less able children within the ordinary-abled group. If the same resources should be devoted the account needs to explain why, and why such differences do not merit the same response as the differences between the ordinarily-abled and disabled. If, on the other hand, differential resources should be devoted, this needs to be explained.

But a full answer to the problems presented by differences in natural ability is not necessary in order to make the principle of educational equality acceptable. The arguments for educational equality we have considered give us two very clear relevant results, which *partially* constitute the ideal on educational equality, regardless of what else that ideal includes.

1. Children of different classes but the same level of natural talent should receive roughly equal educational resources. If we assume that children from wealthy families will generally receive greater educational resources outside school, this supports compensating by expending more in school on similarly talented children from less wealthy backgrounds.
2. More must be spent on the education of disabled students than on ordinarily- abled students, with the rider that significant resources must be spent on all. A full conception will of course be more precise about how much more should be spent on less-able and disabled children.

How do these findings and our discussion help us to evaluate different education policy proposals in practice? I want to suggest three criteria here. But before describing them I want to introduce a new concept which they use. This is the notion of *effective* educational resources.[34] An educa-

---

[34] Thanks to Dan Hausman for suggesting this idea to me.

tional resource is *effective* if it can be used for education by the particular student to whom it is provided. Compare Eric and Ernie. Ernie is deaf, while Eric has fine hearing. Suppose that we spend $100 on a classroom teacher for both. It is true that we are spending $100, but we are spending it all on Eric, since no effective resources are being spent on Ernie: he cannot learn from a classroom teacher alone. When we add a sign-language translator to the classroom we are spending, say, an extra $100 exclusively on Ernie, who, unlike Eric, understands sign language. Of course, the classroom teacher is now as useful to Ernie as to Eric, let us suppose. So we are now spending more money on Ernie than on Eric: but, of course, we are devoting equal effective educational resources to both, since what each has is equally likely to enable them to learn, other things being equal. Providing blind students with braille books or audio tapes is effectively equal to providing sighted students with ordinary books. The notion of effectiveness is not only sensitive to differences in ability, furthermore. To give an example I will use in the next chapter, a Serbo-Croat/Chinese dictionary is an educational resource, but one which is entirely ineffective for a monolingual English speaker, though effective, in the right conditions, for a Serbo-Croat speaker.

It is hard to give a theoretically satisfactory account of effectiveness: but piecemeal cases like those above help to bring out the intuitive idea. It's important to emphasize that, though it may be all we have in practice, the amount of money spent on some resource is a poor proxy for its effectiveness, even when we are thinking of children with the same abilities. Some schools may spend a great deal to make the environment one in which it is possible to learn, while others have to spend little. Still others may spend a great deal of money extremely inefficiently: an incompetent management team can spend a lot of money very ineffectively. So knowing that one school spends twice as much per student on a student population of the same ability profile as that of another school, does not tell us much about the inequalities of effective resources spent on them, unless we know how efficiently the money is spent and how much is spent on educating *vis-à-vis* what is spent on the preconditions of education.

Furthermore, the notion of effective educational resources should not be seen as providing an answer to the bottomless pit problem. Although some students with disabilities can be treated in ways that make equal effective resources an intuitive solution to providing educational equality between them and ordinarily-abled students—the Eric and Ernie case—others, such as those with severe cognitive disabilities, cannot. Nor does the criterion seem to satisfy educational equality between more- and less-able students within the ordinary range of ability.

That said, the notion can help us to explicate three criteria of educational inequality as follows. A schooling system departs from the principle of educational equality when and to the extent that:

(1)  inequalities of effective educational resources spent on children in the school system correlate positively with inequalities of household wealth;

(2)  inequalities of effective educational resources spent on children correlate positively with inequalities of educational attainment of their parents;

(3)  inequalities of effective educational resources correlate positively with the ability levels of students, that is, more talented children get more effective educational resources.

Because the effectiveness of educational resources is so hard to observe, we shall have to use cruder criteria than these in our evaluation of the schemes. In practice, we shall have to ask whether a scheme lessens the gap, or can be expected to lessen the gap, in achievement between children of different social classes; and whether it increases, or can be expected to increase, the amount of money spent on children with learning disabilities. But before we evaluate actual schemes, we need to secure the principle of educational equality by responding to a series of arguments against it.

# 7

# Objections to Educational Equality

The case for educational equality given in Chapter 6 is very powerful. But, as was the case with autonomy, demonstrating the case is simply not enough. We have to show, further, that the objections to the ideal, to the idea that it should be a primary consideration in guiding educational policy, have to be addressed. In this chapter I shall address a series of such objections. The upshot is that educational equality is an ideal which must, indeed, guide the design of educational institutions. The value invoked by opponents of school choice is a legitimate value. Whether it successfully impugns school choice will be discussed in Chapter 8.

## IS EDUCATIONAL EQUALITY INCOHERENT?

The first charge against educational equality is that it is not, in fact, even a coherent value. If it is not coherent—if, in John Wilson's phrase, it does not make sense—then it obviously cannot guide educational policy. Wilson, in his article, 'Does equality (of opportunity) make sense in education?',[1] takes as his target 'equality of opportunity in education', but one of his renderings of this principle is sufficiently close to the principle of educational equality I have elaborated and defended for consideration of his objections to be relevant. His argument proceeds in two stages. First he argues that equality of opportunity in education, insofar as we can make sense of it, is an unappealing goal, and then that it is not even clear that we can make sense of it. Second, he correctly identifies a fallback position for those persuaded by his initial argument, which is something like equality of educational resources: against this position he again argues that it is unappealing insofar as we can make sense of it, and that it is not clear that we can even make sense of it.

---

[1] Wilson, John, 'Does equality (of opportunity) make sense in education?', *Journal of Philosophy of Education*, 25 (1991), 27–31 at 28.

First let us take Wilson's argument for the incoherence of equality of educational opportunity. He claims that it only makes sense to say of someone that they have the opportunity to do X if they have the power to do X:

To see this consider cases where a person is quite unable to do X. Given a particular situation on the football field, a person may seem to have the opportunity to break through the opposing players and score. But he is quite unable to do this: he is too fat or too weak. Or someone leaves the door of a cell open when the prisoner is asleep: does he have the opportunity to escape? Does he have a chance of escaping? Surely we would say not. He has the opportunity only if he has the power. (Wilson, John, 'Does equality (of opportunity) make sense in education?', 28.)

But some pursuits are such that they can be learned by some people and not by others: 'although anyone recognizably human can do *some* learning or learn *some* things, there will be many other things which not everyone has the power or ability to learn. I cannot learn to appreciate certain paintings because I am colour-blind'.[2] Therefore equality of educational opportunity is incoherent.

But the fact alone, that some activities cannot be learned by some people but can by others, does not yield incoherence of equal opportunity. First, we could choose to teach only those activities which can be learned by all, hence preserving equality of opportunity. We could prohibit the learning of those activities not learnable by all. This would be an undesirable policy, both because it would infringe unacceptably upon personal liberties, and because it would deprive society of many of the goods which are both producible by the advantaged and appreciable by the disadvantaged.

Second, the teaching of activities learnable only by some necessarily means only that educational opportunities cannot be the same, not that they cannot be 'equal'. Of two children, one of whom can learn to paint but not to play the violin and the other of whom can learn to play the violin but not paint, we would not say that they cannot have equal opportunity, only that they cannot have the same opportunities. A child living in France and a child living in Japan cannot have the same educational opportunities, but they can have equal opportunities.

It might be argued that we cannot provide equal educational opportunities because some children simply have more abilities than others, and are therefore inevitably advantaged. But even this would yield the impossibil-

---

[2] Wilson, John, 'Does equality (of opportunity) make sense in education?', *Journal of Philosophy of Education*, 25 (1991), 27–31 at 28.

ity, as opposed to the undesirability, of equal educational opportunity only if we could not either handicap the advantaged or compensate the disadvantaged with much greater attention and resources, sufficiently to equalize their prospects. This is doubtful: we can do a great deal to help the disadvantaged, and can, though we should not, do even more to hamper the advantaged.

Equality of educational opportunity, then, does not appear to be an incoherent notion. But in making that case I have indicated that it is not a defensible ideal, for implementing it unconstrained by other principles would violate other greater values, such as the physical and psychological integrity of the person.

We should, then, follow Wilson in turning to a different understanding of the ideal, one which seems more appealing, and is closely related to educational equality as I have understood it. This is the ideal that educational resources be distributed equally. Wilson argues that this notion, too, is incoherent, and that it would be undesirable even if it were not incoherent.

In his argument for incoherence Wilson says that 'the notion of an *educational* resource still contains the concept of uptake. For instance, having a computer is only an educational resource if it is seen and used for learning; that is, if the owner can actually (and will actually) become more educated by his possession of it'.[3] Inequality in the capacity for uptake ensures that the status of a resource as educational is relative to the consumer: so equality of resources is incoherent.

Wilson, in fact, has described two distinct criteria for a resource counting as educational. The parenthetically mentioned criterion for something counting as an educational resource is simply implausible. Consider a nutritional resource. For a peanut to count as a nutritional resource its owner does not have to enjoy nutritional benefits through its use. She might eat it when she is about to be sick. She might forget to eat it, and allow it to waste. She might not like peanuts, and throw it away. In none of these cases is it deprived of its status as a nutritional resource. Nor can it be said that it is not available to her. What is properly said is that she fails to make full use of it as a nutritional resource. Similarly, that the owner does not actually use the computer to educate herself does not seem to justify the claim that it is not an educational resource. It seems only to justify the claim that she fails to make use of it as an educational resource.

Even the claim that a resource is educational only if its owner can actually use it to become more educated is incorrect. A blind person may be unable to use eyeglasses to enhance her eyesight, but this does not mean

---

[3] Ibid., 30.

that they are not an eyesight-enhancing resource. A monolingual English speaker cannot use a Serbo-Croat/Chinese dictionary, but that does not deprive it of the status of an educational resource.

It is not even clear, as Wilson appears to think, that an educational resource needs to be recognized as such for it to count as an educational resource. It seems right to say of someone who has a dictionary but does not understand what it is for that she has an educational resource which she does not know how to use, rather than that she has a resource which is not educational.

Certainly it is questionable why we would want to distribute resources to people who cannot or who do not know how to use them. This, however, does not make the principle of equality of educational resources unappealing. Instead it shows that the principle alone is inadequate to guide the distribution of educational resources. It needs to be supplemented, not rejected.

If the notion of an educational resource does not contain the concept of uptake in the way that Wilson says then equality of educational resources is not an incoherent goal. But is it an admirable goal? Wilson says not because we want educational resources to go 'to those who can make the best use of them'.[4] 'As an ageing philosopher, I can of course be given an Olympic-style pole vault along with everyone else, but it seems pretty pointless if I have no ability to use it; and if there are not enough pole vaults to go round, I cannot complain if I do not get one'.[5]

But this example is inapt for two reasons. The ideal of equality of educational resources is properly limited to students in early life. The advocate of educational equality is not troubled if some people devote more of their resources to education later in life. The principle is aimed at the governance not of complete lives, but of the early part of lives—the time in people's lives when they are learning to be citizens and are not yet autonomous self-governing persons.

The case Wilson gives is one where the recipient 'can do nothing' with the resource provided. But consider a case where the recipient can do something with the resource, but less than another can do. Suppose Charles can learn to play either, but not both, the trombone and the trumpet not excellently, but only moderately well. Fiona can learn to play both excellently. Is it obvious that the person who can make the best use of the resources should get them? Fiona would then get trumpet and trombone, and Charles would get nothing. It is a harsh theory which yields this result.

---

[4] Wilson, John, 'Does equality (of opportunity) make sense in education?', *Journal of Philosophy of Education*, 25 (1991), 27–31 at 29.
[5] Ibid.

A theory which focuses on the resources and asks that each get the best use, mistakes the proper function of distributive principles, which is to distribute goods among persons, not to distribute uses amongst resources.

Wilson finally argues that there are some educational goods, in particular some forms of higher education, 'which cannot be distributed equally without vitiating their nature. . . . We can only get round this, and save the notion of equality of access or resources, at the cost of dismantling all such activities; that is all activities which (by their very nature) are selective, and demand certain standards of attainment and motivation from those who partake in them'.[6]

Wilson depends here on the assumption that there is no acceptable common basis of comparison between educational resources, for otherwise the existence of particular goods which cannot be distributed equally without vitiating their nature would be no barrier to equality of educational resources. Yet there is a very natural way of making such a comparison: by money value.[7] It is not possible for everyone to have an Oxbridge or Ivy League education without vitiating the nature of that education, but it is possible to make available for everyone's education the same amount of money as for the education of everyone else. Of course, as we saw at the end of the last chapter, money is an imperfect measure of the value of educational resources. Comparisons of money spent should be adjusted, for purposes of comparing effective resources spent, to account for such factors as local market conditions, and the efficiency with which the resources are used, in the way suggested at the end of Chapter 6. But the resulting standard is still essentially a resourcist standard, and one that seems sound. This is one natural understanding of the ideal of educational equality which sidesteps the vitiation problem in that it does not require the dismantling of essentially elitist activities.[8]

It is worth noting here that even if educational equality understood this way were undesirable, that would not vindicate Wilson's own preferred

[6] Ibid.

[7] On Wilson's criterion persons with disabilities would be significantly disadvantaged with respect to educational resources, which would make his criterion straightforwardly unacceptable. For that reason, as well as for the sake of simplicity, I am deliberately assuming that people with disabilities are absent from the framework of discussion.

[8] It might be objected that if higher education is included in the calculus it would be very expensive indeed to distribute educational resources equally. There are indeed some kinds of higher education—I am not thinking of Oxbridge, but of medical school—which are so expensive to provide that implementing educational equality would require an implausible level of social resources to be devoted to education. Higher education is, in general, complicated because it is distributed not to children but to adults, and I am not sure that the principle of educational equality should apply to it. Nevertheless, I think that Wilson's distributive criterion would also be inappropriate for the distribution of higher education for the reasons given here.

criterion for the distribution of resources for essentially elitist activities, which is that we 'allocate resources by the criterion of who can best profit from them'.[9] As I suggested earlier this is not just because this is generally a bad criterion. Resources for essentially elitist activities generally have an opportunity cost. An excellent philosophy professor could sometimes have been trained to be an excellent kindergarten teacher. The Magdalene College grounds are conducive to deep thought for undergraduates, but they could equally well be used to teach horticulture to the pupils at the local comprehensive school. In the vast majority of cases it is not clear what it means to ask who can profit from them most. Equality of educational resources gives us a guide as to how to distribute the resources, even on the crude understanding of it that I offer. But the principle of distributing to those 'who can profit most' or 'who can make best use' gives no guidance at all in these cases.

## WHY ISN'T AN ADEQUATE MINIMUM EDUCATION FOR ALL ADEQUATE?

Some philosophers have challenged the idea that material equality is any kind of moral ideal. Harry Frankfurt, for example, has pointed out that when egalitarians make the case for greater economic equality they almost invariably invoke concern for the very poor, those who do not have, in some sense, enough.[10] Instead of equality, he says, justice supports a principle of sufficiency: ensuring that everyone has enough of whatever it is that justice distributes.

In the course of his argument that states should ultimately withdraw from the business of funding schooling, James Tooley has recently followed Frankfurt by claiming that the widespread concern for equality of educational opportunity is misplaced, and that what matters is only that every child should have an 'minimum adequate education'. A policy of radical school choice, which is also desirable on other grounds, can, according to Tooley, accommodate this, rationally defensible value, even when the government pulls out of funding education altogether.[11]

If Tooley is correct in rejecting equal educational opportunity for an adequate minimum education, then his case against state funding of edu-

[9] Wilson, 'Does Equality (of opportunity) make sense in education?', 29.

[10] Frankfurt, Harry, *The Importance of What We Care About* (Cambridge: Cambridge University Press, 1987), chapter 11.

[11] Tooley, J., *Disestablishing the School* (Aldershot: Avebury Press, 1995), chapter 2.

cation is very strong. On reasonable assumptions about the concern parents have for their children and the widespread knowledge that education provides valuable future opportunities, government intervention would be unnecessary to achieve a minimum adequate education for *most*, since all but the very poorest and most irresponsible parents would devote considerable personal resources to their children's education. If an adequate minimum is all we seek, state intervention and funding are necessary only at the margins of the system.[12]

How does Tooley justify his reinterpretation of equality of educational opportunity as requiring only an adequate minimum education for all? He interrogates the work of egalitarian philosophers and tries to show that a careful drawing out of the rational kernel of their arguments shows that not equality, but only adequacy, or satisfaction with respect to some particular good, matters.

Tooley's most important target is John Rawls. Rawls's theory includes two principles of justice, a Liberty Principle, which need not concern us here, and a Second Principle which says the following: social and economic inequalities are to be arranged so that they are both a) to the greatest benefit to the least advantaged, and b) attached to offices and positions open to all under conditions of fair equality of opportunity.

How 'fair equality of opportunity' should be interpreted is, as I pointed out in the previous chapter, much disputed, but Rawls definitively offers what is best understood as a *necessary*, though perhaps not sufficient, condition: 'those who are at the same level of talent and ability and have the same willingness to use them, should have the same prospects of success regardless of their initial place in the social system, that is, irrespective of the income class into which they were born'.[13]

We have seen how fair equality of opportunity supports educational equality: it requires the level of educational resources expended on children in schools to be insulated from family background. Since education is a crucial means to the acquisition of competitive offices and positions, educational inequalities grounded in family circumstances will usually violate fair equality of opportunity.

Why would equality, in this context, require merely an 'adequate minimum'? Tooley interprets Rawls as modifying fair equality of opportunity with the difference principle, which is the principle that social and economic inequalities should be arranged to the benefit of the least advantaged—condition a) above. He says, 'we note Rawls's way around the

[12] Ibid., 35–6.
[13] Rawls, John, *A Theory of Justice* (Cambridge, Mass.: Harvard University Press, 1971), 73.

perceived "problem" of the influence of the family, showing how the principle of equality of opportunity is *tempered by other principles* within his overall theory of justice'[14] and 'we have the notion that fair equality of opportunity, *modified in distinct ways by the difference principle, the principles of redress and of fraternity*, leads to the need for an education for all' (my emphasis in both preceding quotations).[15]

But the difference principle, he argues, is not justifiable *even within Rawls's scheme*. Tooley claims that the considerations offered by Rawls in favour of the difference principle actually support a much weaker principle, that all should have a sufficient, or adequate, level of resources.[16] I shall not review Tooley's exegetical arguments here: I deal with them at length elsewhere.[17] The important point here is that the argument against the difference principle is quite irrelevant to the issue of educational equality, because in Rawls's scheme, contra Tooley, the difference principle *is constrained by* and does not constrain fair equality of opportunity.

Tooley thinks that his argument against the difference principle suffices to defeat equality of educational opportunity because he claims that the difference principle informs fair equality of opportunity: if we substituted a satisficing principle for the difference principle within Rawls's scheme then *it* would inform fair equality of opportunity, yielding the need only for an adequate minimum. But he is simply mistaken about this. According to Rawls, condition b) is *prior to* condition a) in this sense: inequalities of opportunity cannot be justified by their tendency to increase the share of benefits of the least advantaged. When Rawls says that each provision is to be understood in the context of the theory as a whole, he is aiming to mitigate the apparent weakness of fair equality of opportunity. The necessary condition described above says nothing about permissible unequal prospects for those with different levels of talent and willingness to develop and use it. It is, strictly, compatible with a deeply elitist meritocratic society, in which a handful of well-motivated and talented individuals enjoy the vast bulk of the fruits of social co-operation, while a vast mass of slightly less talented and motivated individuals bear almost all the burdens. In the context of the theory, though, this cannot happen, because condition a) ensures that economic inequalities must be arranged so that, consistent with equality of opportunity, they are to the benefit of the least advantaged.

---

[14] Tooley, Disestablishing the School, 22.          [15] Ibid., 25.
[16] Ibid., 28–30.
[17] Brighouse, Harry, 'Why Should States Fund Schools?', *British Journal for Educational Studies*, 46 (1998), 138–52.

Of course, the alternative requirement of a minimum safety net does much less to mitigate the fear of inequality when Rawls's principles operate. However, given that the institution of the family is protected under Rawls's principles, it is fair equality of opportunity that imposes pressures toward material equality. If there are great inequalities of household income and wealth, and children are allowed to grow up in those households, then fair equality of opportunity will be unattainable because children enjoy material advantages which are insensitive to their level of talent and motivation, and have an impact on their life prospects which cannot be effectively mitigated by social institutions such as schooling. So, given the family, fair equality of opportunity will disallow substantial inequalities of household income and wealth.

Where does all this leave Tooley's adequate minimum education? Tooley argues that only children of very poor parents should have their education funded by the state: above the minimum, educational opportunities need not be insulated from family circumstances. But since fair equality of opportunity is the key notion, *prior to* the difference principle or any more defensible substitute, Rawls will still require life prospects to be as insensitive as possible to family circumstances, even if he abandons the difference principle.

In fairness to Tooley, Rawls does allow the possibility of one exception to equality of opportunity: where inequalities of opportunity give those with least opportunity more opportunity than they would under equality. But with respect to educational opportunities and family circumstances it is hard to see how this would ever kick in to justify inequality of opportunity within a generation. How do the superior educational opportunities of some increase the opportunities of others? Sometimes, perhaps, by developing the potential of those who get superior opportunities in ways that enable them to contribute to the opportunities of others. But there is no known mechanism by which inequalities of educational opportunity would achieve this. And, even if there were, there is no reason to think that parental wealth or prudence would play a role.

Furthermore, even if mechanisms could be devised to make inequalities of educational opportunity lead to the greater opportunity of those with least, the inequalities involved would probably undermine the self-respect of the disadvantaged in a way that incentives designed to attract adults to particular occupations do not. Children cannot be presumed to understand the social purpose of inequalities, which will appear to place greater value on the lives of beneficiaries. So while there are good reasons to allow incentive-based inequalities among adults, they do not apply to the distribution of education among children.

Within Rawls's scheme, then, a concern with equal educational opportunity is vindicated. Tooley criticizes Ronald Dworkin along similar lines, arguing that his fundamental moral concerns should lead him only to be concerned with a minimum welfare net. While Dworkin advocates equality of resources, Tooley argues, his opposition to existing inequalities reveals:

that it is not equality as such that Dworkin is particularly worried about. For example he worries that in the United States 'A substantial minority of Americans are chronically unemployed or earn wages below any realistic poverty line, or are handicapped in various ways or burdened with special needs'; or 'the children of the poor must not be stinted of education or otherwise locked into positions at the bottom of society.' But here his problem is not that this minority is earning less than others . . . but that they live in poverty . . . He virtually admits as much . . . when he says: 'We need not accept the gloomy predications of the New Right economists that our future will be jeopardized if we try to provide everyone with the means to lead a life with choice and value'. (Tooley, James, *Disestablishing the School*, 33.)

Tooley regards Dworkin's supplementary argument for equality as inadequate. Dworkin says that *all* viable political theories endorse an abstract egalitarian thesis: that 'from the standpoint of politics, the interests of the members of the community matter, and matter equally',[18] and that equality of resources is the best interpretation of this thesis. But, Tooley says, 'the abstract egalitarian thesis has nothing necessarily to do with equality in this apparently broader sense, only to do with equality of respect for each individual from political institutions'.[19] Dworkin is primarily concerned that persons have an interest in 'leading a life that is, in fact, a valuable life',[20] but, as Tooley argues, this could equally well be spelled out in terms of adequacy as of equality of resources.

I have no interest in defending Dworkin's equality of resources. But Tooley's discussion of Dworkin never goes beyond considering that position. He refrains from asking whether the position Dworkin's more fundamental concerns supposedly point to, adequacy of resources, supports an adequate minimum education for all. This is a serious lacuna: surely it is possible that while equality should be replaced with adequacy with respect to *resources*, the adequacy of resources should be constrained by something like fair equality of *opportunity*. This is Rawls's view, and it is also precisely what I argued in Chapter 6.

---

[18] Dworkin, Ronald, 'Comment on Narveson: In Defense of Equality', *Social Philosophy and Policy*, 1 (1983), 24–40 at 24.
[19] Tooley, *Disestablishing the School*, 34.
[20] Dworkin as quoted (but not cited) by Tooley, *Disestablishing the School*, 35.

## THE PRIMACY OF THE FAMILY AS AN OBJECTION
## TO EDUCATIONAL EQUALITY

The third argument against equal educational opportunity does not question its propriety as a principle, but says instead that the only feasible mechanisms for addressing educational equality undermine values that are more important, even from the perspective of justice, than educational equality. The particular value that I want to consider here is the value of the family. 'Family values' rhetoric has played two distinct roles in recent political attacks on the redistributive state. Authoritarian conservatives have used it to attack the legitimacy of non-traditional familial arrangements and the principles of non-discrimination against women and homosexuals. Right-wing libertarians have also used the rhetoric to attack some of the levelling ambitions of the redistributive state.

The libertarian use of family values rhetoric has resonance in the sphere of schooling because it is widely recognized that the existence of the family does place limits on the achievement of equality of opportunity. As John Rawls acknowledges:

The principle of fair opportunity can only be imperfectly carried out, at least as long as the institution of the family exists. The extent to which natural capacities develop and reach fruition is affected by all kinds of social conditions and class attitudes. Even the willingness to make an effort, to try, and so to be deserving in the ordinary sense is itself dependent on happy family and social circumstances. (Rawls, John, *A Theory of Justice*, 73.)

If we accept background inequalities of income and wealth then the family makes equal opportunity even harder to achieve. Assume the Rawlsian necessary condition for educational equality that I elaborated in the last chapter—that those who are at the same level of talent and ability, and have the same willingness to learn, should have the same prospects of educational success regardless of their initial place in the social system.[21] The family inhibits us from realizing even Rawls's necessary condition. Contrast the financially successful and attentive Lyon family with the poverty-stricken and inattentive Glums. Even ignoring the possibility that their different levels of wealth and attention affect the effort-levels of their respective children, we can predict that, other things being equal, the extra parental attention and additional purchasing power of her parents will give Barbara Lyon better prospects than Ron Glum.

---

[21] Adapted from Rawls, *A Theory of Justice*, 73.

Anti-egalitarians sometimes deny that the family conflicts with equal opportunity, because they understand equal opportunity weakly, as meaning something like 'there is no formal discrimination based on race, class, and sex'. But weak understandings of equal opportunity are mistaken, both in that they fail to do justice to the meaning of the word 'opportunity', and because they neglect the proper moral basis of equal opportunity. Assume that Ron and Barbara have equal opportunities at time t. At $t+1$ Barbara is given $100,000, and no extra restrictions are placed on either of them. Now Barbara seems to have more *opportunity* than Ron, even though neither has been discriminated against on any of the standard bases. At least when we look at the formative stages of a person's life, the resources devoted to them are a good proxy for the level of opportunity they can be said to have.

More tellingly, as we have seen in considering the basic argument, the *moral basis* of equal opportunity supports a strong interpretation. Equal opportunity is desirable as a way of implementing a presumption of the equal moral worth of all persons. This is an individualist criterion: having society devote less resources to someone's life for arbitrary reasons is not much less of an assault on his moral standing than having society license such discrimination on other bases. Yet having less devoted to someone's life simply because he had the misfortune to be born to the Glums rather than the Lyons seems to be an arbitrary reason. So equal opportunity, properly understood, *is* inhibited by the family.[22]

The family is a barrier to educational equality in so far as it makes it difficult to insulate children's prospects from the choice-making ability and level of wealth of their parents. Having acknowledged the conflict, we could insulate the children's prospects by simply abolishing the family. We have seen in Chapter 1 why this is an unacceptable response, and that no participant in the debate on choice advances it. I want to remind the reader of two other kinds of approach to the family. The first, which for want of a better word, I shall call the *fundamental* approach, acknowledges the difficulty of achieving equal opportunity, but includes the liberty to raise one's own family as part of a package of basic liberties which are 'lexically prior' to the principle of equal opportunity. Principle A is lexically prior to principle B if no measure which violates principle A is permissible to serve principle B, but not vice versa.[23] On this view, measures which equalize opportunity are desirable, but they are permissible only in

---

[22] This seems much less arbitrary if good reasons can be adduced for according the family great importance. But that acknowledges the conflict, and resolves it by giving the value of the family priority to equality of opportunity.

[23] Rawls, *A Theory of Justice*, 40–5.

so far as they do not violate the basic liberties which any free society must guarantee, and so residual inequalities of opportunity may be regrettable—because it is regrettable that we cannot devise insulatory measures compatible with the basic liberties—but are not unjust.

Second is what we might call the *institutional* approach. This takes the family to be the most convenient and most effective institutional assignee of our general obligations toward children. It accepts that all adults have extensive obligations toward all children, including but not limited to the obligation to provide them with roughly equal opportunities, but acknowledges that we are ill-positioned to deliver on those obligations directly. Instead, we deliver on them by supporting a social division of labour which assigns special responsibilities for individual children to those who are best positioned to treat those children as required. These are normally those whose activities lead to their birth, or who have made an adoptive commitment, so an arrangement whereby parents have immediate contact with their child is the most efficient way of ensuring that each child gets their due.[24]

Neither of these approaches should be rejected outright, but neither is very satisfactory without further detail. The fundamental response does not specify the content of the liberty to raise one's family. As such it faces the problems we encountered when discussing the idea of parental rights in Chapters 1 and 5. Does this liberty include the right to raise one's family however one chooses? To confer *any* advantages at one's disposal to one's children without regard to the interests of others? To abuse or neglect one's children and their prospects? More needs to be said. Furthermore, it appears to confer on parents absolute responsibility for their own children. Yet if equal opportunity is an ideal at all, it specifies duties *all* of us have to others. We are obliged to ensure that they enjoy roughly equal opportunities as each other and as ourselves. If this is true, the fundamental response assigns to us responsibilities which it gives us no power or permission to fulfil.

It is tempting to draw on the right to freedom of association in defending the right to raise one's own family. But again this does not help. Freedom of association specifies the protected relationships among consenting adults. But the relationships between adults which it most obviously protects—sexual relations—are not protected when they hold

[24] This kind of relationship is spelled out with respect to the relationships among co-nationals in Goodin, Robert, 'What is So Special About Our Fellow Countrymen', *Ethics*, 98 (1987), 663–86.

between adults and willing minors, or even among willing minors.[25] At best, the right to freedom of association suffers similar underspecification to the right to raise one's own family. At worst, it simply says nothing about children at all.

The institutional response acknowledges that all adults have obligations to one another's children, and that where the children are brought up must depend on how well the institutional arrangements serve the children. But it is still incomplete. In the face of considerable anecdotal and statistical evidence that many families do a great deal of damage to the children brought up in them, we need to explain how and why it is that families are convenient places for children to be brought up. In view of the fact that the family palpably inhibits the achievement of equal opportunity, the institutionalist owes an explanation of which obligations the family serves well and why they outweigh equal opportunity. Finally, a practical concern: the position is very hard to accept. Most people think that there is some intrinsic value to the family which is not captured by the idea that the family is merely a convenient institutional assignee. Many opponents of measures designed to implement equal opportunity oppose those measures on principle, because a very serious and independent value is violated.

Without endorsing this third problem as an argument against the institutional response, let us concede it for the sake of argument. In what follows I shall argue that, while acknowledging that the family has distinctive value does rule out some forms of insulation of children's prospects from their parents' level of wealth, it nevertheless permits much more extreme measures to promote educational equality than have been attempted by most successful redistributive movements. The argument clarifies the content and the limits of a purported right to raise one's own family, and suggests the existence of such a right. These same considerations would explain the appeal of the institutional response, if it were not accepted that the family has a distinctive value which cannot be captured by that response.

What we have to see is whether the measures designed to promote educational equality, and in particular the insulation of children's education from the level of success and choices of their parents, jeopardize whatever is important about the value of the family. Some distinctions among kinds of insulation must be explained.

---

[25] That sexual relations among willing minors should not be protected is more controversial than that relations between adults and minors should not be protected. But even if they should be protected it may not be because of the right to freedom of association, but because of non-rights-concerned considerations.

First, insulating children's education from the *choices* of their parents is a distinct aim from insulating them from the *success* of their parents. A grant system which provides all parents with equal money to devote to the education of their child *partially* insulates the child's education from the level of material success their parents enjoy. But if education is not compulsory, parents may refrain from using the voucher. In a grant system without compulsory education a child with no prospects for education would be a victim *not* of her parents' lack of material success, but of their choices with respect to her education.

In fact, *partial* insulation of educational spending from the level of parental success and the quality of their choices is virtually uncontroversial. Most advanced industrial countries provide free public schooling for all whose parents select it, and make some schooling compulsory. Even the most radical advocates of vouchers do not directly challenge the principle of partial insulation. Theoretical defenders of sole reliance on educational vouchers claim that vouchers should be paid for out of public funds, and the political proposals for educational vouchers usually offer these as a reform rather than an abolition of public schooling.

A second distinction among kinds of insulation is between *floors* and *ceilings*. Most voucher proponents, and those defenders of public schooling who countenance legal private schooling, support a floor of resources which can be devoted to the education of children regardless of the means otherwise available to their parents, although Tooley may be an exception.[26] A *ceiling* would set an upper limit on the level of resources that could be spent on the education of particular children. An *absolute ceiling* might specify that no-one may spend more than $10,000 on their child's education; a *relative ceiling* might specify that no-one may spend more than twice as much on their child's education than is spent on the education of the child on whose education least is spent. Again, floors and ceilings only provide partial insulation,[27] since there is scope for differential spending above the floor or below the ceiling.

Standard systems of public education in advanced industrial countries aim to provide partial insulation from both the parents' level of material success, by having state-financed schools which effectively set floors; *and* from the quality of their parents choices, by making education compulsory up to a certain age. But the insulation is, typically, *only* partial, since private schooling and extra-curricular private tutoring are permitted, as is,

---

[26] See Tooley, James, *Education Without the State* (London: Institute for Economic Affairs, 1996).

[27] Unless, of course, both floors and ceilings are in effect and they are set at identical levels.

typically, some level of parental choice with respect to which schools the children attend.

Egalitarian approaches to education are not the only ones that distrust the connection between parental choices and success, and the prospects of children. Recall Wilson's elitist criterion for the distribution of educational resources: that resources should go to those 'who can best profit from them'.[28] Where this principle operates alone, although opportunities will be very unequally distributed, their distribution will not be determined directly by the wealth or preferences of parents. The talented child of poor parents will be inundated with resources, and the talentless child of wealthy parents will be left with nothing: the criterion implies that wealthy parents should be disallowed from devoting educational resources even privately to their untalented children, and that only officials well-positioned to make judgments about who can make good use of educational resources should say who gets what. If egalitarian approaches stand in tension with family values, so do some elitist conservative approaches.

Either form of uncontroversially permissible partial insulation falls far short of establishing either educational equality or equal opportunity— either for material success or for non-competitive intrinsically valuable experiences. *Full* insulation would be necessary, though not sufficient, to guarantee equal opportunity. It is at this point that we are faced with the need to constrain efforts to achieve full educational equality. I shall briefly review the reasons elaborated in Chapter 1 for thinking that parents have the right to raise their own children, and show that these do indeed suffice to block full insulation—the full achievement of educational equality. But I shall then show that the standard measures that social democratic governments have taken, and egalitarians propose, for implementing educational equality do not violate the values underlying the family, and that using a school system to implement educational equality in these ways is permissible.

First, families are the receptacles of many of our best experiences: it is here that lasting and deep bonds of affection find their greatest realization, and for many parents their relationships with their children are the single greatest source of reward in their lives. Second, families persistently matter subjectively to people. Even if there were genuinely better arrangements available for human child-rearing, that does not suffice to justify overriding the very real commitment people have to living in families.

Our interest in ensuring equality of opportunity for our fellow citizens might seem to provide the powerful justification needed for overriding

---

[28] Wilson, 'Does equality (of opportunity) make sense in education?', 29.

people's commitments to living in families. But a third reason for valuing the family is that it contributes massively to the value of our total opportunities. The best relationships between children and parents contribute very significantly to the ability of children to take advantages of opportunities to live well by giving them the internal emotional resources to live a full and good life. Even short of the best relationships, many perfectly good relationships between parents and children contribute to this end. It is not that those who have the confidence which comes from having been loved and cared for in a reflective, respectful, and unselfish manner have more opportunities exactly, so much as that the opportunities, formally understood, that they face have more value because they can make more of them.

Interfering with the capacity of the family to produce fulfilling lives for children might be acceptable if such interference were able to *redistribute* opportunities for fulfilling lives. Some children have poor relationships with their parents; others have good ones, and the inegalitarian consequences of this difference are regrettable. But, since living a rewarding life is not a competitive resource, there is no gain to the person with a poor relationship when the person with a good relationship has that relationship damaged. But we do not know of feasible mechanisms for redistributing those opportunities. Personal relationships are somewhat mysterious and we are confident that, while removing all children from their family homes into orphanages would equalize somewhat our ability to live rewarding lives, it would do so at great cost to those who would otherwise have had more rewarding lives and without gain to those who would not have had them anyway. Destroying the opportunities to live rewarding lives of those with many, does not increase the opportunities of those with few, and we do not know how to redistribute.

The opportunities for a rewarding life that spring from one's relationship with one's parents are, in this way, unlike many other goods such as wealth, and education. We do have fairly reliable mechanisms for redistributing wealth and educational resources without simply destroying everything we try to redistribute.[29]

Of course, the opportunities provided by families are enhanced by the availability of resources: loving parents can do more for their children with more money than with less. And poverty, though not a decisive barrier to

---

[29] It may be that the mechanism for redistribution does destroy, or lead to the non-creation of, some of the resources which would otherwise have been there. But we can nevertheless ensure that those who have least, have more than prior to the redistribution, which is what I am suggesting is not the case with those opportunities for rewarding living which spring from the family.

being a good parent, is a source of frustration to people and can distort their relationships with their children. Resources are by no means irrelevant to how good a familial experience one has.

It might be objected to this account of the value of the family that many families do not contain these goods. Many contain marvellous and lasting realizations of respectful and unselfish love, but many are brutal, violent, and hateful. Families contain the best of human experience, but also contain much of the worst. Acknowledging this, though, does not help us with the determination of public policy unless we believe both that the state, acting on behalf of society, is capable of identifying bad families and providing better for the children of those families. In fact, the state, when it acts properly, is reasonably good at identifying some of the very worst families. There are markers of certain kinds of badness, such as markers of violence and sexual abuse, which can be followed up without doing violence to most family relationships. Since the lived experience and opportunities provided for children in those families are often so poor, the state is able to provide better for them. But, without deep intrusiveness which would jeopardize the ability of any family to provide the goods they do to children, and perhaps even with such intrusiveness, the state cannot gather sufficient information to make the redistributions which would be required by equality of opportunity.

What room does the above account of the value of the family leave for promoting educational equality? The test for any proposed measure is whether it threatens to disrupt the capacity of the family to provide the goods which, if the above account is correct, it reliably provides better than any known alternatives.

There is one class of restrictions and prohibitions which would be likely to damage the capacity of families to deliver the goods, as it were: restrictions on the direct interactions between parents and children. Parents incidentally provide opportunities and education for their children by discussing the internal workings of the Bolshevik party over the dinner table; by teaching them to cook, play cricket, to translate *Georgics IV*, or to use a computer; by discussing homework; by taking them on vacations; by making up stories and reading to them; by listening to *Flanagan and Allen* and watching *Postman Pat* with them.

Why could restrictions or prohibitions on such activities reasonably be expected to interrupt the capacity of the family to provide its benefits? Parents, unconcerned about the welfare of other children, might resent being told by others through an impersonal state how to conduct their interactions with their own children for the sake of equality. This may be a serious problem, though it might equally be the case that such parents draw closer to their children in the face of perceived interference. The problem is better illustrated by the conscientiously egalitarian parent who attempts, for the sake of equality, to make sure that she does not violate the regulations. Such a parent/child relationship loses the spontaneity essential for healthy close personal relationships. It is part of having a close personal relationship with someone else that one does not feel obliged to check one's conversational topics, that one feels permitted to share one's enthusiasms, that one can teach and be taught by the other person. That spontaneity is required for the closeness which, in turn, is required for the benefit to the child of the parental relationship—in comparison with which, the benefits of learning the details of off-spin bowling, Russian revolutionary strategy, and the sex life of bees in Latin are relatively small.

Parents who conscientiously attempted to follow such regulations and restrictions, then, would have to monitor their relationships and ration their attention in ways which could be expected to disrupt those relationships. And, if such restrictions are off-limits, an interest in educational equality supports non-restriction of some other kinds of activities: in particular, commercial purchasing of certain extra-curricular education. If a Latin-speaking parent can teach her child Latin, the non-Latin-speaking parent should be allowed to purchase the same service.[30]

But the account of the family we are working with and the above restrictions on permissible intervention do not support criticism of the standard egalitarian approaches to education. Many indirect strategies for promoting educational equality remain permissible in the light of the value of the family. Consider levelling household income and wealth. As inequality of income and wealth diminishes, so do opportunities to provide differential resources for one's children. Other things being equal, if one family has roughly the same disposable income as another it has roughly the same ability to confer educational benefits. In diminishing the level of income and wealth of a family the state does not interfere with direct interactions, and does not force parents to monitor their beneficent behaviour towards their children. This is not *direct* insulation. The level of material success and choices of their parents still affect children's opportunities; but since levels of material success differ much less than in inegalitarian economies, one source of unequal opportunity is diminished.

---

[30] In the real world, of course, Latin-speaking parents in contemporary Britain or America are likely to be on the whole, wealthier, and hence more able to purchase permitted services, than non-Latin-speaking parents. This concern should be mitigated somewhat by what I say in the next paragraph.

A second, and direct, mechanism of insulation which need not interfere with the capacity of the family to provide its distinctive values, is requiring attendance of some form of school for most of the day, and equalizing the resources devoted to each child's schooling, subject to the requirement that more be spent on less-able and disabled children. This could take the form of providing equally valued vouchers to all parents and prohibiting schools from accepting any supplement to the face value, as I shall suggest in Chapter 9. Or, in a non-choice based public school system, it would involve prohibiting private schools and requiring equal per-pupil funding across schools. Some regulation concerning the distribution of low-ability and at-risk children across schools, and monetary compensation to schools for having higher densities of such children, would also be required.

Such a requirement does not, of course, ensure equal spending on each child's education, since families can supplement or not according to their willingness and ability to pay by purchasing additional tuition. But the length of the school day limits the opportunities for extra-curricular 'top up', and, assuming diminishing marginal returns, if the resources devoted to education during the school day are sufficiently high, then the marginal benefit of the additional tuition is less than it would otherwise be.[31]

Compulsory public schooling is not very controversial. But equalized spending is. Would equalized expenditure on schooling interfere with the family by limiting what parents can do to help their children 'get ahead'? Certainly, while parents can still confer extra educational advantages on their children, a significant part of the time devoted to their children's education is immunized from their interference. But why should this damage parents' relationships with their children? They are bound to the same standard as all other parents, and the matter is, in an important sense, out of their hands. As such, there is no reason for children to resent them: why resent someone for not doing for you something they are not allowed to do? And there is no reason for them to take out whatever frustration they feel about the state of affairs on their children. In this, equal spending on schooling resembles the principle of anti-nepotism. Anti-nepotism limits what parents may permissibly do to advance their children's interests, but is rarely impugned as disruptive of the family, precisely because the limits are justified as preventing unfair advantages, and are the same for all. The

---

[31] If per-pupil spending is effectively equalized, the school day is long enough, and an unregulated private education unavailable, then we can expect well-educated and wealthy parents to try to ensure that per-pupil spending is quite high. This is a standard and generally good argument for making it difficult for the children of wealthy parents to be taught separately from the children of less wealthy parents.

social-democratic approach to education extends the principle of anti-nepotism as far as it can be extended without threatening the value of the family.

## PRAGMATIC LIBERTARIAN OBJECTIONS

Two related concerns will remain. The first is that insulation of the kind that I have described is unacceptably disrespectful to the parents, not because it infringes on their rights over their children but because it curbs their ability to live their lives the way they want to. The second is that the egalitarian approach cedes excessive power from individuals to the state.

The first concern is, I think, without foundation. In enforcing educational equality, the state refrains entirely from commenting on the content of the ways of life of its citizens. In pursuing educational equality the state does not tell us how to live, but ensures that we have roughly equal resources to devote to our lives. Furthermore, when the concern is with educational resources for minors, the lives in question are not ours, but those of our children. It is true that the requirement of autonomy-facilitating education may appear to comment on the content of citizens' commitments, but that measure is justified in a way that makes no comment, and anyway is not at issue here.

The second worry is more serious, but still, I think, misplaced. The modern state is a large bureaucracy, with real tendencies to accrue power to itself. In permitting it to implement educational equality in the ways I have described, we do cede some power to it. But libertarians often describe the state as if it is some outside agency, imposing its independent will on the citizenry. That is a wrong picture of the modern democratic state. The state should be an agent through which the individual members of society act. It is an indispensable instrument for the delivery of some of our most fundamental obligations to others, with information-gathering and processing, and enforcement powers which are essential to doing justice and which no individual or private agency has. The appropriate response to the libertarian worry, therefore, is not to renege on our obligations, but to endeavour to design institutional checks on the power of the state which prevent it from reaching beyond its mandate, and make it more directly accountable to its citizens.

The libertarian response to this exhortation is, I suspect, to express deep scepticism about the possibility of designing such checks. Contemporary libertarians and egalitarians disagree not only about what weight to accord to which political values, but also about the realistic possibility of just institutional design. To vindicate my greater optimism would require a long discussion of the history of the democratic state which would be inappropriate here. But it is worth mentioning that the difference in optimism is a matter of degree. Libertarians are not anarchists, and must believe that it is possible to design a state which limits itself to the effective regulation of what they consider just property relations. Many libertarians display an optimism about the self-sustainability of imperfect markets which easily matches that of egalitarians concerning the state. The state, furthermore, is an ineliminable agent in matters of justice, both for libertarians and egalitarians. It is not good enough that people just happen to get what they have a right to: justice requires institutional guarantees. From the point of view of justice it is not good enough that an individual's rights never happen to be violated: it is essential that we establish institutional forms which *assure* individuals that they can make and execute their life plans without fear of rights violations. The state is an indispensable means for doing this—it plays an essential role in both egalitarian and libertarian justice.

# 8

# Social Justice and Existing School Choice Programmes

I have elaborated, in the previous four chapters, two central criteria for evaluating any set of educational institutions. Education policy should aim at ensuring that every child has a real opportunity to become an autonomous person, and should aim at rough equality of educational opportunity. Equal educational opportunity requires at least the following three things: the quality of the educational inputs in the school system should not reflect the level of wealth of the parents; they should not reflect the decision-making ability of the parents; and children with disabilities should get substantially greater educational resources than children without disabilities.

In this chapter I propose to look at the best evidence available with respect to two quite different choice schemes, and ask of each how it measures up against these criteria. Though none of the evidence is conclusive, it appears that none of them is exemplary with respect to what really matters. But this fact does not, in itself, impugn school choice. There are two reasons for this. The first is that how well a scheme does with respect to some criterion cannot be decisive against it or for it because we have to compare the scheme both with what could be expected if the scheme it replaced had continued, and also with what could reasonably have been expected from alternative feasible reforms. A choice scheme might do very badly with respect to equality, but still represent an improvement on the performance of the previous arrangements, and also be superior to the other reforms which were rejected in favour of it. In that case the absolute weakness of the scheme does not justify its rejection, since it is superior to other options. One consideration I shall advance in favour of choice in the US context—but not, I should emphasize, in the UK context—is that it actually stimulates a dynamic towards equality by helping to shift the bulk of funding away from the local level and toward the state level, where it is politically much more difficult to defend the existing profound inequalities of funding.

The second reason that the weakness of the existing schemes with respect to what really matters does not impugn choice in general, is simply that each scheme has its own specific features, which can be expected to lead to certain objectionable outcomes. The UK scheme, which I shall start with, has quite identifiable mechanisms which are inessential to choice, and which could be expected to promote inequality. These mechanisms are impugned by the evidence, but choice itself is not. The following chapter will be devoted to showing how a choice scheme could be devised which would do well with respect to equality and autonomy, and to exploring potential difficulties with any such scheme.

## THE SYSTEM IN ENGLAND AND WALES

### The Background

The choice-promoting reforms of 1988 were introduced into a system which had been more or less stable since 1944. The one major national reform was the raising of the school-leaving age from 15 to 16 in the 1970s, though throughout the 1960s and 1970s there was also a strong movement at the local authority level away from selective and toward comprehensive secondary education. Under the 1944 *Education Act*, both primary, or elementary, and secondary schools were to be administered directly by Local Education Authorities (LEAs) which were directly accountable to locally elected bodies—for the most part County Councils, which also had responsibilities with respect to housing, local planning, basic municipal and welfare services. Schooling was compulsory from the ages of 5–15. Secondary education was, in most LEAs, organized on a selective basis: academically-oriented grammar schools were available for the 20 to 25 per cent of children who passed an exam take at ages 11 or 12, while the other 75 to 80 per cent would attend secondary modern or technical schools, which would prepare them for apprenticeships but not for University entrance. A dramatic shift toward so-called comprehensive schooling, in which all children would be educated in the same school, occurred on an authority-by-authority basis in the 1960s without any change in the law: this was possible because the 1944 Act was sufficiently ambiguous to allow for comprehensive schooling.

Although the LEAs administered the schools and assumed authority for such decisions as whether to 'go comprehensive', the system was very much a national system. Schools were funded out of locally-levied taxes on home-owners (rates), but funding of schools did not vary according to the tax-base, since rates were supplemented by the central-government administered rate-support grant, according to a formula which ensured that poor authorities would be able to spend just as much on their schools as wealthy authorities. LEAs had a strong management and leadership function, but had little funding discretion.

Parental choice had, as we have seen, a significant formal place in the system, and, unlike in the US system, schools were deliberately differentiated along various lines. Among elementary schools within any Authority, there would be secular schools but also Roman Catholic and Church of England schools, which were brought into the state system by the 1944 Act, with the churches having a limited share in management with the LEA. Among secondary schools there would typically be single-sex as well as mixed schools, and again, some Roman Catholic and Church of England schools. Though access to a Grammar School was available only to children who had passed the relevant exam, and the presumption was that a child would attend its local school, parents could opt for alternatives on the basis of such reasons as: family associations, religious affiliation, preference for single-sex or mixed schools, and special facilities at the school. But choice was not absolutely to be respected: it could be denied on the grounds that it would incur unreasonable public expenditure, lead to overcrowding, or impose on the child an unreasonably long journey to or from school.

The formal role permitted to parental preference was never, however, a decisive aspect of the system. The vast majority of children attended the school to which the authority allocated them, and parents by and large did not attempt to exercise the choice available to them. Furthermore the choice of a parent had to be backed up by formal reasons, reasons which could be overridden by other reasons offered by the local authority. The process was less like consumer choice than like litigation, except that the LEA was the judge and was also one of the parties in the litigation. Although parental choice had a formal place, it could not be considered a significant aspect of the organization of the system.

## The Choice Reform

The Conservative party won the 1979 general election with a small majority, which it increased in 1983, and stayed in power until 1997. A succession of Education Secretaries implemented a series of piecemeal reforms primarily aimed at strengthening the private sector. But the *Education Reform Act* of 1988 aimed to transform completely the delivery of education in the UK. By this time, the vast majority of secondary schools were comprehensive schools, but otherwise the system was still as established in the 1944 Act. The three major reforms were as follows:[1]

1. The establishment of a national curriculum which all schools would be bound to follow. Mathematics, science, and English were to be the core subjects, with a modern foreign language, technology, history, geography, art, music and physical education as foundation subjects, and religious education as a basic subject. Assessments of achievement would be done at ages 7, 11, 14 and 16, through teachers' reports and a series of nationally administered tests.

2. The establishment of local management of schools. School budgets were to be turned over to the management teams in the schools themselves, and 80 per cent of the budget was to be determined solely by the number and ages of the pupils in the school. Schools were allowed to admit students up to their physical capacity. Open enrollment was introduced, allowing schools to seek out pupils and attract a large applicant pool.[2]

3. Two new forms of schools were established: City Technology Colleges, which would be sponsored by local businesses and run by independent trusts; and Grant Maintained (GM) Schools, which would be established by having existing schools opt out of the control of the local authority on the basis of a parental ballot. Grant Maintained Schools would be run by a governing body without any local government appointees, and funded directly by the central Government. The GM Schools had increased discretion over admission, and a 1993 *Education Act* encouraged GM schools to specialize, as well as allowing some private schools to 'opt in' to GM status.

The government's intention and expectation was that numerous schools would take up the Grant Maintained option. A substantial proportion of public education would then be provided by schools which were largely self-governing and subject only to centralized regulation. A quasi-market

---

[1] See Chitty, Clyde, *The Education System Transformed* (Manchester: Baseline Books, 1992) for a valuable account of the reforms. Also Whitty, Geoff, Power, Sally, and Halpin, David, *Devolution and Choice in Education* (Buckingham: Open University Press, 1998), especially chapter 2.

[2] The *Schools Standard and Framework Act* (UK) of 1998, introduced by the Labour government, altered the situation with respect to admissions. Every admission authority within the LEA—each state-aided (religious) school, each Grant-Maintained school, and the LEA itself—must consult with each other and agree on a common admissions process and on the criteria to be used for admissions. A single national Adjudicator's office was established to adjudicate disagreements where they arise. But there remains scope for the agreement to allow both Grant-Maintained schools and LEA schools to have a great deal of discretion on admissions.

would be created, in which schools competed with one another for funds by competing for pupils.

In fact relatively few schools have taken the option. By 1997 there were over 1,000 grant maintained schools, with only about 700,000 pupils—10 per cent of the school age population—being educated in the grant maintained sector.[3] This is not an insignificant number, but it is not massive, nor is it growing substantially—the vast majority of opt-outs took place in the first few years of the reform. However, the 1993 Act has increased the discretion of these schools over admissions, and in light of the discretion awarded even to local authority schools it makes sense to call the overall reform a choice reform.

## The Evidence

In presenting the evidence concerning the UK choice reforms I shall concentrate on a study by Sharon Gewirtz, Stephen J. Ball and Richard Bowe entitled *Markets, Choice and Equity in Education.*[4] As its title suggests, their study concentrates on the effects of the reforms on educational equality—there appear to be no studies that attempt to measure the reform's effects on autonomy, for reasons which should be fairly apparent, though I shall have some comments to make about autonomy in the light of the study. Gewirtz *et al.* looked at the operation of the new reforms in 'three overlapping local education markets in one English city—London'. Their research looked at both the demand side: the ways in which parents went about choosing schools; and the supply side: the way that schools went about attracting and selecting pupils. Their data consisted of interviews of parents, interviews of administrators, governors, and teachers in the schools, interviews of administrators at the LEAs involved, and various materials pertaining to school enrollments, choices, school performance indicators, and LEA planning meetings.

There are two problems with the Gewirtz *et al.* study from my point of view. First, the data was collected from 1991–4, some time after the reforms had been introduced, but before the effects of the reforms were in any way settled. It is clear from the study that various schools are still undergoing transitions not only in terms of their student-base, but more importantly in terms of their institutional culture in the light of the

---

[3] Whitty, *et al.*, *Devolution and Choice in Education*, 19.

[4] Gewirtz, Sharon, Ball, Stephen, and Bowe, Richard, *Markets, Choice and Equity in Education* (Buckingham: Open University Press, 1995). For a more comprehensive discussion of the effects on equality of choice schemes in general see Whitty, *et al.*, *Devolution and Choice in Education*, especially 115–25.

reforms. Many teachers and administrators greeted the reforms without enthusiasm, but, since they were in place, recognized an obligation to change the behaviour of the school to suit the new environment, and this process was still going on during the study. The second problem is that they do not have access to the fine-grained data which would most help us to make confident conclusions about equality. From this perspective the ideal study would be quantitative, and would demonstrate either an improvement or decline in educational achievement, or test scores, for the least able and poorest students relative to the most able and wealthiest children, and demonstrate this change to be stable over a long period of time. This is not to fault the design of the Gewirtz *et al.* study—the researchers's interests were not exactly the same as mine, and they used the most feasible methods suited to their purposes.

What were their findings? On the demand side they found a distinct difference, correlating strongly with the social class and educational background, in the considerations given by parents to support their choices. They distinguish three classes of chooser. 'Privileged, or skilled', choosers, or better educated parents, were better able to understand the public sources of information, including the information offered by the schools themselves. They display 'a marked scepticism about the attempts at impression management involved in the production of school prospectuses and in the organization and choreographing of open evenings and school tours'.[5] They are much more likely to take control of the process of choice, and less likely to allow their children to make the choice themselves. They also display a consistent concern with the social origins of the likely peer group, and an interest in having the child among bright children. Semi-skilled choosers are seeking a good school, but are less aware than the skilled choosers of the need to find a good match between the school and their child: as Gewirtz *et al.* put it, 'the process of school choice is abstract, more a matter of finding the "good" school rather than the "right" one'.[6] Finally there are the least well-educated, the 'disconnected' choosers. 'While the skilled/privileged choosers often ended up with two possible schools from their process of elimination and comparison, the disconnected almost always began with, and limited themselves to, two. These would be schools in close physical proximity and part of their social community.'[7] The disconnected choosers do not talk about child personality or teaching methods, but focus on 'factors such as facilities, distance, safety, convenience, and locality'.[8]

---

[5] Gewirtz, *et al.*, *Markets, Choice and Equity in Education*, 32.
[6] Ibid., 44.          [7] Ibid., 45.          [8] Ibid., 47.

Gewirtz *et al.* conclude that the unequal sophistication of parents as choosers in the educational marketplace bodes ill for educational equality. *Prima facie* we would expect that the worse choosers would get worse schools for their children, and that the privileged children of privileged choosers will tend to congregate together in schools where they can transmit advantages to one another. It should be easier to teach them than the children of the less-skilled choosers, and if school budgets are responsive almost exclusively to the age and number of pupils in the school, we would expect the per-pupil allocation of effective educational resources to be greater in the schools with more privileged pupils.

But, although Gewirtz *et al.* do not point this out, these are only *prima facie* expectations. As I shall suggest in the next chapter, they could be confounded by the appropriate kinds of regulation on the supply side. However, as Gewirtz *et al.* find, the supply side has also responded to the reforms in a way that would lead us to expect inequality. School management teams have responded in different ways, some embracing the need to market their school with enthusiasm, others embracing it as a necessary evil in the light of the changed environment. But the incentives are clear, and schools are all pursuing, to a greater or lesser degree, the more desirable pupil base: students who are identified as able, well-motivated and middle class, and especially girls and children with South Asian backgrounds. These are the pupils viewed most likely to improve the test scores which will serve as the performance indicators which will be used to attract further desirable applicants in the future. Even management teams deeply committed to some sort of comprehensive ideal are forced by the logic of the market and the content of their ideal into this sort of marketing: a comprehensive school without able pupils and middle class pupils is not a comprehensive school, but a lower-tier school in a selective system. The behaviour on the demand and supply sides interact to produce inequality: when schools have discretion over admissions and are not rewarded materially for admitting students who are difficult to teach, they will naturally aim for the more easily teachable students; and if the parents of the more easily teachable pupils are able to identify the best schools for their children we can expect inequalities to emerge.

The unequal capacities of parents as choosers are not the only factors that can be expected to lead to educational inequality under the reforms. Because structural features encourage schools to advertise themselves primarily to the most easily 'educable' students, there appears to have been a decline in the resources devoted to students with special educational needs. Schools which seek to do well by students with special needs face the following dilemma, nicely summarized by one of Gewirtz *et al.*'s interviewees, a school governor:

The school has an enormous intake of SEN [special education needs] . . . But that's another thing; you work hard, you develop an area, you get known as a good school for SEN and so what happens?—you're flooded with SEN kids which don't drag the resources with them that they need and so disproportionately affect the resourcing of the school.   (Gerwitz, Sharon, *et al.*, *Markets, Choice and Equity in Education*, 141–2.)

Because there is a prejudice in the population that schools which contain disproportionate numbers of children with disabilities cannot educate academically more able children well, and because children with special needs do not bring with them all the resources that will have to be devoted to them in the school, schools face a disincentive to provide well for those students. The prejudice against schools which attract students with special educational needs is exacerbated by the manner of publication of exam results: schools are required to publish raw scores in school leaving examinations, without making any reference to the level of attainment of those students when they entered the school, so that children with special needs pull down the 'grades' by which the school will be evaluated.[9] In keeping with these incentives, the study found that 'it is provision in those schools which have the greatest numbers of children *requiring* learning support which is most vulnerable because such schools tend to be the ones which are undersubscribed and so financially less secure' and that teachers were routinely redeployed away from special needs departments even as numbers of students with special needs increased.[10]

The evidence, then, is that at least during this transition period we cannot expect the 1988 reforms to do well with respect to the value of educational equality. However, even if Gewirtz *et al.*'s findings were reproduced in other areas of the country there are still three reasons to be guarded about thinking that the evidence against the reforms is decisive. First, there is no evidence concerning the efficiency effects of the reforms: if, as the proponents of choice argue, efficiency is enhanced, the improved educational benefits for the least advantaged students may compensate somewhat the expected inequalities. Even with respect to students with special needs, since no objective measures are available of how well the children are educated, it could be that efficiency-effects produce a net benefit for the children, though this would, given the evidence they describe, be extremely surprising. Second, it may be that the differentiation of the parents as choosers is an artifice of the newness of the reforms. It would not be surprising if the privileged choosers easily accommodate to the new system, but it also would not be surprising if the disconnected choosers

---

[9] Gewirtz, *et al.*, *Markets, Choice and Equity in Education*, 167.       [10] Ibid.

should become more sophisticated over time. Effective choosing is a skill that can, to some extent, be learned. Choice proponents typically argue for transparent information provision. It could be that, as the system passes through the transition into a fully-fledged choice system, transparent information will become readily available, and the ability to choose effectively will be more widely learned. Finally, and most importantly, the Gewirtz study is not a comparative study between the egalitarianism of the new system and that of the old. The researchers determinedly refuse to evoke nostalgia for the old system, but they do not assess how badly the previous system did with respect to equality. Yet they quote Kenneth Clarke's ironic comment, that when the comprehensive schools replaced academically selective schools in the 1960s 'selection by mortgage replaced selection by examination and the eleven-plus route was closed for many bright working-class boys and girls'.[11] In the pre-1988 arrangements schools were already segregated by the class backgrounds of the pupils, not because of conscious choices made by school admissions teams, but because of the *de facto* class-based segregation of the catchment areas for the schools. Those who needed to, and could, exercised choice by purchasing houses in the catchment areas of desired schools, by exiting the system into the private sector, or by using their talents at working the system to have their children accepted to the school of their choice. The people who can take best advantage of the new reformed system are precisely the same people who could take best advantage of the previous system: to impugn the reforms thoroughly we need evidence that the old system or some alternative reforms would have done better.

As I said, there is no evidence, quantitative or qualitative, on how well the different systems safeguard the prospective autonomy of children. The most immediately relevant features of schooling are the stance toward religious education and the provision for the compulsory 'collective act of worship'. Although not a national curriculum subject, religious education is compulsory and officially, has the same standing as the national curriculum subjects, though unofficially it does not seem to. 'Agreed syllabi' are determined at the level of the Local Education Authority, by the Standing Advisory Council on Religious Education (SACRE). The SACRE is composed of representatives from four interests: the Church of England, the 'other religions', the LEA and the teachers. The agreed syllabus, and any revisions to it, have to be unanimously endorsed by the SACRE. Although, formally, this arrangement would horrify American secularists, political pressure and the need for consensus ensure that the

---

[11] Ibid., 9–10.

outcomes are rarely objectionable. Take, for example, the Norfolk County Council statement: 'In County and Voluntary Controlled Schools the aim is not to make pupils religious but to inform them about religions and the part they play in people's lives, as individuals and as members of other communities and societies'.[12]

The insistence that schools include in the school day a collective act of worship which should be mainly Christian in character is even more shocking to those of secularist inclinations. The 'Christian character' is negotiable, and schools can adopt a religious character more congruent with the actual faiths of their students in consultation with the SACRE. But, of course, acts of worship of any character, potentially threaten the autonomy of students when they are officially supported.[13] But neither the collective act of worship, nor the requirement of religious education, are new to the system: both were written into the 1944 Act, and in fact, little else but them were mandatory.[14] If the religious education and act of worship provisions represent threats to autonomy, the previous system was just as culpable as the reformed one.

It might be suggested that the availability of choice of religious schools in itself jeopardizes the opportunities for autonomy of the children for whom they are chosen. I shall show when discussing the Milwaukee voucher programme that this is not necessarily the case. What matters is not whether the child attends a school over which some organized religion has some control, but what kind of curriculum they will encounter in that school. But, regardless, again this issue is not relevant to assessing the 1988 reforms, since religious schools were already available as a choice for parents in the pre-1988 system, and the new system has not led to any kind of proliferation of religious schools. The greatest threat to the opportunity for autonomy in both the old and the new system is not the threat of religious indoctrination, but the lack of class and cultural heterogeneity in the schools themselves, neither of which appears to have changed a great deal.

[12] Norfolk County Council, *Information for Parents: The National Curriculum* (Norwich, 1996).

[13] Acts of worship which are organized by students as extra-curricular activity, even in consultation with teachers who are acting completely outside officialdom, have a quite different status, and, at least in secondary schools, probably merit protection precisely on the grounds that children's prospective autonomy is important.

[14] The phrase 'Christian in character' was not in the 1944 Act, but this because it was unnecessary, since most school administrators would not have imagined organizing acts of worship of any other character.

## THE MILWAUKEE PUBLIC CHOICE PROGRAM

*The Background*

The system of public schooling in the US is far more decentralized than in the UK. A Federal Department of Education devises various programmes which it offers incentives for states and school districts to participate in, and provides subsidies for schools with very high densities of poor children. Schools are also governed by the court system which imposes various demands for racial integration. Each of the fifty States also has its own department of education, which again offers programmes and imposes certain regulations. But the basic level of organization is the school district, of which there are some 20,000 in the fifty States. The districts vary greatly in size: the Los Angeles Unified School District covers a population of some 2 million people; whereas many rural districts contain just a single small k-12 school. Although this varies by State, the district typically does all the hiring; chooses the curriculum, often within constraints laid down by the State; engages in collective bargaining with unions; and provides the major portion of the funding for the schools. One obvious consequence is that funding varies dramatically both across States and within States. In 1996 average per-pupil spending was $9,787 in New Jersey, $7,168 in Pennsylvania, and $6,621 in Wisconsin; but $4,297 in Alabama, $4,001 in Mississippi, and $4,497 in Louisiana.[15] In the 1989–90 school year per-pupil spending in Manhasset NY was $15,084, compared to $7,229 in New York City NY; in 1988–9 it was $7,725 in Princeton NJ, but $3,538 in Camden NJ.[16] Of course, per-pupil expenditures are not a perfect proxy for effective educational resources. The differences across States especially also reflect differences in the cost of living and varieties in the labour market: it may just be less expensive to buy the services of a high quality teacher in Alabama than in New Jersey. But the same does not hold for differences within States: especially when, as is the case in many metropolitan areas, inner city and suburban school districts are competing for labour in what is basically a single local labour market.

It is also true that what matters is effective schooling rather than expensive schooling, and of course some schools with low per-pupil expenditure are better than some schools with high per-pupil funding. A number of

[15] Shokraii, Nina H., and Youssef, Sarah E., *School Choice Programs: What's Happening in the States* (Washington, DC: Heritage Foundation, 1998).
[16] Kozol, Jonathan, *Savage Inequalities* (New York, NY: Harper Perennial, 1992), 236–7.

factors undermine the effectiveness of expenditure: managers and teachers vary in competence; many rural and small school districts lack the economies of scale available to larger districts; schools face different numbers of students with varying degrees of special needs. But inner city schools in the US are typically underfunded, and face far more serious and expensive problems than their better-funded suburban counterparts. Given the conditions they face and the profile of the student bodies, the less-well funded schools are less likely to be effective schools.

A final feature of the system of education delivery in the US is relevant here. Unlike in the UK system, all public schools are strictly secular. This has not always been the case: the public schools were to a considerable extent Protestant schools, albeit unofficially so, when they were first instituted, and the development of a vibrant system of private Roman Catholic schools was a response to this fact. But in the second half of the twentieth century the schools have become exclusively secular. However, an elaborate system of accommodation of the demands of religious parents has been developed, so that the children of religious parents are often systematically exempted from practices and aspects of the curriculum to which their parents object. This is what Meira Levinson calls the strategy of 'accommodating the private', whereby diversity is maintained in the site of the public school by ensuring that children will actually be exposed to that level of diversity tolerable to their parents.[17]

### The Milwaukee Vouchers

The Milwaukee voucher programme was initiated in the spring of 1990.[18] Students may attend private schools in the Milwaukee Public Schools (MPS) area. Vouchers were only available to children who come from households with household income at 1.75 times the federal poverty level or below, and who had not attended a private school in the previous year— though, of course, after the first year, participation in the programme in the previous year did not disqualify students. Participants were initially restricted to 1 per cent of the total MPS school population, rising to 1.5 per cent in 1993. Transportation costs were not the responsibility of the schools, but in some cases the MPS would assist in transportation. Schools could not charge parents any additional fees for attendance, but they could charge

[17] Levinson, Meira, 'Liberalism versus Democracy? Schooling Private Citizens in the Public Square', *British Journal of Political Science*, 27 (1997), 333–60 at 346.

[18] Details of the scheme can be gathered from the Wisconsin Department of Public Instruction. Its web site contains the instructions for parents and answers many questions about the details of the scheme. See http://www.dpi.state.wi.us

reasonable fees for extra-curricular activities, towels, school uniforms, etc. The 'voucher' comes in the form of a cheque, payable to the parents, which is sent directly to the choice school four times a year and must be signed over by the parents to the choice school. Initially choice schools were permitted to have only 49 per cent of their attendees be choice students: this cap was raised to 65 per cent starting 1994–5. The 1997–8 value of the voucher was $4,894, which is the State equalization aid per-pupil which would otherwise have been sent directly to the Milwaukee public school district: the total amount sent to the choice schools is deducted from the grant made to MPS. Choice schools were, and still are, subject to strict non-discrimination requirements: they must not discriminate on the basis of race, special educational needs, past academic performance, or past behaviour. If a school is oversubscribed it must select from the choice pool randomly, with the small exception that it may prefer a student whose sibling already attends the school. Although there is no discrimination against children with special educational needs, schools are only required to provide special services that can be provided with 'minor adjustments', and parents are directed to discuss this matter with the schools they are applying to.

Major changes to the programme were made in 1995, although they were fully implemented only in 1998–9. These changes do not affect the findings of the studies I shall discuss, all data for which was collected prior to 1995: one of the changes was the elimination of funding for the collection of evidence and data. However, the most important change was the extension of the programme to include religious schools. This measure was blocked by court action until June 1998, when the Wisconsin Supreme Court found that it did not violate the separation of church and state and that the measure could go ahead pending further appeal: the US Supreme Court refused to hear a further appeal in November 1998, so the change is now permanent. One crucial element of regulation on religious schools is that they are not permitted to require that choice students participate in any form of religious service if their parents object. Other changes were the removal of caps on the proportion of students in a school who were funded by the state: schools are now permitted to be populated 100 per cent by choice students. The cap on the total number of choice students was also raised dramatically to 15,000, and k-3 students were permitted to use the system even if they had attended a private school in the previous year. The non-discrimination requirements remained as, importantly, did the restriction of the programme to students from households with income of 1.75 times the poverty line or below.

In its first years the programme was small: in 1993–4 only 742 students participated, and as late as 1997–8 there were only 1,500 students in twenty-three secular schools. However, with the introduction of religious schools and the lifting of the caps, the programme has increased in size dramatically. In 1998–9 there were eighty-seven schools participating, with 6,200 students. Thirty secular schools enrolled about 2,200 students, while fifty-seven religious schools enrolled about 4,000 students. Around $28.6 million in state aid was therefore diverted from MPS to the participating choice schools.

## The Evidence

At the outset of the reforms, the State appointed a team of researchers from University of Wisconsin, Madison led by John Witte to monitor the voucher scheme.[19] Studies were carried out annually for the first five years of the scheme, until the State stopped collecting the relevant data. The methods are extremely sophisticated, and I shall restrict myself largely to reporting their most relevant findings. Since 1995 the data they used have been publicly available, and one team led by Paul Peterson has used the data to challenge some of Witte's findings: my report incorporates Witte's comments on that challenge. The findings are relevant, again, only to the issue of educational equality, there being no obvious method of evaluating the opportunities to become autonomous. However, the introduction of religious schools to the scheme, and their widespread use, naturally raises issues concerning autonomy, so I shall discuss those separately. Unlike the UK study, though, the restricted and targeted nature of this voucher scheme makes it possible to compare the performance of the schools involved in the scheme with the public schools as they standardly work: it is hard to believe that, given its small size in its first few years, the MPCP could have had significant effects on the performance of the MPS schools so quickly as to render the comparisons worthless.

The first question for Witte was, who used the scheme. Here his findings are consistent over the years: the choosing families were very poor, as one would expect given the target group, with household incomes of under $12,000, and 60 per cent of households on AFDC (Aid to Families with

---

[19] My main source here is Witte, John F., 'Achievement Effects of the Milwaukee Voucher Program', a paper presented at the 1997 American Economic Association meeting, 4–6 January 1997. Other sources include Witte, John F., Thorne, Christopher A., and Sterr, Troy, *Fifth Year Report: Milwaukee Parental Choice Program* (Madison: Department of Public Instruction, 1995); Witte, John F., Thorne Christopher A., and Pritchard, Kim, *Private and Public Education in Wisconsin: Implications for the Choice Debate* (Madison, Wi.: UW, Madison, 1995); Witte, John F., and Thorne, Christopher A., 'Who Chooses? Voucher and Interdistrict Choice Programs in Milwaukee', *American Journal of Education*, 104 (1996), 186–91.

Dependent Children); 75 per cent of households were headed by a single female; and 74 per cent of the pupils were black, and 19 per cent Hispanic. The parents were typically very unhappy with MPS, and the children were typically performing badly, in terms both of academics and behaviour. The average choosing parent, however, had a higher level of educational achievement than the average MPS parent, and had higher educational expectations for their children.[20]

What were the educational outcomes of the scheme? It is important to note why this is an important question for our purposes. Given the class backgrounds of the users of the scheme, if, controlling for the higher education level of the parents, test scores were significantly better for the choice children than for the relevant children in MPS, that would at least be *prima facie* evidence that the scheme is good for educational equality. Of course, it would represent an inequality between the choice students and the similarly disadvantaged MPS children, but it would represent an improvement for the overall class of children, making them more equal with their competitors in the suburbs.

Witte proceeded by using data taken from the performance of the children in the Iowa Tests of Basic Skills, focussing on the normalized national percentile rankings in the reading ability and comprehensive mathematics part of the tests. Initially he compared Choice students with MPS students, hampered by the fact that most MPS students took the tests only at grades 2, 5, and 7, rather than every year, the exceptions being students qualifying for Chapter 1 aid, which is designed to help children from poor families. Subsequently, spurred by the challenge to his findings, he compared the Choice students with the students who, rejected from their preferred choice school because of oversubscription, continued in MPS.

Correcting for differences in social class of the subjects, and taking into account as far as possible the high attrition rates from Choice schools, Witte found, consistently, no difference in the math scores between the Choice and MPS students. MPS students displayed a weak advantage in the reading tests, but that advantage is not statistically significant once the missing years of test data are corrected for. In other words, on the basic comparison made by the study, the voucher scheme yielded no improvement in educational outcomes.[21]

However, one factor this comparison cannot correct for is possible selection bias. Since many of the students in the MPS sample had the option of using the choice scheme but did not take it up, there could be a

[20] Witte, 'Achievement Effects of the Milwaukee Voucher Program', 4.
[21] Ibid., 7.

difference in their background situation, manifested in the fact that their parents did or did not choose to take up the system, which would bias the outcome of the study. A comparison between Choice students and Rejects—students whose parents sought to use the scheme, but who, on being randomly rejected from their preferred school, remained in MPS schools—would correct for any such difference. The comparison between Choice and Reject students yields remarkably different results from the comparison between Choice and MPS students. In reading, the two groups of students are virtually identical. But in the mathematics score, there is a stark contrast. The Choice students initially do 2 per cent better than the Reject sample. But when a full set of controls is introduced, improvements are 3.5 per cent after one year, 4.4 after two years, rising to 8.5 and 10.9 per cent after three and four years. Those Choice students who stay in the choice schools long enough seem to do dramatically better than the reject sample who remain in the MPS schools.[22] These results have prompted Paul Peterson, one of the researchers whose secondary analysis prompted Witte to review the scheme, to claim that 'if similar scores could be achieved for all minority students nationwide it could close the gap separating white and minority test scores by somewhere between one third and one half'.[23]

There are reasons to be more cautious about drawing strong conclusions about MPCP from the Choice/Reject comparison. Witte points out that the reject group is tiny, and that of the 27 students in the Reject group fully five of them scored very poorly with 1, a score which usually just reflects a failure to fill in the dots in the test. Remove these students from the comparison, and the remarkable improvement disappears. Even if the results are taken to be significant, furthermore, it is not clear why they should be taken to support much extension of the choice scheme: after all, since the MPS students did as well as the Choice students they, too, did better than their Reject classmates. Perhaps the children of parents who exercise choice have needs that are better met in the private schools, but the public schools do just as well with other students.

---

[22] Witte, 'Achievement Effects of the Milwaukee Voucher Program', 9.

[23] Greene, Jay P., Peterson, Paul E., Du, Jiangtao, Frazier, Curtis L., and Boeger, Leesa, *The Effectiveness of School Choice in Milwaukee: A Secondary Analysis of the Data from the Program's Evaluation* (Cambridge, Mass.: Harvard University, 1996), 4. Greene *et al.*'s secondary analysis has been taken as canonical by some of the partisans for school choice. Editorial pieces in the *Wall Street Journal* and other publications routinely refer to the Peterson 'results' without mentioning either Witte's study or the problems we are about to survey with the findings. A recent Heritage Foundation publication heralds the Peterson findings as 'the fifth-evaluation of the program', as if the Witte study did not exist. See Shokraii and Youssef, *School Choice Programs: What's Happening in the States*, 146.

Although, as I have said, there are no studies concerning the respective opportunities for autonomy of children in the choice schools and the MPS schools, the major legal battles over the MPCP have been fought on grounds related to this issue, not the equality issue. This is because the teachers' unions—primarily the Wisconsin Education Association and its Milwaukee affiliate—and other forces opposing vouchers considered a legal challenge based on separation of church and state grounds to be the most promising strategy for blocking reform. Section 18 of Article I of the Wisconsin State Constitution states that no one 'shall be compelled to attend, erect or support any place of worship or maintain any ministry without consent . . . nor shall any money be drawn from the treasury for the benefit of religious societies or religious or theological seminaries'. The Wisconsin Supreme Court found that the scheme, even when it included private religious schools, did not violate this provision; and the US Supreme Court has refused to hear the case.

Now, strictly speaking, the issue of the separation of church and state is not identical with the more fundamental moral question of ensuring that all children should have a real opportunity to become autonomous. Separation of church and state could be adhered to in the form preferred by its strictest advocates, and that would be no guarantee of the opportunity for autonomy—children could be indoctrinated in secular dogmas in the public schools or could, of course, be withdrawn from the public schools and indoctrinated in religious dogma. However, the separation of church and state is not a value in itself—it is a constitutional guarantee which matters only because it is important that matters of religious conscience should be exempt from the coercive power of the state. Although many proponents of choice will disagree with it, the account I have given in Chapters 4 and 5 suggests that this, in turn, matters because each individual has a right to become an autonomous person. For my present purposes I want to assume this, since I want to argue that state funding of religious schools need not violate what really matters, the right of all children to a real opportunity to become autonomous.

First, it is worth commenting on the current understanding of the constitutional provision of the separation of church and state in this context. A great deal of public money is already used in the US, to subsidize private religious organizations. According to *The Economist*, in 1995 about 57 per cent of the $144 billion made in contributions to tax-deductible charities in the US went to churches.[24] Assuming an implausibly low average marginal tax rate of 20 per cent, and that each contribution would have been

---

[24] 'Tax-exempt and loving it', *The Economist*, 4–1– January 1997, 17.

diminished by the amount that was saved via the tax-deduction, the Federal government indirectly subsidized churches to the tune of about $16.5 billion, even without counting the state and local tax exemptions churches often receive. The US Supreme Court's *Nyquist* decision permits individual States to allow parents to deduct expenditures on their children's private and religiously sectarian schooling from their tax returns. This practice amounts to an indirect subsidy to the religious schools.

These subsidies are admittedly indirect. But there is no difference from the *moral* point of view between a direct and an indirect subsidy. Indirect subsidies exercised through permitting tax deductions will doubtless be used in a different way from direct subsidies, and will have different outcomes in terms of what gets supported. It is also worth noting that indirect subsidies through tax credits tend to help the wealthy pursue their religious goals, whereas vouchers tend to help the poor. Tax credits only benefit those wealthy enough to pay taxes, whereas vouchers are given equally to all—or, in the cases of the Cleveland and Milwaukee programmes, they go only to the poor.[25] But the morally significant feature is that funds which would otherwise have gone to some other public purpose are being diverted to religious schools. Whatever the legal issues, it would be morally inconsistent for the Court to rule out vouchers for private religious schools, on the grounds of the separation of church and state, while upholding *Nyquist*.

Perhaps, as some people argue, *Nyquist* and the tax-deductions for contributions to churches violate the separation of church and state too. I doubt it. The purpose of separation is not to insulate religious organizations from publicly generated funds, but to ensure that no government action is motivated by the desire to favour some religious organizations over others or none at all. As long as all *bona fide* religious and non-religious groups that meet reasonable regulations are included in a scheme, the spirit of church/state separation is intact.

As I have argued, the real problem is *not* state/church separation, but the right to prospective autonomy of children of religious parents. Does religious school choice have to abandon a commitment to this right of children? Whether the MPCP represents that, depends on two things: the effective curricula of the religious choice schools and of the MPS schools; and the material conditions in the two kinds of schools: how safe and secure are the children? There are, as far as I know, no reputable studies on these questions. But it is easy to imagine public school districts in which the real curriculum is weak with respect to the prospective autonomy of chil-

---

[25] MPCP currently grants vouchers only to households which are at 175 per cent of the official poverty line or below.

dren, and in which children have relatively low levels of physical security; whereas some religious private schools participating in choice schemes do well in both these areas. Certainly, there are few public schools in which children receive the kind of exposure to religious and critical ways of thinking about the world which I sketched in Chapter 4, while such a curriculum can be found in some Catholic schools run by religious orders, as opposed to Catholic Diocesan schools.[26] The Wisconsin statutes governing the choice schools do not regulate the curriculum: even the requirement that children be exempt from religious worship is based on parental preference, and express preference at that. But the statutes were designed by political forces entirely uninterested in personal autonomy, and it cannot be argued that because this scheme displays no concern with this value, choice in general will violate the right to prospective autonomy.

## CONCLUDING COMMENTS

The two major schemes we have looked at do not appear to do well with respect to educational equality in their own terms. However, the British scheme has various features which are clearly non-egalitarian, but which are not in any sense essential to choice. The latitude given to schools over their admissions process and the funding formula in particular, would lead one to expect that the system will diverge from the ideal of educational equality. But oversubscribed schools could be required to select randomly among applicants, as the MPCP schools are, and the funding formula could be changed to make less easily educated children more attractive to schools, and to provide material incentives to achieve a prescribed social and educational mix of students. The MPCP is very carefully targeted, and although it does not seem to improve the situation with respect to equality, it does not seem to worsen it either, and this despite the fact that considerably less money is being spent on the Choice children than on the children in the MPS schools: the choice schools receive *only* the per-pupil state equalization funds whereas the MPS schools receive, in addition, the locally-raised funds. Furthermore, it is possible to speculate that the introduction of the religious, primarily Catholic, schools to the scheme will help with respect to equality.

---

[26] This distinction is important: diocesan schools have different governance structures and different curricula from the schools run by the religious orders, which are significantly more independent from the church. See Dwyer, James, *Religious Schools vs. Children's Rights* (Ithaca, NY: Cornell University Press, 1998), chapters 1 and 2.

# 9

## School Choice For Social Justice?

### THE PROPOSAL

Surveying the evidence on actual choice schemes suggests that it should be possible to design a choice scheme that implements reasonably well the fundamental values that I have argued should govern the design of educational institutions. There have been several attempts to outline such a scheme. I shall use here the most detailed such attempt, offered by Herbert Gintis—and incorporated, in less detail, in his and Samuel Bowles's cluster of economic proposals to 'recast egalitarianism'—as a skeleton for a more elaborate proposal. Gintis's main aim is to design a choice scheme that implements educational equality, so I shall supplement his proposals with more speculative suggestions drawn from my own tentative choice proposal, and I shall also add detail to other aspects of his proposal where it seems necessary.[1] Using my own and Gintis's work I shall show how a series of standard practical objections to school choice can be met or deflected, and shall then look into serious difficulties with accommodating the values of autonomy and educational equality: suggesting, however, that these difficulties will be encountered with differing degrees of seriousness by any system of delivery. I shall then look at a new kind of commodification objection, and finally consider very briefly some of the alternative directions in education policy.

Bowles and Gintis are primarily concerned with offering a reform that will enhance both efficiency and equality at the same time. They point out that schooling constitutes a large part of the economy, and that if the preferences of consumers are frustrated in this area of the economy, that con-

---

[1] See Gintis, Herbert, 'The Political Economy of School Choice', *Teachers College Record*, 96 (1995), 492–511. I want to emphasize that the proposal offered in this chapter is modelled on, but not identical to his, and encourage the reader to scrutinize his proposal. For earlier left-wing advocates of choice see Jencks, Christopher, *Education Vouchers: A Report on Financing Education by Payments to Parents* (Cambridge, MA: Center for the Study of Public Policy, 1970); and Coons, John and Sugerman, Stephen, *Education By Choice: The Case For Family Choice* (Berkeley, CA: University of California Press, 1978).

stitutes a large *prima facie* inefficiency. However they 'elide the not small problem of possible differences in interest between the parents and the child',[2] and in doing so they take the satisfaction of preferences of *parents* to be the proper measure of efficiency. As we have seen, this assumption, though appropriate for some idealizations, is indefensible in practice. But so, of course, would be taking the satisfaction of the preferences of children as the standard for efficiency. For our purposes, the difficulties of understanding efficiency in this context need not detain us, since we shall be assessing the proposal with respect only to equality and autonomy. I just want to note that there is a difficulty.

My proposal, working from the Bowles/Gintis model, has the following central features:

1. Parents/guardians choose the schools their children attend.
2. Schools can be established by private, for profit and not-for-profit, firms, public institutions, associations of teachers, and local community groups. For Gintis it is essential that schools face a hard budget constraint, and in particular that for-profit schools be admitted into the market place, so that ineffective, or 'sink' schools—those that fall below some threshold level of popularity—cannot struggle along, continuing to provide a poor education to students at considerable cost to the government. Competitive pressure, according to Gintis, 'generates the information necessary to judge firm performance'[3] that cannot be generated when firms are subject solely to democratic control. There is no need, however, for all schools to be for-profit, and some may be run by governmental agencies, as long as their performance is compared with those of independent schools: Gintis's model is the market in higher education in the US, where public and private institutions coexist despite considerable differences in the missions of the different kinds of institutions.[4] Gintis is right that there has to be some mechanism that will ensure that failing schools are rapidly closed. However, much of the relevant information can, it seems, be generated without subjecting schools to the need to make a profit, or even to face competition. We can look directly at test scores, the socio-economic background of students, retention and truancy rates, and survey the parents who are much more easily identifiable than the consumers of many other goods. The problem with schools is typically not so much gathering relevant

---

[2] Bowles, Samuel, and Gintis, Herbert, 'Efficient Redistribution: New Rules for Markets, States, and Communities', *Politics and Society*, 24 (1996), 307–42 at 322.

[3] Gintis, 'The Political Economy of School Choice', 503.

[4] I'm grateful for clarification on this matter in a personal communication from Gintis, 22 January 1999.

information as preventing political coalitions from conspiring to save failing schools. This may be overcome by the appointment of independent inspectorates that are empowered to force the closure of schools that fail to meet certain standards of success.

3. The participating schools are funded publicly, the per-pupil amount being set according to the educational needs of the student and 'such economic factors as the local price level', taking into account the competitiveness of the local labour market. Participating schools would be strictly prohibited from charging additional tuition, or 'top-ups'.[5] This ensures that participating schools cannot effectively price themselves out of the reach of working-class parents, and thus become exclusive private schools for middle and upper class children receiving a government subsidy. As in the MPCP, schools might be permitted to charge tuition for certain extracurricular activities that students could not be required to participate in, but even these additions would have to be strictly limited.

4. School management teams should aim to achieve heterogeneity in the school population. There are two quite distinct approaches to achieving this. One approach favours making mandatory a certain mix of socio-economic backgrounds and ability levels, thus giving schools extremely limited discretion over admissions, and requiring them, as in the MPCP, to use a lottery when oversubscribed, with two exceptions: a rule that a sibling of a child already in the school would automatically be accepted, and a weighting in the lottery to help the school achieve a prescribed mix of socio-economic classes and of levels of educational ability.[6] The limited discretion and the weighting in the lottery are aimed at preventing schools from becoming effectively selective by social class or academic ability; the sibling rule is justified by reference to the potential time and travel costs incurred by parents having to take their children to different geographic areas, and by the fact that if the first child is admitted in the standard way then the sibling rule should not affect significantly the mix of socio-economic backgrounds in the school.

Bowles and Gintis favour an alternative approach, preferring a system of incentives grounded in the value attached to the voucher for each child: 'decentralized incentives for racial, class, gender and other

---

[5] Gintis, 'The Political Economy of School Choice', 504; Brighouse, Harry, 'The Egalitarian Virtues of Educational Vouchers,' *Journal of Philosophy of Education*, 28 (1994), 211–19 at 214.

[6] Brighouse, 'The Egalitarian Virtues of Educational Vouchers', 214. See also Walford, Geoffrey, 'Diversity and Choice In Education: An Alternative View', *Oxford Review of Education*, 22 (1996), 143–54, who argues for reform of the system in England and Wales to require oversubscribed schools to admit by a lottery constrained by a sibling rule.

integration of schools could also be written into the system by making the value of the voucher to the school depend on the demographic and economic characteristics of the family, perhaps in relationship to the current composition of school enrollment'.[7] Schools would have a great deal of latitude, but otherwise undesirable students would be made more desirable because they would bring more money to the school, up to the point at which desired heterogeneity had been achieved. Without committing himself, Gintis, when writing alone, even canvasses a third possibility: that ability levels may be exempted from the heterogeneity incentives: 'it is plausible that . . . elective admissions policies would help *all* ability levels, since each school could then tailor instruction to the particular needs of its clientele'.[8] To the objection that the aspirations of students with less ability would be diminished by stratified schooling, he responds that 'it is certainly reasonable to think that schools dedicated to serving all students of a given range of ability levels could instill [sic] self-confidence and high aspirations in these students'.[9] While there is evidence that less-able students benefit educationally from mixed-ability environments in public schools as we know them, this evidence does not imply that they could not benefit more, from more homogenous ability level schooling in the presence of substantial innovation.[10] It is important to emphasize that Gintis countenances having schools divided only by ability levels and not also by socio-economic status, so that schools would still have incentives to avoid segregation by class. It is notable that the Charter school movement in the US has been motivated partly by the sense of parents of children with various forms of educational disabilities that their children are not well served in the regular classroom, and a good number of Charter schools do specialize in the education of students with particular learning disabilities. If the level of the voucher were sensitive to differences in ability level there may well be a movement away from heterogenous ability level schooling unless there were countervailing incentives, since considerable economies of scale could be achieved by schools specializing in particular disabilities or ability levels.

I am not going to choose between the three approaches here. But I must emphasize the relevant criterion for selecting among them. Many progressive educators will balk at Gintis's permissiveness concerning

---

[7] Bowles and Gintis, 'Efficient Redistribution', 324.

[8] Gintis, 'The Political Economy of School Choice', 505.       [9] Ibid.

[10] For an empirical study suggesting that tracking harms the less-able student see Oakes, Jeannie, *Keeping Track: How Schools Structure Inequality* (New Haven, CT.: Yale University Press, 1985).

selection for ability level. But the objectionability of selection for ability is based on our actual experience of it, not the mere fact of it. Our experience of selectivity by ability level is that more-able students are selected, and then more resources are devoted to their education. They are doubly advantaged: once by being more able, and again by having more attention devoted to the development of their talents. This is *not* what Gintis countenances: he is suggesting that low-ability students and students with disabilities should be placed in situations where more resources and attention can be devoted to developing their talents, than to developing those of more- able students. Suppose twenty hearing-impaired children are placed in twenty different classrooms: each requires their own sign-language interpreter. Suppose, instead, that they are placed in a single classroom: they can now have a single signing teacher who is a specialist in the subject she is teaching, plus all the other resources that would otherwise have gone to the salaries of the nineteen other interpreters. By hypothesis each student has the same amount spent on them as in the first scenario, but each has far more educational resources devoted to them. The criterion for choosing among the options I have set out can not be our prejudice about selection, but which option best serves the educational interests of the less-able and disabled students.

5. Public regulation would govern staffing levels, condition of physical plant, curriculum, admissions and financing. Curriculum regulation would include the recommendations I have made with respect to autonomy-facilitation in Chapter 4. Schools would have to meet whatever regulation was in place in order to be accredited and participate in the scheme: though obviously the regulation would have to be relaxed enough to allow for differentiation and competition.

6. Quantitative measures of the performance of participating schools would be made, and disseminated to the public in readily understandable form. Such things as retention rates, teacher accreditation levels, the ratio of expenditure on bureaucracy to classroom teaching, and test scores would be provided by a government-empowered independent body. The test-score performance measures would be given in terms of value-added: scores of children entering the school would be compared with the scores of those same children leaving the school. This is essential, since the raw scores of children in the school are no indication of the effectiveness of the school: parents not sophisticated enough to understand this will be misled by the raw score information, while parents who do understand it are simply not getting any information from the raw scores.

7. Increased competition among schools to attract parents may have the effect of diminishing the informational value of students' credentials, through erosion of standards and grade inflation. To offset this, Bowles and Gintis, whose proposal is designed for the US, insist that 'any program of enhanced competition between schools should include strengthened national certification of competencies'.[11] Insulating the credentialing process to some extent from the influence of individual schools is important not only to secure the informational value of credentials for employers and higher education institutions, but also to enable parents to make more informed decisions about the effectiveness of schools.

This measure runs against the trend in both the US where there is no tradition of anonymous credentialing, and in the UK where credentialing used to be done entirely anonymously, but increasing emphasis has been placed on portfolios and classroom teacher-graded examination. So it is worth mentioning that national standards and anonymous testing have one efficiency-enhancing effect that is extremely important, regardless of whether vouchers or choice is adopted. Clear national standards and some amount of anonymous testing yield significant benefits in the classroom. When the classroom teacher is entirely responsible for assigning the grade to her students, two possibilities adversely affect her relationships with parents and students: their fears or hopes that her feelings about their overall behaviour might affect her grading of them; and her fear that they will pressure her with respect to their grades. While classroom teacher grade-assigning sets up an incentive for parents and students to pressure directly for better grades—thus wasting her time and energy—anonymous grading sets up an incentive for them to pressure for better and more teaching. Including the results of anonymous testing as a major part of student credentialing can thus be expected to improve classroom discipline, allowing more resources to be put into education and fewer into maintaining the preconditions for providing education.

The balance sheet on anonymous testing is not entirely positive, though, and it is only fair to mention the drawbacks. When both the school and the student expect to be judged by exam performance, they will devote considerable resources and effort to good performance. This will lead schools to teach to the exam, neglecting those aspects of the curriculum that are not going to be tested. There is less time in the school day for the exploration of individual interests, and it may be that

---

[11] Bowles and Gintis, 'Efficient Redistribution', 324.

a love of learning for its own sake is less likely to develop in a high pressure atmosphere. All of these concerns have been frequently expressed by both teachers and parents in the UK since the introduction of the National Curriculum.

## SOME PRACTICAL ISSUES.

A series of practical objections are routinely made to school choice proposals, so I want to deal with some of the most common here.

### Failing Schools

First there is the problem of what to do with failing schools: schools that fail to attract enough students to function effectively. In a choice system where regulation allows schools to expand rapidly to meet increased demand, as any viable choice system would have to, it can be expected that some schools will be sufficiently undersubscribed not to be economically viable. What happens to them?

The obvious, and apparently callous, answer, is that they will close. In a standard public schools system failing schools can hobble along, delivering poor education to children who remain in them and whose parents are either not savvy enough or not wealthy enough to find them alternative schooling, and presenting a substantial barrier to educational equality. One reason that Gintis and Friedman both consider it so crucial that market entry should be available to for-profit schools, is that the profit motive provides a mechanism whereby the providers of failing schooling exit the market of their own accord. If all schools were for-profit, there would be no need to consider the problem of failing schools.

However, under the proposal outlined above there is a need to consider the problem, since there are not-for-profit and government-run schools. Furthermore, even if the system consisted solely of for-profit schools, school failures would represent a problem: even if it is worse than the school to which children are transferred on its closure, the closure of a failing school mid-year may be worse for the education of the transferred students than its artificial maintenance till the end of the year. This is why it may make sense to establish a fund, to be administered by an independent body, to ensure that failing schools can be maintained until the end of the year that they fail.

Readers shocked by the callousness regarding failing schools should consider the alternatives. One is to provide government subsidies to schools that too few people want to attend for them to be viable. This is often a politically attractive option within a public or state system, since even unviable schools can often generate significant lobbies in their defence. But the cost is great: not only is there an opportunity cost in the form of the wasted subsidies but, more importantly, the students may receive a worse education than they otherwise would. The other alternative is to intervene in the schools and attempt to improve them. This is a viable alternative only if it is assumed that external authorities are capable of identifying failing schools and have both the political will and competence to improve them. I suspect that under any politically feasible system-wide choice scheme there will be some efforts at outside intervention of this kind. But it is worth noting that they are, also, not costless: the intervention is, presumably, costly in itself, and the students who remain in the school are subject to the inadequate educational practices until the intervention works. In some cases this alternative may be the right one: but in many it will be more costly than letting the school close.

These considerations assume, of course, that schools that are massively undersubscribed are on the whole educationally less effective than more popular schools. I shall consider an objection based on the poor choosing abilities of parents later in this section. But even if parents are by and large much better choosers than opponents of choice assume, good schools may sometimes be unpopular. It is tempting to allow that an independent body be empowered to identify and 'save' such schools. However this is risky, since such a body could not be guaranteed to protect only those schools that deserved saving. It is also costly, since the expertise of those managing and teaching in effective but unpopular schools may be sought by other less effective schools if they are released to the labour market.

## Physical Plant

A related problem is that, in the familiar public schools, there are great capital costs associated with the establishment of a new school. School buildings are heavily used, and are expensive to build. If, as some opponents and defenders of markets in education suggest, schools are constantly entering and exiting the marketplace, and face dramatically fluctuating rolls depending on the demand for them, how would the physical plant be managed? Gintis suggests two alternatives, both of which are feasible, and both of which help to lower the minimum feasible size of schools. The first is to have the government own the physical plant and make it available to schools on a rental basis. The second is to force schools to share physical plant, 'such as classroom, athletic facilities, and specialized instruction resources'.[12]

Both options, notice, give the government a significant regulatory role, and the first option would involve the government in a degree of forecasting what plant would be needed. Both suggestions reject the identification of the school with the physical building, which identification limits the apparent feasibility of having markets operate effectively.

*Transportation*

If transportation costs are picked up by the families, then choice is, again, more readily available to wealthier families than less wealthy families. If they are included in the voucher, then schools that attract students from significant distances will have to suffer loss of real income. For these reasons it makes sense to have a standard of 'reasonable transportation costs' that would be set by reference to the locations of the schools *vis-à-vis* the local populations, and have those costs paid by the government. Parents could be expected to pay additional costs when they have a large selection of schools that fall within the 'reasonable' range, but choose to go outside that area.

*Schools as Centres and Crucibles of Community*

Schools do not typically function solely as places where children are educated. They are often centres of the local community, places where fêtes and political meetings are held, polling stations established, recreation centres located. It may be much more attractive to entrepreneurs establishing schools to set them up in the suburbs than in the inner cities, thus depriving inner city neighbourhoods not only of the ability to send their children to local schools, but also of a much needed anchor of community life. Of course, economics will help with this: physical plant will be cheaper to rent in deprived neighbourhoods, so that especially profit-seeking firms will have a countervailing reason to use inner city sites. The incentives to establish a prescribed mix of social classes should also work in favour of inner city locations, at least when inner city parents display strong preferences for local schools, as the evidence suggests that they do. However, these may not be sufficient to offset the problem, and it is compatible with choice that special incentives and rewards be provided to ensure that sufficient schools are built, or school buildings used, in the inner city.

[12] Gintis, 'The Political Economy of School Choice', 497.

A distinct concern is that schools are crucibles of community. In the American neighbourhood school, or the true comprehensive school in Britain, children are supposed to mix with people who are unlike them, not only in ability level and social class, but also in religion, interests, and political outlooks. Future employers mix with future employees, future political representatives with future constituents, future rabbis with future priests. The children gain from the exposure, and, for some people just as importantly, the community gains stability from the level of mutual understanding achieved. My response to this concern is simple: I doubt that this ideal has been achieved better in many places or at many times than in schools run according to choice principles which are required to provide autonomy-facilitating education. I have expressed doubts about the legitimacy of using community promotion to guide the design of educational institutions in Chapter 3, but that is not part of my response here: I simply doubt that any neighbourhood-based system of schooling has achieved the ideal very well where private schooling is a live option, and where neighbourhoods are segregated along class, and often along ethnic, lines.

## Rural Areas

In the US at least, school choice has been offered primarily as a reform option in urban areas. The rural US poses spectacular problems for offering a system of school choice that could plausibly provide the benefits claimed for choice by its proponents. Population densities are so low, and therefore distances to travel so great, that in a great many areas it is barely feasible to provide a single school, let alone a multiplicity of schools from among which parents can realistically choose.

The feasibility of a choice scheme does depend to some extent on geographical factors, and it seems reasonable for that reason to encourage co-operation among schools in areas of sparse population. Nevertheless, it also seems reasonable to allow a degree of choice: as, for example, Minnesota has done, with its open enrolment policy, so that where the 'natural' geographic catchment areas for two schools overlap, those schools can be made to feel the consequences of their perceived success and failure. The sparse population problem faces the working of many other markets, which need to be regulated differently in rural than in urban and suburban areas. Choice should certainly be regulated differently in rural areas, or possibly not even presented as an option for parents; but this is a specifically geographical issue, not one that impacts on the broader arguments for choice.

*Poor Choosers Revisited*

The most serious of what I dub the practical problems with implementing
a school choice scheme that meets the demands of liberal justice is the
problem that some or even many parents are poor choosers. Even if all
choosers were good choosers, there still may be serious problems, as we
shall see in the next two sections. But for the moment let us look at the
problem of poor choosers.

Gewirtz, Ball, and Bowe, as we saw in the last chapter, distinguished
three levels of chooser: privileged, semi-skilled, and disconnected
choosers. They claim, reasonably enough, that each level corresponds
pretty closely with the social class and level of education of the parent.
This correspondence matters, because it could be expected to lead to a tendency for the quality of education of children to track their social class.
But if enough people are bad enough choosers, regardless of their social
class, school choice will not have the most important efficiency benefits
claimed for it: these depend on the idea that parents left to their own
devices will exert the kinds of pressure on schools that will benefit all children. In a study of an inter-district transfer programme in St Louis, Amy
Stuart Wells found similar results to those of the Gewirtz *et al.* study.
Interviewing seventy-one African-Americans—thirty-seven children and
thirty-four of their parents—in 'inner-city' St Louis, some of whom transferred, and others of whom remained in the St Louis schools, she found
that the non-choosers frequently simply went along with the preference of
their children to remain in the city schools: in other words, like Gewirtz *et
al.*'s disconnected choosers they frequently left the choice up to their uninformed children. But Wells also found that among those exercising the
choice to leave the district schools, few had reliable information on how to
make their choice:

Not one of the transfer or return [children returning from county to city schools]
parents interviewed actually went to visit a county district before listing their top
three choices on the transfer application . . . while transfer parents were attempting to 'maximize' on educational utility, much of their cost-benefit analysis was
based on a perception that county is better than city and white is better than
black, not on factual information about the schools.   (Wells, Amy Stuart, 'The
Sociology of School Choice', 40.)

A study by Valerie E. Lee *et al.* of the attitudes toward choice of parents
in Detroit found that academic concerns did not rank at the top of their
list of concerns. Parents, especially those who favoured choice, ranked
concern that schools be safe and that they share the parents' values, above

an interest in the academic programmes available in and performance of the schools.[13]

I believe that the evidence cited poses serious problems for proponents of unregulated, or virtually unregulated choice schemes, such as Milton Friedman. They could claim that the poor quality of choosing is an institutional effect of the fact that for so long most parents have had no effective ability to choose among schools, and so not only have individuals not learned how to choose, but the institutional culture that underlies good choosing has not yet developed. Allow free reign to the market for long enough, and people will learn how to choose well: local and educational versions of such publications as *Consumer Reports* and *Which Magazine* will emerge to promote a culture of effective choosing.[14] The problem is, in other words, merely transitional. There are good reasons for doubting that the problem is merely transitional. In an unregulated choice scheme, especially one introduced in the US, where the institutional culture of public education militates so strongly against the kinds of grading and scoring that would be necessary for making informed choices on grounds of educational effectiveness, the most optimistic observer would expect the transition to be very long indeed. But even if the problem is merely transitional, it is serious: during the transition many millions of children will not get as good an education as could otherwise have been provided. These children's interests count, and transition costs even to a superior system, are sometimes of a kind that justifies retaining an inferior system.

Herbert Gintis, acknowledging that school choice proponents 'tend to minimize the importance of the problem of uninformed parents',[15] suggests that regulation can 'considerably attenuate'[16] the problem by allowing for the appointment of guardians to exercise school choice when parents are found to be incapable of making considered choices for their children. This may be appropriate, and *would indeed* do something to attenuate the problem of educational inequality arising from the fact that some parents are completely incompetent choosers. But it could not help with the problems raised by Gewirtz *et al.* and Wells. Their claim is that poor choosing is extremely widespread, and if it is as widespread as they say then to salvage the efficiency benefits of school choice would effectively negate its principal aim by removing parents from the equation: a

[13] Lee, Valerie E., Croninger, Robert G., and Smith, Julia B., 'Equity and Choice in Detroit', in Fuller, Bruce, and Elmore, Richard (eds.) *Who Chooses? Who Loses?* (New York, NY: Teachers College Press, 1996), 70–94 at 84.

[14] See Tooley, James, 'Choice and Diversity in Education in Education: A Defence', *Oxford Review of Education*, 23 (1997), 103–16, at 107.

[15] Gintis, 'The Political Economy of School Choice', 499.       [16] Ibid., 500.

large minority, or even a majority, of parents would be replaced by guardians.[17]

However, there are other features of the regulation already included in the proposal above, and especially in the Bowles/Gintis version of Gintis's proposal, that should help to mitigate the problem a good deal. Schools in the scheme are forced to submit to external inspection, a substantial part of which is based on anonymously graded assessments of childrens' performance, but which also includes auditing of their books and establishment of the ratios of their expenditures on administration and classroom teaching, etc. This information would be published prominently and rendered in a form that is reasonably easy to understand. Parents in the US studies have no comparable data on which to base their choices, and have no way of getting access to such data: with that data they would be significantly empowered to choose well. In the British case some, though by no means all, of what I suggest has been done, but there has not been an effort to educate parents in how to make comparisons and consider their choices: and this is no surprise given the political agenda and free-market prejudices of the government that introduced the reforms. Poor choosing should be relegated to a problem at the margins of the system with sufficiently aggressive regulation of, and public education about, choice.

## ACCOMMODATING EQUALITY WITHIN A CHOICE SCHEME

I want to turn now to two problems that emerge from the need to establish democratic regulation of a choice scheme that incorporates the values of educational equality and autonomy, and that are independent of the problem of poor choosing: we face them even if parents are by and large well-informed and effective choosers. First, the problem with equality.

It is likely to be publicly acknowledged that the disabled need to be granted more resources in order for them to have the same level of opportunity, and there is significant public support for the current policy of devoting considerably more resources to the education of students with disabilities than to those of students without disabilities. This public support is facilitated by some degree of trust that experts can tell who has and who does not have disabilities.

But on the proposal above—especially Gintis's version on which schools have discretion to aim for homogenous ability levels among the

[17] This is not meant as a criticism of Gintis, as should become clear in the following paragraph.

student body—it is not only disabled students who must be granted larger vouchers: less-able students within the normal range should be supplied with larger vouchers than more-able students. But it is notoriously difficult to establish who are the less-able and who are the more-able students within the non-disabled range, and there is much less public trust in the 'experts' who claim to be able to differentiate them. Furthermore there is much less public support, and it would be much harder to generate public support, for a regime of publicly devoting differential resources to the education of the less-able, but not disabled, students, or for badly behaved students.

One solution might be to allow the schools to devote more resources to the less-able once the students pass the school gates. But if parents have the capacity to monitor what is going on, those whose children are, quite properly from the perspective of equality of opportunity, receiving fewer resources within the school gates, say in the form of less attention from teachers, will feel that they are being cheated, because their child is receiving back in educational resources less than they are contributing to the school in the form of the money value of their voucher.

A second problem is that, regardless of the conception of educational equality we are working with, there are serious problems for parents trying to monitor how far resources are being devoted to their children within the school. Even if each student is supplied with roughly the same materials, they are not likely to be supplied with the same amount of valuable attention. With the best will in the world the teacher cannot be sure that he is even coming close to an equal distribution of attention. Parents, who are not in the classroom, cannot know at all. Sometimes parents will know and will resent that the teacher deliberately withheld assistance from their child, and will see this as shortchanging even though, in fact, the decision was pedagogically well-motivated.

This is not to say that educational equality is impossible to achieve through a voucher system, but the considerations here do suggest that there will be serious difficulty in winning majority political support for the implementation and maintenance of a system designed to achieve it.[18]

[18] There is a separate question about the needs of children being different. Boys get far more attention in the co-educational classroom than girls do, and naughty boys get the most attention of all. Despite, or because of, the informal and formal constraints on teachers being able to discipline students informally in the classroom, discipline implementation in the form of security guards, and assistant principals, exhausts enormous amounts of resources in contemporary public schools, which resources are being devoted mostly to a very few students. Is this lavishing of resources on very few students unfair? I am not sure— the point here is that it is liable to appear as an inequality of resources which will be unjustifiable to parents whose vouchers are 'worth' more than the resources being devoted to the education of their children.

ACCOMMODATING AUTONOMY WITHIN A CHOICE SCHEME

Whatever the difficulties with meeting an equality constraint, voucher schemes are liable to have even more serious difficulties with a constraint requiring that all children receive an autonomy-facilitating education. The problem is not that parents may be incapable of, or uninterested in, advancing the educational success or opportunities of their children. This is a problem, but it is not the one that matters here. The objection that the liberal will press is nicely expressed by Elizabeth Anderson: a voucher system

effaces the distinction between the freedom of the parents and the autonomy of the children. Many parents fear that training in argument, reasoning and imagination, in conjunction with certain kinds of knowledge . . . will enable their children to defy parental authority and challenge their parents' religious and moral ideals. A voucher system would enable parents to satisfy their ideal-based desires to indoctrinate their children rather than educate them to exercise their own judgment.　(Anderson, Elizabeth, *Value in Ethics and Economics*, 163.)

Bowles and Gintis deliberately evade this question when they say, 'we shall elide the not small problem of possible differences of interest between the parents and child'. But this is, as they know, and as we have established at length in Chapters 1, 4 and 5, a false assumption. In some crucial cases their interests diverge, and the design of the curriculum should reflect this. Every child has an interest in being able to be an autonomous person, which interest all adults have an obligation to provide for, regardless of parental preferences. How can a choice system be constrained to ensure that autonomy-facilitating education is provided?

Elizabeth Anderson's claim that vouchers efface the distinction between the freedom of the parents and the autonomy of the children is not exactly true. As we have seen, it is possible, in principle, to maintain and respect that distinction by implementing a regulation requiring that all accredited schools have a programme of autonomy-facilitating education. But there are practical difficulties with doing this. It is important to assign responsibility for monitoring the implementation of curricular regulations. One of the advantages of a voucher scheme is that parents, those closest to the individual child, can, at least to some extent, directly monitor the education he or she receives.[19] But this advantage depends on the coincidence of interests of parents and children. Where the interests diverge parents are

---

[19] This advantage plays a crucial role in Bowles and Gintis's case for vouchers, though a less crucial role in Gintis's more extensive defense of school choice.

no longer suitable monitors. This is not to say that all, or even most, parents are interested in depriving their children of access to this kind of education, just that those parents who are so interested are ill-suited to monitoring its implementation.

Even those parents who *are* interested in monitoring will have difficulty doing so. The methods by which we teach children how to be critically evaluative are complex, and success is hard to measure. Even suppose that the aim were to ensure that children become autonomous—which, on the account I have given, it is not. Success is not measurable by standardized tests. It is not even measurable by looking at the content of the ways of life they select, since most ways of life that can be lived autonomously can also be lived heteronomously. And the process of turning a child into an autonomous person does not always seem to reflect the end of autonomy very clearly. Sometimes we present them with information about other ways of life, and expose them to other people's critical thinking about those ways of life. But sometimes we might try to get them to entertain the thoughts they would have if they were a member of a cult so as to make the contrast. And, of course, autonomy promotion would be liable to infuse the curriculum, or at least substantial parts of it. For example, at Central Park East Secondary School in New York the curriculum is integrated to provide for effective reflection by the students on the different elements of what they are taught, and even the running of the school reflects a commitment to developing autonomous democratic citizens. Students are examined in part by a public 'exhibition' in which they are expected to defend a portfolio of work they have developed over thee years, which examination is supposed to enhance their sense of initiative and responsibility for their own intellectual and personal development.[20]

The monitoring difficulties are compounded by the fact that the policy we are concerned with is not one of *autonomy promotion*, but of *autonomy-facilitation*, the problems of measuring which are even greater. Even if we knew how to measure whether or not someone had selected their way of life autonomously, finding out that they had not would not tell us whether we had failed in facilitating autonomy, since they might have learned how to live autonomously, and then rejected that option. So even parents who wanted autonomy for their children would be hard pressed to ensure that the classroom experience was doing what they want. It would also be difficult to distinguish autonomy-facilitation and autonomy promotion in practice. It is hard to see how a teacher could impart the skills associated with autonomy without simultaneously communicating some norms

[20] See Meier, Deborah, *The Power of Their Ideas* (Boston, MA: Beacon Press, 1995), for a description of the practices at Central Park East.

concerning the virtues of autonomy. In teaching a child to play cricket one cannot teach the skills without also communicating enthusiasms and a sense that the game is worth playing, and similarly someone teaching the skills associated with autonomy is likely to communicate that autonomy is worth applying. This does not mean that all children will become autonomous, nor that there is no meaningful distinction at the level of justification between an autonomy-facilitating and autonomy-promoting policy, but it does mean that in practice the policies will be difficult to distinguish, to the detriment of attempts to monitor what is being taught.[21]

The difficulties with monitoring the implementation of autonomy-facilitating education are not problematic exclusively for advocates of vouchers, however. The natural response to these problems from the voucher proponent is to shift a burden of justification back onto the liberal *opponent* of vouchers. What alternative kind of educational governance can do *better* at guaranteeing autonomy-facilitation? Direct democratic governance has its own problems. First of all, if autonomy-facilitating education is an obligation that we owe to our future fellow citizens, then it is not a matter over which democratic discretion can properly be exercised. That is, to use Ronald Dworkin's terminology, it is a choice-insensitive policy, in the sense that a democratic decision to withhold it would be illegitimate.[22] So the justice of mandating autonomy-facilitating education by no means automatically supports democracy as the central direct mechanism for governing schools. Second, the monitoring problems raised above appear to be as severe under direct democratic governance as under vouchers: it is no easier for concerned liberal citizens to monitor than for concerned liberal parents. This very important point is too often neglected. When raising a problem with the efficiency of a system it is not enough to point out a source of inefficiency. One has to point to alternative institutional forms that lack that source and do not introduce equivalently bad sources. But the character of the difficulty of monitoring the delivery of autonomy-facilitating education seems to make it as hard for the state as for citizens to overcome it.

Liberal opponents of vouchers may claim that democratic governance is nonetheless more likely to ensure autonomy-facilitating education. The idea is that democratic deliberation fosters the valuing of autonomy by enticing citizens to engage in public rational defence of their own views, and hence to rationally evaluate their own views. Once one engages in rational evaluation one begins to recognize its value. Furthermore, demo-

---

[21] I'm grateful to Erik Wright for pointing out this difficulty.
[22] See Dworkin, Ronald, 'What is Equality? Part 4: Political Equality', *University of San Francisco Law Review*, 22 (1987), 1–30.

cratic governance provides assurance to those who, though they are not completely averse to having their children engage in critical reflection on their ways of life, are reluctant to have that happen unless they can be somewhat confident that the children from other sectarian faiths are doing the same. Someone who might use a voucher to withdraw their children from autonomy-facilitating education might nevertheless vote for autonomy-facilitating education for all.[23]

I suspect that both these claims are true, but are also beside the point. We have seen that voucher proponents can accept the need for practical democratic regulation, and would make autonomy-facilitating education a condition of accreditation. While democratic control is not direct, it is present, and as such it can contain the advantages referred to.

## COMMODIFICATION REVISITED

A further case against choice concerns the stable *reproducibility* over time of a system providing autonomy facilitation and implementing educational equality.[24] One of the key considerations in designing any social programme is whether it will be stable and long lasting. Two programmes that appear to do equally well at implementing given social goals can differ in the kinds of political coalition-formation they put into process, and can therefore differ in their long-term reproducibility even when they do not appear to differ in their short-term success at achieving the goal.[25]

[23] A standard argument for direct democratic governance of schools is the speculation that democratic participation enhances autonomy. While it doesn't seem unreasonable to think that participation enhances autonomy there are two problems with this as an argument for democratic school governance. First, democratic governance does not guarantee participation, and typically participation in school board elections in the US, let alone in the kind of deliberative process that could contribute to autonomy, is very low indeed. Second, while it seems reasonable to think that participation does generally enhance the autonomy of *participants*, they are not the people whose autonomy matters with respect to determining how schools should be governed. The autonomy-enhancement we should care about with respect to schooling is that of the students, who are not likely to be significant participants in the democratic process of governance, and in my view shouldn't be. There is no particular reason to think that democratic participation leads people to make decisions which enhance the autonomy of *others*.

[24] I am grateful to Erik Wright for making this case clear to me. My rendering of it is partly, but only partly, based on comments which can be found in his 'Equality, Community and "Efficient Redistribution"', *Politics and Society*, 24 (1996), 353–68 especially at 360–4.

[25] For a sophisticated history of the development of the welfare state in the Scandinavian countries, which highlights the differences in institutional design, see Gøsta Esping-Anderson's excellent *Politics Against Markets* (Princeton, NJ: Princeton University Press, 1986).

There are several reasons for fearing that a scheme of the kind I've described will be politically unstable. First, if, as Gintis and I both suggest, bodies that are independent of the government are allowed to establish and run schools, this will give rise to new political lobbies. Firms, and especially for-profit firms, running schools may lobby against the kinds of regulation that are necessary for effective information provision, which they will experience immediately as costly. Firms running schools, furthermore, have more immediate contact with their consumers than most other firms, and may be more effective in harnessing the efforts of the public in their cause than many other firms. Second, since many parents are not concerned with autonomy or with equality, they will seek to undermine or get around the legislation enforcing it. The establishment of a weak right to choice may, in itself, corrode the sense of parents that they have an obligation to think about justice when they participate in democratic politics, so accustomed will they be to thinking exclusively of the interests of their own children. It could even be argued that vouchers appear to embody the idea that the parent is the presumptive arbiter of their child's interests. By contrast, a democratically accountable regulatory body that is simultaneously the provider of the service directly paid for through taxation, appears to embody the idea that each member of society bears a responsibility to ensure that justice is done to each child. The argument concerning reproducibility need not deny that the two ideas may be compatible, and may even both be true, which is why the autonomy objection is not, in fact, a principled objection to voucher schemes as such. It would say, though, that having the latter idea rather than the former idea embodied in our public institutions is more likely to make autonomy-facilitating education and educational equality reproducible over time.

This commodification objection is speculative of course. One can, furthermore, make counter-speculations: if we take the state out of direct delivery of education it is quite possible that, for example in the US context, sectarians who currently resent and fear the state might be assured in ways that relax their guard against their children's exposure to diverse moral outlooks and ways of ratiocinating about them. Similarly, it may be that in a choice scheme regulated for equality, parents who, fearing that their children are not even getting an adequate education, currently go to extremes to ensure that they get the best possible education, would relax their efforts, assured that one does not have to seek the best education in order to be assured of an adequate education.

I want to be clear that the commodification objection cannot be evaluated properly in the absence of empirical evidence, and that the empirical evidence may differ according to the background institutional context. It may be more difficult to sustain an egalitarian voucher scheme in a society where markets dominate the delivery of other social goods, like health care, than in societies with a tradition of non-commodified delivery of basic welfare goods. But the evidence would have to show that choice schemes that are well-designed to implement educational equality and facilitate personal autonomy cannot, in the long run, retain those features of their design that enable them to do this. So the commodification objection cannot, I think, be decisive, in the absence of a great deal of supporting empirical evidence.

## ALTERNATIVE REFORMS

I have said that the case for choice cannot be evaluated fully without making comparisons with other feasible alternative reforms that would attempt to implement educational equality and a real opportunity for autonomy. I do not have the space to make such a comparison in the kind of detail needed to make the full evaluation, especially since what constitutes a feasible alternative reform differs across different countries in which school choice reforms are proposed. However, I would like to look briefly at some reforms that could move education delivery in the two countries I have focused on, the US and the UK, in the direction of justice, and discuss the relationship of these reforms to school choice.

Before doing so, I should emphasize that one of the greatest barriers to the realization of the two principles I have suggested is one that is not addressed by the decision whether or not to have choice, or, in fact, by any education reform proposals. This is poverty. In the contemporary US especially, though also in the UK, the prospective autonomy of children growing up in the urban inner cities is jeopardized by the poverty, violence, and social decay that surrounds them; it would be laughable to counter this only with an autonomy-facilitating curriculum. Children cannot reasonably be expected to become autonomous if they lack the good health, circumstantial stability, and physical security to take up educational opportunities. Even when the skills associated with autonomy are developed, circumstances of great physical and mental stress, such as those caused by poverty and violence, constitute serious barriers to their use. Promising an autonomy-facilitating education to children for whom the government has not even secured basic preventative health care is, at the very best, reprehensibly naïve. Similarly, no amount of effort to equalize education within the schools can be expected to be successful when significant number of children grow up in poverty, lack basic health care and physical security, and lack the level of attention that can only provided by most of us when we have a living wage and job security. The state should do a great deal—far more than the US government currently does, and more even than the UK government does—to ensure that all children enjoy good health care provision, circumstantial stability, and physical security, both because these are prerequisites of autonomy and educational equality, and because they are, independently, important for well-being.

## The United States

### Funding Sources and Distribution

Schools in the US are funded mainly through a local real estate tax, supplemented by state allocations and various forms of federal funds. That local taxation is the major source of funding generates massive inequalities among public schools, and also helps to mask those inequalities. Reforms that shift the major sources of funding from local to state and federal taxation, distributed more evenly, would assist greatly in implementing the ideal of educational equality.[26] It is worth mentioning, though, that in practice the establishment of choice schemes, and especially state funded voucher schemes, represents a step in this direction. The savage inequalities of funding are politically defensible only as long as the local district is seen as the 'natural' source of funding and authority: the inequalities appear as the consequence of different levels of willingness to fund education. This is a false impression, not because unequal funding is more a consequence of unequal ability than unequal willingness to pay, but because the state draws up the districting rules: it is the state that decides what constitutes a district and that gives the governing body taxing authority. The savage inequalities are designed by that state, but the way they are designed obscures this fact. When, as has been the case with voucher schemes and open enrolment schemes, the state takes up the task of directly funding the schools, inequalities of funding become politically indefensible.

### Housing Policy

In this book I've focused almost entirely on the institutions of education delivery. But this is partly an artifice of the philosophical concerns and the

---

[26] See Kozol, Jonathan, *Savage Inequalities* (New York, NY: Harper Perennial, 1992) for an extended argument to this effect.

public debate. One of the greatest sources of unequal educational opportunity, and of limited opportunities for autonomy, is the *de facto* segregation of residential neighbourhoods by race and class. In many districts education activists concerned with justice would do well to lobby their County Boards for an integrationist housing policy, so that the entirely understandable parental preference that their child attend their local school results in integrated public schooling. It would, in addition, make it more likely that children of parents who never attended higher educational institutions would nevertheless have access to adults who did, and that children would, in their out-of-school lives socialize with people from significantly different backgrounds.

*Districting Rules*

Secession of school districts from one another should be made much more difficult. Under the current system whereby the local regressive real estate tax is the major source of school funding, wealthy communities can 'take their money and run' by seceding from poorer communities. Ironically, some choice proposals, forcing school districts to pay for parental choice for schools in other districts, would make secession less relevant by making the borders between districts more permeable. Proponents intend these measures to drive down the cost of schooling through inter-district competition, but egalitarians might explore ways of harnessing the positive aspects while providing incentives for higher spending.

*Student-body Composition*

Egalitarians might lobby state and federal agencies to provide incentives for class integration of schools. For example, schools in districts allowing public school choice might get federal per-pupil allocations calibrated to the household income of the pupil's home. Poor children would be worth more to the school, wealthy students much less, with bonuses given to the school if it achieves a previously stated balance).

*Autonomy*

'Diversity' has become a slogan for progressives who care about tolerance of different ways of life. But there is nothing intrinsically important about diversity: we have an obligation to tolerate how other people live, but there is no reason to promote more diversity than already exists, or than would exist as a consequence of the freely-made choices of individuals. The rhetoric of 'diversity' is sometimes incoherent and often misunderstood by potentially supportive constituencies. The values that matter are toleration and autonomy, not diversity *per se*. Progressives should be explicit in their policy formation and presentation, that they do not see *any* children as essentially tied to the sub-cultures they are born into, but see *all* children as potentially autonomous citizens who should become able rationally to make their own choices from among the diversity of cultures that present themselves.

## The United Kingdom

The basic choice structure of the UK education system is now virtually unchallenged. Even the most determined opponents of the 1988 reforms have now, albeit reluctantly, accepted that the reforms will define the system for the next generation or so. There is a dearth of anti-choice reforms in public discourse. However, there are a series of options of amending the reforms that could be expected to improve the situation with respect to justice.

### Removing Discretion on Admissions

As I have already mentioned, Geoffrey Walford recommends that schools be forced to use a lottery to determine their admissions when they are oversubscribed, in the manner of the Milwaukee Public Choice Program. This could be expected to have one bad effect, in that it would lead schools to advertise even more heavily for attractive pupils, in the hope of raising their proportion of attractive applicants and thus their chances of randomly selecting those students. But, if the Gewirtz *et al.* study is correct, there is already a great concentration on such advertising, so this effect should be more than offset by the effects on student composition.

### Expensive Students

As we saw in Chapter 8, the additional funding available for students who are difficult and/or expensive to educate is not sufficient for there to be an incentive for schools to want to admit them. The tendency, then, will be for such students to congregate in particular schools that are thereby rendered unattractive to the parents of more easily educated children. This tendency is exacerbated by the form in which examination league tables are published, which is not sensitive to the starting point of students entering the school. Furthermore, while what extra funds there are for students with disabilities can be accessed through getting an individual 'statement' for the child, statementing is controlled by the Local Authority, which is also the source of the funds, and therefore has a powerful incentive to keep statementing to a minimum. Teachers of non-statemented students with disabilities or other special needs are faced with the distasteful choice between diverting resources from other students, abandoning the needs of the needy student, or volunteering extra and unpaid effort. In this way society displaces the moral and material burden of ensuring educational equality onto teachers.

Greater resources should therefore be made available to schools for students with special needs, and the 'statementing' authority should be independent of the funding authority. Published information on exam results should be in a 'value-added' form, and should be adjusted in a fine-grained way to take account of what is known about the potential detriment to learning of particular disabilities. If the practice of educating students with special needs in the same school settings, or even the same classrooms, as other students is valued, it might nevertheless make sense to provide incentives for schools to specialize in the education of students with particular disabilities, so that they are encouraged to take advantage of potential economies of scale.

*Housing Policy*

As in the US, housing policy is a key to education policy. A determined policy of integrating neighbourhoods by class and race, by placing mandates on new developments and by designing appropriate subsidies and incentives for existing neighbourhoods, would help to integrate schools as well as the larger educational context, to the benefit of the least-advantaged students.

*Reforming the National Curriculum*

Unlike the US, the UK has, in the national curriculum, a tool that can be used for the widespread implementation of autonomy-facilitating education. Whitty *et al.* describe the national curriculum, rightly, as 'the one symbol of a common educational system and an identifiable entitlement that people can struggle to alter, rather than leaving all provision to emerge from the individual exercise of choice (or non-choice) in the market place'.[27] The recent interest in developing a citizenship education aspect of the national curriculum provides a context to argue for the autonomy-facilitating education and education for legitimacy that I outlined in Chapter 4.[28]

[27] Whitty, Geoff, Power, Sally, and Halpin, David, *Devolution and Choice in Education* (Buckingham: Open University Press, 1998), 139–40.

[28] A national curriculum can, of course, go awry: how it will look depends on what kinds of political pressure are applied. For an excellent discussion of the efforts of conservatives to influence the history component of the national curriculum in Britain see Crawford, Keith, 'A History of the Right: The Battle for Control of National Curriculum History 1989–1994', *British Journal of Educational Studies*, 43 (1995), 433–56.

*Private Schools*

I have not mentioned private schools up until now. These, especially the ancient, so-called 'Public Schools' such as Winchester and Eton, are probably the most important symbols of educational inequality in the UK. Egalitarians used to argue for their abolition. This position is rarely heard, having been replaced by the call for the end to their charitable status, which call is, at the time of writing, still not attracting the legislative attention of Britain's left-of-centre government. I do not see any reform of the system that will undermine the elite private schools short of a very radically egalitarian choice scheme that sets per-pupil spending so high that the elite schools cannot resist joining it and submitting to its regulation.[29]

## CONCLUSIONS

I have refrained so far from adopting a firm position on school choice. I have tried to outline and argue for the principles of justice that should guide the design and reform of educational institutions. In the light of these principles, and the evidence regarding choice schemes, I think it is fair to say that support for choice is usually overenthusiastic, whereas opposition to choice is usually overcritical. I've tried to show that social justice in education allows a good deal of scope for having parents choose among schools for their children. The standard bureaucratic model of public or state schooling has not delivered justice in education in either of the countries I have focused on, and there are reasons to think that an appropriately designed choice scheme could do better. Social justice also, however, places principled constraints on the scope of that choice, which limits must be institutionalized in any just choice scheme. The schemes we have surveyed both have some of these limits partially built in, but both of them, and especially the British scheme, allow a great deal of scope for injustice.

However, showing that a scheme could be designed that would in principle protect social justice in education is a far cry from showing that the best feasible choice scheme would yield, or move us towards, social justice in education. The social and political context in which some reform is passed has a crucial influence not only on how that scheme is modified

---

[29] See Brighouse, Tim, *Private Schooling: What is and What could Be* (Keele: University of Keele Department of Education, 1992) for a proposal of this kind which would effectively efface the distinction between private and public schooling.

during the legislative process, but also on what effects the scheme will have in practice and on how it will evolve. Both the countries I have concentrated on have experienced two decades of increasing income and wealth inequality, and the political rhetoric in both countries has simultaneously abandoned commitments to the well-being of the least-advantaged members of society. The Labour Government in the UK came to power in 1997 well aware of many of the flaws I have outlined in the choice scheme, and made no effort to rectify most of them, despite having an unassailable majority and an almost certain guarantee of ten years in office. In the US, fundamentalist Christianity remains a strong cultural force, and even a remarkably strong political force. While most elected and electable politicians regard the so-called Religious right with suspicion or contempt, the peculiar structure of the electoral system in the US ensures that Republican politicians rarely dare to anger the fundamentalist and similar constituencies. The religious right may wield sufficient power to prevent the kind of regulation of the curriculum that I have recommended: without it school choice cannot serve the interest of children in being able to be personally autonomous.

In this context, it may seem that school choice is bound to be a Trojan Horse working against the interests of children. Public education as we know it may, for all its faults, be a bulwark against the inegalitarian tendencies of the market and the inclinations of fundamentalists to control their children's lives.

But it is hard to be confident in making predictions about the feasibility of reforms, and especially their long-term ability to generate the desired effects. Such predictions rely on assessments of the structural conditions into which the reform is introduced; judgments about whether desirable legislation can be passed in the current political conditions without being amended in unacceptable ways, and judgments about whether the internal design of the reform and the external conditions into which it is introduced will continue to interact to produce the desired effects. None of these judgments can be made with certainty, and the uncertainty of each compounds the uncertainty of the overall judgement.

It is worth bearing in mind, however, that many public education systems, like, for example, the British, have already been transformed into choice systems. Not only is it doubtful that choice can be reformed out of these systems, but few political actors or policy commentators argue that it should. The issue in these systems is not about choice, but how to redesign choice to better realize social justice. I hope this book helps with that task, by explaining what social justice requires, and suggesting reforms that could help realize it.

In the US, choice is a very limited formal part of the system. This is changing, and I believe that it will continue to change with or without the intervention of people who are concerned with social justice. Opposition to choice is, too often, *de facto* support for an indefensible *status quo*. Some choice schemes should, of course, be opposed: in particular, schemes that have the government pay for private schooling without regulating the curriculum and without prohibiting top-ups, can be expected to undermine rather than to further social justice in education.[30] But choice should often be amended, or redesigned, rather than opposed.

It is also important to emphasize, once again, that even in the bureaucratic model choice has a crucial role, underacknowledged by critics of choice. Wealthy parents can always exercise choice by buying houses in the appropriate neighbourhoods, or by opting for private education. The parents most able to improve schools for everyone already have no incentive to do so: they can always opt out at a cost they find affordable. But poorer parents do not have the same option: their only options for improving bad schools are the costly routes of political lobbying and voting for ever higher levels of property tax on themselves. In the US, deeply religious parents can exempt their children from public schools, and typically do so by selecting very inexpensive schools that provide curriculums that depart considerably from the ideal that every child will have a realistic opportunity to become autonomous. Choice may worsen this situation, if the right kind of regulation of choice schools cannot be achieved. But choice may also improve matters, both by disarming the religious entrepreneurs who exploit deeply religious parents' feelings of alienation—feelings that might be mitigated by the introduction of choice—and because opinion polls routinely show that even those who strongly support public funding of private schools believe that those schools should, in return, be made strongly accountable to the government.

I have, furthermore, identified one mechanism whereby choice can be expected to improve the situation with respect to educational equality. Choice schemes involving public funding in the US have always shifted the funding sources away from the most local level toward the state or even the federal level. The greater the proportion of public schooling funded directly by the state or the federal government, the less inequality of fund-

---

[30] I would qualify this statement: if the value of the voucher is sufficiently high, then there may not be a threat to educational equality among the ordinarily-abled, and there could even be a threat to educational inequality. If the value were set at, say, the average tuition level of the ten most expensive elite private schools, the elite status of those schools may rapidly be challenged. The worry about regulation of curriculum would remain, however.

ing will be experienced. Whereas unequal funding seems to be publicly defensible when it comes from local sources, it is politically unsustainable when it comes from a distant source. In this way the movement for choice has actually been serving the goal of educational equality. Inequality could, of course, be diminished without introducing choice: but only by challenging directly the deep-set principle of local control that underlies the savage inequalities in the US system. These are easier to challenge indirectly, by using choice.

In the UK, then, choice is not going to go away. The task is to reform it in line with social justice, not to abolish it. In the US, matters are more complicated: increased choice of kinds that are politically achievable may help with respect to educational equality, but may harm the prospects for autonomy of the children of deeply religious parents. If so, policy-makers face trade-offs between the two principles of social justice in education I have defended. I have not offered a principle for managing such trade-offs, but I hope that it is obvious that large gains in the achievement of one principle would offset small losses in the achievement of the other.

My main aim in the book, however, has not been to take sides on the issue of choice, but to offer a theory of social justice for education policy. In many countries, including the two I have focused on, the education systems as they stand do not do well with respect to social justice when that is properly understood. So social justice cannot legitimately be a basis for defending the *status quo* against the introduction of choice measures, unless there is good evidence that those measures will make things worse. But opponents of choice cannot rest content with the *status quo*: they have to advocate feasible reforms that will improve the justice of the education system. And many such reforms are as compatible with choice as they are with non-choice. The long-term stability of any choice scheme firmly based in considerations of justice is, of course, open to question, and any choice reforms aimed at social justice should be carefully monitored to ensure that they are achieving their goals. But the same is true of non-choice-based reforms. The lesson of this chapter, I think, is that the ultimate problem with implementing social justice in education may well be that it is hard to get political support for it, whether or not it is attached to school choice. Ultimately, it is not up to philosophers to judge what reforms can move us in the direction of social justice and to win political support for them: those are the tasks of citizens, activists, politicians and policy-makers. I hope that this book has made the task a little easier by providing compelling arguments for the principles of educational equality and personal autonomy.

# BIBLIOGRAPHY

ALMOND, BRENDA, 'Education and Liberty: Public Provision and Private Choice', *Journal of Philosophy of Education*, 25 (1991), 193–202.

ANDERSON, ELIZABETH, Value in Ethics and Economics, (Cambridge, MA: Harvard University Press, 1993).

—— 'What is the Point of Equality?', *Ethics*, 109 (1999), 287–337.

ANGUS, MAX, 'Devolution of School Governance in an Australian State School System: Third Time Lucky?', in Carter, David G., and O'Neill, Marnie H. (eds.), *Case Studies in Educational Change: an International Perspective* (London: Falmer Press, 1995).

ANDRE, JUDITH, 'Blocked Exchanges: A Taxonomy', *Ethics*, 103 (1992), 29–47.

ARNESON, RICHARD, 'Equality and Equal Opportunity for Welfare', *Philosophical Studies*, 56 (1989), 77–93.

—— 'Neutrality and Utility', *Canadian Journal of Philosophy*, 20 (1990), 215–40.

—— 'Against Rawlsian Equality of Opportunity', *Philosophical Studies* (forthcoming).

ARONOWITZ, STANLEY, and GIROUX, HENRY, *Postmodern Education* (Minneapolis, Minn.: University of Minnesota Press, 1991).

BARRY, BRIAN, *Theories of Justice* (Los Angeles, CA: University of California Press, 1989).

—— *Democracy, Power and Justice* (Oxford: Oxford University Press, 1989).

—— *Justice as Impartiality* (Oxford: Oxford University Press, 1995).

BATES, STEPHEN, *Battleground: One Mother's Crusade, The Religious Right, And The Struggle For Control Of Our Classrooms* (New York, NY: Simon and Schuster 1993).

BERLIN, ISAIAH, *Four Essays on Liberty* (Oxford: Oxford University Press, 1969).

BOWLES, SAMUEL, and GINTIS, HERBERT, 'Efficient Redistribution: New Rules for Markets, States, and Communities', *Politics and Society*, 24 (1996), 307–42.

BRIGHOUSE, HARRY, 'The Egalitarian Virtues of Educational Vouchers', *Journal of Philosophy of Education*, 28 (1994), 211–19.

—— 'Is There Any Such Thing As Political Liberalism?', *Pacific Philosophical Quarterly*, 75 (1994), 318–22.

—— 'Neutrality, Publicity, and State Funding of the Arts', *Philosophy and Public Affairs*, 24 (1995), 36–63.

—— 'Against Nationalism', *Canadian Journal of Philosophy*, Supplementary Volume 22 (1996), 365–405.

—— 'Egalitarianism and Equal Availability of Political Influence', *Journal of Political Philosophy*, 4 (1996), 118–41.

BRIGHOUSE, HARRY, 'Is There a Neutral Justification for Liberalism', *Pacific Philosophical Quarterly*, 77 (1996), 193–215.
—— 'Civic Education and Liberal Legitimacy', *Ethics*, 108 (1998), 719–45.
—— 'Why Should States Fund Schools?', *British Journal for Educational Studies*, 46 (1998), 138–52.
BRIGHOUSE, TIM, *Private Schooling: What is and What could Be* (Keele: University of Keele Department of Education, 1992).
—— *A Question of Standards: the need for a local democratic voice* (London: Politeia, 1996).
BUCHANAN, ALLEN, 'Justice as Reciprocity versus Subject-Centered Justice', *Philosophy and Public Affairs*, 19 (1990), 227–52.
BURBULES, NICHOLAS C., 'Equal Opportunity or Equal Education?', *Educational Theory*, 40 (1990), 221–6.
BURTT, SHELLEY, 'Religious Parents, Secular Schools', *Review of Politics*, 56 (1994), 51–70.
—— 'In Defense of Yoder: Parental Authority and the Public Schools', in Shapiro, Ian, and Hardin, Russell (eds.), *NOMOS 38: Political Order* (New York, NY: New York University Press, 1996), 412–37.
CALLAN, EAMMON, 'Political Liberalism and Political Education', *Review of Politics*, 58 (1996), 5–33.
—— *Creating Citizens* (Oxford: Oxford University Press, 1997).
CARL, JIM, 'Unusual Allies: Elite and Grass-roots Origins of Parental Choice in Milwaukee', *Teachers College Record*, 98 (1996), 266–85.
CHITTY, CLYDE, *The Education System Transformed* (Manchester: Baseline Books, 1992).
CHRISTIANO, THOMAS, *The Rule of the Many* (Boulder, CO: Westview Press, 1995).
CHUBB, JOHN, and MOE, Terry M., *Politics, Markets, and America's Schools* (Washington, DC: Brookings Institution, 1989).
CLUNE, WILLIAM H., and WITTE, JOHN F. (eds.), *Choice and Control in American Education: Volume 1* (London: The Falmer Press, 1990).
COHEN, GERALD A., 'Back to Socialist Basics', *New Left Review*, 207 (1994), 3–16.
—— 'Incentives, Inequality and Community', in Darwall, Stephen (ed.), *Equal Freedom* (Ann Arbor, MI: University of Michigan Press, 1994).
COONS, JOHN, and SUGERMAN, STEPHEN, *Education By Choice: The Case For Family Choice* (Berkeley, CA: University of California Press, 1978).
COWEN, TYLER, *In Praise of Commercial Culture* (Cambridge, MA: Harvard University Press, 1998).
CRAWFORD, KEITH, 'A History of the Right: The Battle for Control of National Curriculum History 1989–1994', *British Journal of Educational Studies*, 43 (1995), 433–56.
CROMPTON, JOHN L., 'Economic Impact Analysis of Sports Facilities and Events: Eleven Sources of Misapplication', *Journal of Sports Management*, 9 (1995), 14–35.
CULLITTY, GARRETT, 'Moral Free Riding', *Philosophy and Public Affairs*, 24/1 (1995), 3–34.

CURREN, RANDALL R., 'Justice and the Threshold of Educational Equality', *Philosophy of Education*, 50 (1995), 239–48.

DWORKIN, GERALD, *The Theory and Practice of Autonomy* (Cambridge: Cambridge University Press, 1988).

DWORKIN, RONALD, 'What Is Equality? Part 2: Equality of Resources', *Philosophy and Public Affairs*, 10 (1981), 283–345.

—— 'Comment on Narveson: In Defense of Equality', *Social Philosophy and Policy*, 1 (1983): 24–40.

—— *A Matter of Principle* (Cambridge, MA: Harvard University Press, 1985).

—— 'What is Equality? Part 4: Political Equality', *University of San Francisco Law Review*, 22 (1987), 1–30.

DWYER, JAMES, *Religious Schools vs. Children's Rights* (Ithaca, NY: Cornell University Press, 1998).

EDWARDS, TONY, and WHITTY, GEOFF, 'Parental Choice and Educational Reform in Britain and the United States', *British Journal of Educational Studies*, 40 (1992), 101–17.

ESPING-ANDERSON, GØSTA, *Politics Against Markets* (Princeton, NJ: Princeton University Press, 1986).

FINN, CHESTER, MANNO, BRUNO, BIERLEIN, LOUANN, and VANOUREK, GREGG, *Charter Schools in Action: The Final Report* (Washington, DC: The Hudson Institute, 1997).

FLIEGEL, SEYMOUR, *Miracle in East Harlem: The Fight for Choice in Public Education* (New York, NY: The Manhattan Institute, 1993).

FLUERBAEY, MARC, 'Equal Opportunity or Equal Social Outcome?' *Economics and Philosophy*, 11 (1995), 25–55.

FRANKFURT, HARRY, *The Importance of What We Care About* (Cambridge: Cambridge University Press, 1987).

FRIED, CHARLES, *Right and Wrong* (Cambridge, MA: Harvard University Press, 1978).

FRIEDMAN, MILTON, 'The Role of Government in Education' in Solo, Robert A. (ed.), *Economics and the Public Interest* (New Brunswick, NJ: Rutgers University Press, 1955).

—— *Capitalism and Freedom* (Chicago, IL: University of Chicago Press, 1962).

GALSTON, WILLIAM, *Liberal Purposes* (Cambridge: Cambridge University Press 1991).

GAUTHIER, DAVID, *Morals By Agreement* (Oxford: Oxford University Press, 1986).

GEWIRTZ, SHARON, BALL, STEPHEN, and BOWE, RICHARD, *Markets, Choice and Equity in Education* (Buckingham: Open University Press, 1995).

GINTIS, HERBERT, 'The Political Economy of School Choice', *Teachers College Record*, 96 (1995), 492–511.

GOODIN, ROBERT, 'What is So Special About Our Fellow Countrymen', *Ethics*, 98 (1987), 663–86.

GREENE, JAY P., PETERSON, PAUL E., DU, JIANGTAO, FRAZIER, CURTIS, L., and BOEGER, LEESA, *The Effectiveness of School Choice in Milwaukee: A Secondary*

*Analysis of the Data from the Program's Evaluation* (Cambridge, MA: Harvard University, 1996).

GUTMANN, AMY, 'Children, Paternalism and Education: A Liberal Argument', *Philosophy and Public Affairs*, 9 (1980), 338–58.

—— *Democratic Education* (Princeton, NJ: Princeton University Press, 1987).

—— 'Democracy and Democratic Education', *Studies in Philosophy and Education*, 12 (1993), 1–9.

—— 'Civic Education and Social Diversity', *Ethics*, 105 (1995), 557–79.

HARGREAVES, DAVID, 'Diversity and Choice in School Education: A Modified Libertarian Approach', *Oxford Review of Education*, 22 (1996), 131–41.

HASSLER, JOHN, *Staggerford* (New York, NY: Ballantine Books, 1985).

HENIG, JEFFREY R., *Rethinking School Choice: Limits of the Market Metaphor* (Princeton, NJ: Princeton University Press, 1994).

HILL, THOMAS JR., *Autonomy and Self-Respect* (Cambridge: Cambridge University Press, 1990).

HIRSCH, ERIC D. Jr., *The Schools We Need and Why We Don't Have Them* (New York, NY: Doubleday, 1996).

HIRSCH, FRED, *The Limits to Social Growth* (Cambridge, MA: Harvard University Press, 1976).

HIRSCHMAN, ALBERT O., *Exit, Voice, and Loyalty* (Cambridge, MA: Harvard University Press, 1970).

HOLLIS, MARTIN, 'Education as a Positional Good', *Journal of Philosophy of Education*, 16 (1982), 235–44.

HOWE, KENNETH R., 'In Defense of Outcome-Based Conceptions of Equal Educational Opportunity', *Educational Theory*, 39 (1989), 317–36.

—— 'Equal Opportunity is Equal Education', *Educational Theory*, 40 (1990), 227–230.

—— 'Equality of Educational Opportunity and the Criterion of Equal Educational Worth', *Studies in Philosophy and Education*, 11 (1993), 329–37.

JENCKS, CHRISTOPHER, *Education Vouchers: A Report on Financing Education by Payments to Parents* (Cambridge, MA: Center for the Study of Public Policy, 1970).

—— 'Whom Must We Treat Equally for Educational Opportunity to Be Equal?', *Ethics*, 98 (1988), 518–33.

JORDAN, JOEL, 'Is Voucher Mania Defeated', *Against the Current*, 48 (1994), 3–5.

KANT, IMMANUEL, *Groundwork to a Metaphysics of Morals* (New York: Harper and Row, 1964).

KOZOL, JONATHAN, *Savage Inequalities* (New York, NY: Harper Perennial, 1992).

KYMLICKA, WILL, *Liberalism, Community and Culture* (Oxford: Oxford University Press, 1990).

—— *Multicultural Citizenship* (Oxford: Oxford University Press, 1995).

LEE, VALERIE E., CRONINGER, ROBERT G., and SMITH, JULIA B., 'Equity and Choice in Detroit', in Bruce Fuller and Richard Elmore (eds.), *Who Chooses? Who Loses?* (New York, NY: Teachers College Press, 1996), 70–94.

LEVINE, ANDREW, *Rethinking Liberal Equality: From A Utopian Point of View* (Ithaca, NY: Cornell University Press, 1998).

—— 'Rewarding Effort', *Journal of Political Philosophy* (forthcoming).

LEVINSON, MEIRA, 'Liberalism versus Democracy? Schooling Private Citizens in the Public Square', *British Journal of Political Science*, 27 (1997), 333–60.

LOMASKY, LOREN, *Persons, Rights, and the Moral Community* (Oxford: Oxford University Press, 1987).

MACINTYRE, ALISTAIR, *After Virtue* (London: Duckworth, 1981).

MCMURTRY, JOHN, 'Education and the Market Model', *Journal of Philosophy of Education*, 25 (1991).

MARGALIT, AVISHAI, and HALBERTAL, MOSHE, 'Liberalism and the Right to Culture', *Social Research*, 61 (1994), 491–510.

MARSHALL, GORDON, SWIFT, ADAM, and ROBERTS, STEPHEN, *Against The Odds* (Oxford: Oxford University Press, 1997).

MARTINEZ, VALERIE, GOODWIN, KENNETH, and KEMERER, FRANK, 'Who Chooses and Why: A Look at Five School Choice Plans', *Phi Delta Kappan* (May 1994), 678–88.

MEIER, DEBORAH, *The Power of their Ideas* (Boston, MA: Beacon Press, 1995).

MILL, JOHN STUART, *On Liberty* (New York, NY: Norton 1975).

MILLER, DAVID, *On Nationality* (Oxford: Oxford University Press, 1995).

MOE, TERRY M. (ed.), *Private Vouchers* (Stanford, CA: Hoover Institution Press, 1995).

MOLNAR, ALEX, *Giving Kids The Business* (Boulder, CO: Westview Press, 1996).

NORFOLK COUNTY COUNCIL, *Information for Parents: The National Curriculum* (Norwich, 1996).

OAKES, JEANNIE, *Keeping Track: How Schools Structure Inequality* (New Haven. CT: Yale University Press, 1985).

O'NEILL, ONORA, 'Opportunities, Equalities and Education', *Theory and Decision*, 7 (1976), 275–95.

—— *Constructions of Reason* (Cambridge: Cambridge University Press, 1990).

OLNECK, MICHAEL R., 'Terms of Inclusion: Has Multiculturalism Redefined Equality in American Education?', *American Journal of Education*, 101 (1993), 234–60

PARIS, DAVID, *Ideology and Educational Reform* (Boulder, CO: Westview Press, 1995).

RANSON, STUART, 'Markets or Democracy for Education', *British Journal of Educational Studies*, 41 (1993), 333–52.

RAWLS, JOHN, *Political Liberalism* (New York, NY: Columbia University Press, 1993).

—— *A Theory of Justice* (Cambridge, MA: Harvard University Press, 1971).

RAZ, JOSEPH, *The Morality of Freedom* (Oxford: Oxford University Press, 1986).

—— 'Multiculturalism': A Liberal Perspective', *Dissent* (1994), 67–79.

SANDEL, MICHAEL, *Liberalism and the Limits of Justice* (Cambridge: Cambridge University Press, 1982).

SCHRAG, FRANCIS, 'Diversity, Schooling and the Liberal State, *Studies in Philosophy and Education*, 17 (1998), 29–46.

SEN, AMARTYA, *Inequality Re-examined* (Cambridge, MA: Harvard University Press, 1992).

SHAPIRO, IAN, *Democracy's Place* (Ithaca. NY: Cornell University Press, 1996).

SHOKRAII, NINA H., and YOUSEF, SARAH E., *School Choice Programs: What is Happening in the States* (Washington, DC: Heritage Foundation, 1998).

SILVERS, ANITA, 'Reconciling Equality to Difference: Caring (f)or Justice for People with Disabilities', *Hypatia*, 10 (1995), 30–55.

STILLMAN, ANDY, 'Half a Century of Parental Choice in Britain?', in Halstead, J. Mark (ed.), *Parental Choice and Education* (London: Kogan Page, 1994).

STRAIN, MICHAEL, 'Autonomy, Schools, and the Constitutive Role of Community: Toward a New Moral and Political Order for Education', *British Journal for Educational Studies*, 43 (1995), 4–19.

TAYLOR, CHARLES, *Sources of the Self* (Cambridge: Cambridge University Press, 1990).

TITMUSS, RICHARD, *The Gift Relationship* (London: George Allen and Unwin, 1971).

TOOLEY, JAMES, *Disestablishing the School* (Aldershot: Avebury Press, 1995).

—— *Education Without the State* (London: Institute for Economic Affairs, 1996).

—— 'Choice and Diversity in Education: A Defence', *Oxford Review of Education*, 23 (1997), 103–16.

VAN PARIJS, PHILLIPPE, *What, if Anything, Justifies Capitalism?* (Oxford: Oxford University Press, 1996).

WALDRON, JEREMY, *Liberal Rights* (Cambridge: Cambridge University Press, 1992).

—— 'Money and Complex Equality' in Miller, David, and Walzer, Michael (eds.), *Pluralism, Justice and Equality* (Oxford: Oxford University Press, 1995), 144–70.

WALFORD, GEOFFREY, 'The 1988 Education Reform Act for England and Wales: Paths to Privatization', *Educational Policy*, 4 (1990), 127–44.

—— 'Diversity and Choice in School Education: an alternative view', *Oxford Review of Education*, 22 (1996), 143–54.

—— 'The Common Good: reply to Brighouse', *Oxford Review of Education*, 23 (1997), 517–21.

WALZER, MICHAEL, *Spheres of Justice* (Oxford: Martin Robertson, 1983).

WELLS, AMY STUART, *Time to Choose* (New York, NY: Hill and Wang, 1993).

—— 'The Sociology of School Choice' in Rasell, Edith, and Rothstein, Richard, *School Choice: Examining the Evidence* (Washington, DC: Economic Policy Institute 1993) 29–48.

—— (Principal Investigator), *Beyond the Rhetoric of Charter School Reform: A Study of Ten California School Districts* (Los Angeles, CA: UCLA School of Education, 1999).

WHITTY, GEOFF, 'Social Theory and Education Policy: the legacy of Karl Mannheim', *British Journal of Sociology of Education*, 18 (1997), 149–63.

—— POWER, SALLY, and HALPIN, DAVID, *Devolution and Choice in Education* (Buckingham: Open University Press, 1998).

WILSON, JOHN, 'Does equality (of opportunity) make sense in education?', *Journal of Philosophy of Education*, 25 (1991), 27–31.

WITTE, JOHN F., 'Achievement Effects of the Milwaukee Voucher Program', a paper presented at the 1997 American Economic Association meeting, 4–6 January 1997.

—— and THORNE, CHRISTOPHER A., 'Who Chooses? Voucher and Interdistrict Choice Programs in Milwaukee', *American Journal of Education*, 104 (1996), 186–91.

—— —— and PRITCHARD, KIM, *Private and Public Education in Wisconsin: Implications for the Choice Debate* (Madison, WI: UW, Madison, 1995).

—— —— and STERR, TROY, *Fifth Year Report: Milwaukee Parental Choice Program* (Madison, WI: Department of Public Instruction, 1995).

WRIGHT, ERIK O., 'Equality, Community, and "Efficient Redistribution"', *Politics and Society*, 24 (1996), 353–68.

WYLIE, CATHY, *Self-Managing Schools in New Zealand: the Fifth Year* (Wellington: New Zealand Council for Educational Research, 1994).

# INDEX